The Leaders
We Need

LEADERSHIP FOR THE COMMON GOOD

HARVARD BUSINESS SCHOOL PRESS

CENTER FOR PUBLIC LEADERSHIP
JOHN F. KENNEDY SCHOOL OF GOVERNMENT
HARVARD UNIVERSITY

The Leadership for the Common Good series represents
a partnership between Harvard Business School Press and
the Center for Public Leadership at Harvard University's
John F. Kennedy School of Government. Books in the series aim to
provoke conversations about the role of leaders in business,
government, and society, to enrich leadership theory and enhance
leadership practice, and to set the agenda for
defining effective leadership in the future.

OTHER BOOKS IN THE SERIES

Changing Minds
by Howard Gardner

Predictable Surprises
by Max H. Bazerman and Michael D. Watkins

Bad Leadership
by Barbara Kellerman

Many Unhappy Returns
by Charles O. Rossotti

Leading Through Conflict
by Mark Gerzon

Five Minds for the Future
by Howard Gardner

Through the Labyrinth
by Alice H. Eagly and Linda L. Carli

The Leaders We Need

And What Makes Us Follow

Michael Maccoby

HARVARD BUSINESS SCHOOL PRESS
BOSTON, MASSACHUSETTS

Copyright 2007 Michael Maccoby

Printed in the United States of America

11 10 09 08 07   5 4 3 2 1

Library of Congress Cataloging-in-Publication Data

Maccoby, Michael, 1933-
  The leaders we need : and what makes us follow / Michael Maccoby.
     p. cm.
  ISBN-13: 978-1-4221-0166-7 (hardcover : alk. paper)
  ISBN-10: 1-4221-0166-5
  1. Leadership. 2. Leadership—Psychological aspects. 3. Context effects
(Psychology) 4. Transference (Psychology) I. Title.
  HM1261.M317 2007
  303.3'4—dc22

                                     2007017284

The book is dedicated

to those leaders who are making

this world a better place.

Contents

x   *Contents*

Acknowledgments

THIS BOOK GREW out of two articles, written for different readers. One, "Toward a Science of Social Character," was written for psychoanalysts and psychotherapists, to help them understand the changes they are facing in the personality and problems of their patients.[1] I first tested out the theory of a shift from the bureaucratic to the interactive social character in meetings of the Academy of Psychoanalysis and the International Forum of Psychoanalysis. Mauricio Cortina, a psychiatrist, made valuable contributions to my thinking, especially how changes in psychotherapy were matching the change in social character.

Later, I introduced this theory of a changing social character in a research seminar on collaborative organizations led by Charles Heckscher, a sociologist who has been extremely helpful with his encouragement and criticism of a draft of this book. I benefited greatly from the interaction with members of the seminar, whose research enriched my understanding of the changes taking place in the knowledge workplace: Paul S. Adler, Lynda M. Applegate, Mark Bonchek, Nathaniel Foote, Jay R. Galbraith, Robert Howard, John Paul MacDuffie, Saul A. Rubinstein, Charles F. Sabel, and Barry Wellman. Their research and earlier versions of some of the material I've developed in this book were published in *The Firm as Collaborative Community*, edited by Heckscher and Adler.[2]

The second article, "Why People Follow the Leader: The Power of Transference," published in the *Harvard Business Review,* was written for business leaders to help them understand how to deal with changes in the motivation of their followers.[3] That article describes how the shift in social character requires a revision of Freud's theory of transference—the projection on to others of unconscious emotional attitudes shaped by infantile and childhood relationships. My editor, Diane Coutu, encouraged me to write the article, and as always, she was a brilliant and demanding guide and partner.

Jeff Kehoe, a senior editor at the Harvard Business School Press, read the article and suggested I expand it into a book on leaders and followers. Over a period of two and a half years, Jeff helped me first to craft a book proposal and then became an indispensable critic and speaking partner as I wrote the book. He has been the kind of editor writers wish for but seldom find, someone who understands and appreciates what the writer is trying to say and challenges him to stretch himself.

Others have also been helpful. Mike Wolff, editor of *Research Technology Management,* edited and published articles I wrote for "The Human Side," which tested out some of the ideas I've used in this book. Paul Griner read and corrected the descriptions of healthcare organizations in chapter 7. Phillip Cleary, Mike Feinberg, Rick Frechette, Reinhart Koehler, Dave Levin, Ed McElroy, Laura Rico, Susan Schaeffler, Henry Simmons, and Gary Smuts all responded generously to my questions about their lives and work.

The Harvard Business School Press sent a draft of the book to five anonymous reviewers who wrote useful criticism and gave their approval for publication. I thank them for the care they took, and I believe their suggestions improved the book.

I am also grateful to Bob McLean, an inspirational bridge-builder who has led the Washington Metropolitan Dialogue, a group of business, religious, government, and educational leaders supporting each other to improve relations in the city. Bob has been an enthusiastic supporter of my studies of leadership.

I appreciate the time, thought, and useful criticism contributed by Nora Maccoby, Max Maccoby, Erik Berglof, and Richard Margolies.

Thanks to my assistant, Maria Stroffolino, who prepared the many drafts of this manuscript, and to Monica Jainschigg, my careful and exacting copy editor.

Most of all, I am grateful to Sandylee Maccoby, who has been a very helpful critic and loving companion. She brightens every day we're together, and I'm fortunate to be married to her.

—Michael Maccoby
  Washington, D.C.
  April 2007

Who's a Leader?

THE NEED FOR LEADERS is urgent—to mobilize human intelligence and energy to grapple with historic threats such as global warming and weapons of mass destruction, and also to respond to vast opportunities to improve life on this planet. Only effective political leadership can show the way to achieve health care for all Americans, to gain energy independence through alternative nonpolluting technologies, or to fix public education so that it prepares children of every background for a demanding global economy. Only a persuasive national leader can gain support at home and abroad for policies that protect our society from its enemies. Only exceptional business and organizational leaders can provide employment and produce the goods and services essential for a strong economy. Yet despite the thousands of books and articles on the subject, we haven't improved on classic writings about leadership. To start with, even the best recent writers on leadership stumble over the definition of a leader, and a good definition is the beginning of understanding the kinds of leaders we need and how they'll gain followers in the context of our time.

John Gardner, a former secretary of Health and Human Services and noted leadership thinker, described very well what bureaucratic leaders do, but like a number of writers on the subject, his definition is inadequate. He defines a leader in terms of tasks: setting goals, motivating people, evaluating them.[1] This definition doesn't distinguish a leader from a manager or even from some leaderless teams that set their own goals and motivate each other. Other writers tell us the defining task of a leader is visioning.[2] Certainly, many leaders have been visionaries, but lots of people with visions have no followers; some of them have ended up isolated—and even in mental hospitals.

James McGregor Burns's brilliant treatise on leadership is full of rich historical vignettes.[3] Burns has given us the useful distinction of transactional versus transformational leaders. By his definition, a transformational leader raises people to higher moral levels, changing them in a positive way. But this definition implies that monsters like Hitler, Stalin, and Mao weren't transformational leaders—even though millions of people worshipped them and millions were changed by them, mostly for the worse. Even if a leader is just defined as someone who gets people to change, this wouldn't distinguish a leader from a manager who shakes up an organization by redesigning roles and incentives. It wouldn't even distinguish a leader from a skillful psychotherapist.

There is only one irrefutable definition of a leader, and that is *someone people follow*. This may seem too simple a definition for many academics, but once accepted it opens the door for plenty of hard thinking. Once we agree that anyone with followers—liberator or oppressor, transformational visionary or transactional problem solver—is a leader, then we have to answer two difficult, essential questions about leadership.

The first is: why do people follow this person? Much is written about leaders, but much less about followers. This book is about the leaders we need and also about the attitudes toward leaders and leadership that are being formed in a new historical context. How will leaders gain these followers? This is not just a question of using well-known techniques; we'll see in this book that would-be followers are no longer moved by what worked in the past.

Of course, there are and always have been leaders who force people to follow them and make the alternative unpleasant—imprisonment or execution by despots; firing by managers. In fact, most of the organizational leaders I've met are followed grudgingly, without enthusiasm or trust. But those leaders won't inspire anyone to meet the challenges of our time.

The second question: *How* do people follow the leader? Do they follow blindly? Do they do what they are told to do? Do they imitate the leader? These are typical follower behaviors in the bureaucratic-industrial world. But in the emerging era of knowledge work in which technical and professional specialists work across organizational and national boundaries, we'll see that leaders are most effective when they and their followers become collaborators who share a common purpose.[4]

Leadership always implies a relationship between leader and led, and that relationship exists within a *context*. Leaders who gain followers in one context—which could be historical, cultural, or organizational—may not attract followers in a different context. A well-known example is Winston Churchill, the indispensable leader who was willingly followed when Britain was attacked by Germany, but was rejected by his countrymen before and after World War II. Another example is the Confucian benevolent despot Lee Kwan Yu, who led Singapore, a poor city-state, to glittering prosperity. But he's not a leader who'd be followed in the democratic West.

Who are "the leaders we need"? They are the leaders motivated to achieve the common good who have the qualities required to gain willing followers in a particular culture, at a historical moment when leadership becomes essential to meet the challenges of that time and place. In short, they are the leaders needed within their contexts. To understand leadership in context, we have to place ourselves within that culture and get inside the heads of the people a would-be leader is trying to mobilize (i.e., the followers). Furthermore, we should have intellectual tools for understanding these qualities, which add up to the leader's *personality*.

In the global marketplace of our time, the leadership context has changed from that of fifty years ago, when corporate bureaucracies rode along in stable, predictable markets. Then, managers were needed to plot a steady course; innovative leaders could be seen as disruptive and were often sidelined. Now, in the context of continual change brought about by knowledge workers, leadership is needed not only at the top, but also throughout companies. Furthermore, different types of leaders are needed to integrate projects and teams of technical professionals working across department and national borders: strategic, operational, and network or bridge-building:

- Strategic leaders communicate a vision with a compelling sense of purpose.

- Operational leaders build the organization and infuse the energy that transforms visions into results.

- Network/bridge-building leaders facilitate the understanding and trust that turns different types of specialists into collaborators.

These leadership roles are most effectively filled by different types of people in terms of their intellectual skills and personalities. Furthermore, these leaders need to *understand* each other in order to work together; and most importantly, they need to understand the diverse mix of people they want to follow them.

The reader should know that my approach to the study of leadership is shaped by my academic training and professional experience as a psychoanalyst and anthropologist who for over thirty-five years has studied and counseled leaders in business, government, universities, and unions. As an anthropologist, I view leadership within a cultural context, a system that weaves together modes of work, political institutions, family structure, and values. As a psychoanalyst, I focus on the way personality determines how we relate to others, especially at work. Erich Fromm's idea of social character, which integrates anthropological context with a psychoanalytic approach to personality, is an essential concept for developing what I call Personality Intelligence, the ability to understand people.

Although I don't subscribe to all of Freud's theories, in this book I do make extensive use of his concept of unconscious transference, and I build on his theory of personality types. Transference helps to explain why people sometimes idealize leaders, projecting onto them comforting childhood images of protective parents. And it also explains why they sometimes turn against these leaders, seeing them as inept or neglectful parents. In chapter 3, we'll examine how changes in the experience of childhood and a shift in the social character cause different perceptions of parents and peers resulting in dramatically different attitudes to leadership.

In my teaching and consulting work, I've met many inspiring young leaders with strong values and high aspirations for the common good. This book expands on what I have taught to and learned from them, and I hope that it will strengthen their Personality Intelligence and their ability to become the leaders we need.

CHAPTER 1

Introduction

Leadership in a New Context

IN TIMES OF GREAT CULTURAL CHANGE, such as the present, people need leaders to take them to a positive future. But what makes leaders successful depends not only on their message and their skill in getting it across, but also on their grasp of what followers want from them. Throughout history, people have not always followed the leaders they needed. Sometimes they have been forced to follow oppressive dictators. Sometimes they have idealized and willingly followed Pied Pipers. This book is about why people follow leaders and what it takes to become the kind of leader we need today in a time of profound change in organizations, work, family life, and the social character—a time when both opportunities to improve life and threats to life have never been so great.

The cultural change we're experiencing is at least as far-reaching as the Industrial Revolution that drove people from farms into factories and bureaucracies, and changed their work from handling tools to mastering machines. It can be compared to the changes wrought by Genghis Khan and his Mongol followers nine hundred years ago.[1] The Mongol invaders smashed feudal ties in eastern Europe and began to build an innovative culture in China. The new Chinese technologies—gunpowder, the compass, printing—spread to the West and became tools for an era of exploration and conquest, the rise of a new entrepreneurial class, the beginnings of capitalism, and profound changes in values and emotional attitudes. At the height of the Renaissance, in the sixteenth century, Niccoló Machiavelli and William Shakespeare described how leaders gain power in ways that still influence our thinking.

But our thinking about leadership has not kept up with events. A fast-moving current of technology and social revolution moves some people to a new practice of life and leaves others in its wake. People relate to each other in new ways with identities that didn't exist in previous generations. Everyone is in some way touched by what happens in places that once seemed far away. Work moves to low-wage countries, but there is even more of an impact from the information and communication technology that continues to wipe out millions of factory and transactional service jobs, replacing them with work that calls for more brainpower and interpersonal skills. Bureaucratic hierarchies are pulled and stretched into complex systems, and the new roles demand flexibility from employees.

Persistent tension and anxiety keep people on edge. Corporate executives who once felt invulnerable now need to worry that someone else's innovation will blindside them and send their companies into a tailspin. Information about highly competitive international markets, global warming, terrorist threats, natural disasters, and weapons of mass destruction, all funneled through radio, television, and the Internet, send people instant and alarming images of events they can't control. Individuals have information at the touch of a mouse that before was available, if at all, only to privileged experts; yet they struggle to parse its meaning. At the same time that people yearn for protective and soothing leaders, they have become skeptical about leaders in general and distrustful of their motives and competence.[2]

The social changes have also upset historic patterns of family relationships. The liberation and empowerment of women has transformed workplace, family, and the way men and women view each other. The whole experience of growing up has been shaken up and with it, the dynamics that shape the deep-rooted emotional attitudes that drive people's values—what we can call the *social character*.

Social character is a key concept at the center of my research. It can be thought of as a kind of macro personality, describing the emotional attitudes and values shared by people whose personality has been formed in a particular culture or social class. It's a concept that clarifies how cultures shape human nature. And in this age of globalization and cultural change, I believe it's an essential concept for understanding the leaders we need and why people will follow them. Yes, we all share needs and strivings for self-protection, sustenance, and relatedness—love and work, self-expression and self-worth. But these needs play out differently, shaped by culture, acting through institutions of family, school, workplace, and places of worship. Yes, we each have a unique personality, and our genetic patterns are as different as snowflakes. Yes, we take on different identities, some of which are membership cards for interest groups. However, despite these differences, most people who have grown up and adapted to the norms of similar institutions share ways of almost instinctually relating to their work and to others. We all think that the way we feel and act in social relationships is human nature, yet those in other cultures who feel and act differently think the same thing. We and they are both wrong; human nature is always formed and expressed through the social character.[3]

With such radical changes in the context in which people live and work and in the social character, it is not surprising that how people view their leaders—what they want and need from them—has also changed. Our theories of leadership were formed in other contexts. Leaders, especially those in the most advanced organizations, can no longer gain followers in the old ways. In particular, how we have been taught to think about organizational leadership—a one-size-fits-all manager in a bureaucratic hierarchy with uniform roles—is now misleading. The bureaucratic theory of leadership assumes a psychology of followers that no longer describes a growing number of working people, especially in our dominant organizations and global companies.

I argue that in the evolving knowledge organization, it's more useful to know how different personality types fit specific leadership roles, and how they can get people to collaborate with them. I'll explain why changes in social character and the knowledge-creating workplace make it essential to raise our understanding of personality, not just intellectually but also experientially, to develop what I call *Personality Intelligence*.

To describe the leadership we need, we can't extrapolate from the past. People have changed—both would-be leaders and potential followers. People today respond to different qualities in leaders than they did a generation ago. Take corporations in the 1970s. Most managers were white men who were raised in families with one male wage earner, the father. Today there are fewer of these families than those headed by a single woman.[4] While many top leaders have come from traditional families, most people now entering the workforce have not. Likely, they were raised by parents who both worked and shared authority in the family, and this will be even more likely for their children. As I'll discuss in chapter 3, it appears that many people raised in nontraditional families feel stronger ties to sibling figures than to parental-type bosses.

Furthermore, women now hold key leadership roles, and that makes a big difference for workplace psychology. Instead of hierarchies of men following father figures, would-be leaders face a diverse group of followers who may project any number of images—mother, sibling, friend—onto them.

During the past few years, whenever I've met groups of managers, mostly in their late thirties or early forties, in workshops on leadership in the United States and Western Europe, I've asked for a show of hands from those born into families with a single male wage earner. It's usually about 75 to 80 percent. Then I ask how many now live in this type of traditional family. It's usually about 10 to 20 percent, mirroring the historic shift in the role of women and the makeup of families.

Because people are less likely to idealize leaders as father substitutes and they're more critical of parental figures in general, you can't lead in ways that worked in the past, especially in the advanced industrial democracies. Yes, fear or pervasive anxiety may, in psychoanalytic terms, regress people for a while so that they project a protective parental image onto a leader who exploits their fear. This is what Freud called *transference*. It causes us to idealize a leader and ignore his or her faults, and it dulls our own critical faculties. But once that protective image cracks, the new social character asserts itself and we become skeptical about all leaders. This is particularly dangerous in our present time of disruptive change, when we desperately need leaders to inspire diverse groups of people to pull together for the common good.

This book will help readers understand why people follow different leaders in different times and circumstances, including the present time, and it will show how the leaders who are needed in a given context must engage the social character of followers. I'll also explain why people sometimes follow the wrong leaders. After illuminating the dynamic nature of the leader-follower relationship, I'll provide a useful typology of the different kinds of leaders we now need, how they can engage followers, and how they need to develop themselves. But first, a brief account of how I came to the views of leadership and followership presented in this book will be useful.

STUDIES OF FOLLOWERS AND LEADERS

Over the past forty years as an anthropologist, psychoanalyst, and then a consultant to business, government, educational, healthcare, and union leaders in North America, Europe, Asia, and Latin America, I've interviewed a global spectrum of people at work: peasant farmers; entrepreneurs; workers in factories and offices; professionals; civil servants; military and Foreign Service officers; elected and appointed national and local officials; World Bank managers; and corporate managers, executives, and CEOs. Actually, I began to study leaders as an undergraduate at Harvard in the 1950s, interviewing political and academic leaders for *The Crimson*, the daily student newspaper. After receiving a doctorate in 1960, I joined Erich Fromm in Mexico to train as a psychoanalyst and study a village where entrepreneurs were beginning to change the culture and institutions that formed the social character.[5]

After returning to the United States in 1968, with a grant from Harvard, I led a study of managers in high-tech companies and initiated projects to improve the quality of working life at Harman International Industries and AT&T. Because of these projects I was hired to consult to companies, unions, and government agencies. Through these studies and consulting work I was able to observe that the attitudes and values in industrial societies—the social character—were changing, mirroring the historic transformations of work and family that started in the 1960s and that are still playing out today.

What most causes the social character to change is the dominant mode of production in a culture, the way of working in the most competitive and dynamic businesses. Those people with the skills, emotional attitudes, and strong values that fit this mode of work are the ones who do well, become models for others, and influence how the next generation is raised. Parents and schools strive to prepare children to become like the people who are making it in the world of work. And the successful innovators, the entrepreneurs who create the new modes of work, lead efforts to change education to develop the next generation for the new workplace. This was the case a century ago as innovators like Andrew Carnegie, John D. Rockefeller, and Henry Ford financed foundations to influence education. And it's happening again today with innovators like Bill Gates, Don Fisher, Eli Broad, Michael Dell, Oprah Winfrey, and others.[6]

In this way, we might say that social character changes by a process of *social selection*, an analogy to natural selection. The difference is that while in natural selection certain traits determine biological reproduction—that is, which offspring survive—in social selection, the traits of the most successful people are reproduced in the educational and work practices that shape the social character.[7]

FARMING–CRAFT SOCIAL CHARACTER

To understand the changing social character, consider the differences between traditional peasant farmers, workers in the industrial bureaucracies, and the technical-professional knowledge workers of today. In Mexico, the social character of the most prosperous villagers Erich Fromm and I studied was adapted to work that had changed little for centuries here and in villages throughout the world. The successful farmers were just like their parents and ancestors: self-sufficient and rooted in the land they farmed, hardworking, cautious, and conservative, with a strong sense of dignity based on independence and self-reliance. Respectful themselves, they expected to be respected by others. Used to the repetitive tasks of the seasons, they were patient as nature took its time to make their plantings grow, but also fatalistic, emotionally prepared for unpredictable calamities—droughts and disease, shifts in market prices. Often cheated by middlemen and politicians, they trusted only family members. A close-knit family with paternal authority reinforced by a patriarchal religion made for a strong economic unit that provided security for the old as well as the young.[8] Village decisions were typically made by consensus among the heads of family, mostly men but also some women.

These people were suspicious of all leaders as out to use them for their personal gain. Leaders were followed only in times of crisis, as when, in the Mexican Revolution of 1910–1920, villagers in the state of Morelos hired Emiliano Zapata to protect their lands from being grabbed by owners of large sugar-planting haciendas in collusion with the federal government. However, some of the farmers I interviewed did follow entrepreneurs who seduced them with visions of getting rich if they would sell their land to build weekend houses for rich people from Mexico City and transform their village into a tourist attraction. These entrepreneurs also persuaded villagers to invest in schooling, roads, and electricity to support changes that connected their village more closely to the modern world.

Reading studies of peasants in other parts of the world and working with George M. Foster, the University of California at Berkeley expert on peasant life, I learned that the social character of these *campesinos* was typical for peasants in Latin America, India, China, and eastern Europe. And the villagers' behavior conformed to what appears to be a general law about why free people want to follow a leader who pulls them out of their comfort zone. They will do so if they feel they need the leader to rid them of threats and oppression, or to help them get rich—in other words, conscious self-interest.

INDUSTRIAL–BUREAUCRATIC SOCIAL CHARACTER

Back in the United States in the 1970s, the success of a project I led to improve productivity and the quality of working life at Harman Industries propelled me to study organizations at the heart of the industrial world, among them Volvo and AT&T's Bell System, which included Western Electric and the regional telephone operating companies, giants then at their height of power and importance. These were prototypical bureaucracies, with uniform roles structured in a pyramidal hierarchy.

The personality of bureaucratic managers is described in chapters 3 and 4 as inner-directed, obsessive, and father-oriented, with values of loyalty, stability, and expert knowledge. But the only leaders that workers at AT&T and other industrial bureaucracies wanted to follow were not the bureaucrats who managed with carrots and sticks, but those exceptional managers who allowed them to experiment with how they performed their work, listened to their ideas, and coached them. But these companies did not usually place such people in leadership positions. More likely, they promoted people who were themselves good workers and were most like themselves.

However, it was in the rural Tennessee Harman factory where I learned that people did not always conform to popular academic theories of motivation.[9] Many workers there were also farmers and homemakers who took factory jobs only to supplement the uncertain income from farming. The prevailing theories taught in business schools predicted that workers like these would be on a low level of Abraham Maslow's needs hierarchy and be motivated solely by money. Other academics like Frederick Herzberg disagreed and argued that almost all factory workers would be motivated by more challenging work.

Yes, challenge did motivate some workers, especially those with a bureaucratic social character who sought a career in the company and wanted to show off and also improve their skills, but many rural workers with a farming-craft social character were most motivated by the prospect of going home early to do what they considered their real work on the farm or running a household: cooking and cleaning, preserving fruits, making clothes, raising children. This was more important to them than earning more money at the factory. And when they were given the opportunity to have a say in designing their jobs, with the promise that they could share the time saved and leave work early, the workers doubled their productivity. One group of women on an assembly line actually rejected the offer of more challenging work: since the work had become automatic, they passed the time chatting about friends and family. More challenge would force them to concentrate on work rather than enjoying gossip.

Another, more positive exception I saw in the late 1980s was at a Toyota factory at Nagoya, Japan, where the workers promoted to foreman roles were natural leaders who already had followers because they helped others and created group harmony. This was one example of Toyota's extraordinary ability to combine social intelligence with technical excellence.

It's not that the academics were all wrong. Rather they formed their theories within one context, one type of workplace with one type of social character; and then they overgeneralized. We will see in chapter 2 that this is still the case for popular academic theories of motivation and leadership that neglect the psychology of followers.

KNOWLEDGE WORK AND A NEW SOCIAL CHARACTER

In the mid-1970s, in the budding information age, my study of managers at Hewlett-Packard (HP), IBM, Intel, Xerox, Bell Laboratories, Schlumberger, the Jet Propulsion Laboratory, and Texas Instruments revealed an emerging mode of production involving teams of knowledge workers creating new technology.[10] Companies needed high-energy project leaders to fire up the engineers who had been raised in a slower-moving bureaucratic world.

I called the most effective leaders *gamesmen* because they treated their work like a game they were driven to win. They began to break up the bureaucratic hierarchies with a spirit of competition. The obsessive, craftsman-like engineers followed them because they stirred up excitement and heady feelings of being part of a winning team.

At that time, computer programmers operated at the fringes of technology companies like IBM and HP, whose main products were hardware. Managers and engineers saw programmers as oddballs, nerds who worked odd hours and dressed like perpetual adolescents. But the software revolution of the 1980s and 1990s transformed some of these social character mutants into charismatic visionary leaders like Bill Gates, Steve Jobs, and Larry Ellison who formed cultlike organizations around revolutionary products.[11] Employees followed them because they promised riches and a role in a great adventure that would change the way people lived and worked.

In this period, the mode of production evolved, as did the experience of growing up. In the 1980s, for the first time, I met the new social character in knowledge work, fields like telecommunications, finance, health care, consulting, entertainment, professional services, and government. The surveys my colleagues and I gave to managers and professionals showed that their numbers were growing. Unlike the bureaucratic social character, the *interactive* social character is focused less on status and autonomy, more on teamwork and self-development.[12] The strengths of *Interactives* lie in their independence, readiness for change, and quick ability to connect with others and work in a self-managed team. Many of them, especially those who have grown up playing video games with people around the world, feel at home in the global economy. As long as the rules are clear, and the purposes meaningful, they'll play the game at work, take responsibility for their decisions, and keep learning to stay sharp and marketable, but they don't want to follow autocratic, insensitive bosses who don't listen.

However, their weaknesses, like those of all social characters, are the obverse of their strengths. Not expecting loyalty from organizations, they aren't committed to a company, even though they'll commit to a meaningful project. Comfortable with technology and the Internet, it's easy for them to escape to alternative worlds, second lives, and assumed identities. Quick to Google the answers, they overweigh superficial knowledge. While the bureaucratic social character could be annoyingly stubborn and self-righteous, the Interactives can be inauthentically ingratiating and self-marketing.

This psychological shift changes the relation of leaders to followers. For the interactive social character, bonds of affiliation are often stronger with colleagues than bosses. Unlike bureaucratic employees of large companies a generation ago, the interactive social character does not idealize the boss and questions the very need for a leader. These people won't be led by father figures, only by role models who engage them as colleagues in meaningful corporate projects, ideally creating a collaborative community.[13] But only if they are led toward goals they find meaningful by leaders who understand them will organizations be able to meet the challenges of our time.

WHAT KIND OF LEADERS ARE NEEDED NOW?

I've seen at first hand and by reading history that the kind of leaders needed always depends on the context—the challenges of the time and the social character of the people who are being led. Here's an example. Right after I wrote *The Leader*, Samuel Carnegie Calian, then president of Pittsburgh Theological Seminary, invited me to participate in a discussion on the book with academics and business executives; he also asked me to talk at morning chapel on my favorite leader in the bible. I chose Moses for two reasons, one more trivial and the other more profound.

The trivial reason is that Moses is the only biblical leader with a management consultant—his father-in-law Jethroe, who counsels him that he'll exhaust himself trying to judge all the many disputes among his people. He needs to delegate to lieutenants whose judgment he trusts and only deal with the tough cases that can't be resolved by one of them. Of course, that's still standard good advice for someone managing many people.

The profound reason is that Moses took people who were slaves in Egypt and afraid of freedom and not only liberated them but also taught them how to be free. Once in the desert, the people who had followed Moses to escape from the backbreaking work of building the pyramids complained: "We don't know where our next meal is coming from. Why have you brought us here? We were better off in Egypt. At least we knew we'd have food to eat." The Talmudic rabbis believed that Moses took two generations, forty years, to transform these ex-slaves into a free, self-reliant people. He needed time to teach them the law and burn it into their psyches, to turn the fear of

Pharaoh into the fear of God, to prepare them for freedom. Social character changes much more slowly than changes in the social environment. But Moses was not just forging a new social character—he also gave his followers the norms and processes to sustain a free and just society, and the hope that they could be God's chosen people if they lived according to His commandments.

Moses not only led slaves to freedom physically; he transformed a slave mentality. He not only took people to a new place; he took them to a new state of mind. He transformed their social character. Moses was the leader the people needed, not only to become free in body, but also in spirit.

IT'S NOT ALWAYS MOSES WHO LEADS

But people sometimes want the wrong leaders. Another biblical example comes from the Book of Samuel, a righteous judge leading the Israelites. Because they had been defeated by the Philistines and were afraid, the people wanted a warrior-king to protect them. Samuel warned that a king would enlist their sons as soldiers and grab their daughters to serve him as cooks and bakers; he would take their fields and tax them. Samuel predicted the people would regret their decision, but they'd be stuck with it. They would cry out, but the Lord wouldn't hear them. And so it happened.

Most Americans grow up believing that, notwithstanding a setback here and there, things will always turn out well in the end. Isn't that our history? But there's nothing inevitable about progress, and like the Israelites who wanted a king, people don't always get the leaders they need. Inept, grandiose, or corrupt leaders hastened the fall of civilizations like Athens and Rome. We've seen sadly in the last few years that people don't always get the leaders they need in corporations. And skillful bureaucrats continue to move up the ranks of business and government where they become poor leaders or petty dictators. Rakesh Khurana has shown brilliantly how corporate boards have recruited media stars who, after giving a short-lived boost to the share price, weaken a company.[14] Even innovative entrepreneurs like Henry Ford can become puffed up by success and then lead their companies toward disaster. Recently, great companies like Westinghouse, AT&T, and HP have been led astray by inept leaders.

Why do people follow bad leaders? Sometimes they have no choice. A Mao, Stalin, Castro, or Saddam Hussein sweeps to power in a revolution against corrupt and inept leaders. People are forced to follow. And sometimes people flock to a demagogue, like Juan Perón or Huey Long, who makes big promises he can't keep. Sometimes people follow bad leaders because they're frightened or hopeless and believe the leader's promise of protection and a better future. In his book *Escape from Freedom*, Fromm analyzed Hitler's appeal to the German people.[15] According to Fromm, Hitler's first followers were small shopkeepers and low-level functionaries who shared a social character that was extremely patriotic, hardworking, parsimonious, stubborn, and moralistic. But their sense of self, their pride as successful people, had been crushed. They were humiliated by defeat in World War I and the loss of their father figure, Kaiser Wilhelm, and their hard-earned savings had melted away in the heat of postwar inflation. Also, the licentiousness in art and behavior in the Weimar Republic of the 1920s disgusted these rather traditional and moralistic people. Angry and seeking a champion, they were drawn to Hitler.

Based on questionnaires filled out by German workers and employees in 1930, Fromm concluded that the original supporters of Hitler had authoritarian personalities; they admired strong leaders and identified with them, and they were contemptuous of weakness, including their own. Hitler appealed to both their resentment and ambition. He offered power to the powerless, revenge against those who had humiliated Germany, and, tapping into historic anti-Semitism, he blamed the Jews for the cultural decadence. He promised a return to greatness for the "racially pure" Germans.

Once Hitler had taken over, other Germans who did not fully support his destructive vision followed the crowd to share in the spoils. With his early successes and their growing prosperity, Germans began to idealize Hitler. And many of those who did not agree with the Nazis were silenced by fear of the Gestapo, whose spies were everywhere. The regime tolerated no criticism, and those journalists and labor leaders who first resisted Hitler were taking a huge risk of being sent to concentration camps, even being executed for treason. On the basis of his study, Fromm predicted that while only 10 percent of Germans would be fervent Nazi supporters, no more than 15 percent had a strong enough democratic social character to resist Hitler. The majority, 75 percent, would follow as long as Hitler held power.[16]

WHAT'S AT STAKE

In the new context, understanding people becomes essential both for leaders and followers. Unless leaders understand the cacophony of personalities in this global economy, they won't create the collaboration needed for economic innovation, political-military security, and environmental protection. And unless we understand would-be leaders, we risk being seduced by demagogues who won't improve the world but will make things worse. We can't afford that. Let's be clear, it's not always easy to see behind the mask a clever leader wears, especially in an age of media manipulation and manufactured identities. To avoid being seduced by Pied Pipers, our grasp of personality—our Personality Intelligence—needs a lot of improvement. To recognize the person giving the spiel, and to be better able to predict how would-be leaders will act when in power, we need to understand their personalities. Correspondingly, with a better understanding of social character, would-be leaders for the common good will be better able to gain willing followers.

In the bureaucratic world, trust in the leader resulted from paternalism, from an idealization rooted in unconscious father transference. (I'll describe these dynamics in chapter 3.) In the new context, organizational leaders are willingly, even enthusiastically, followed not because of unconscious attachments (although these never fully disappear) but because they are good role models who articulate meaningful purpose, are transparent in their communications, encourage dialogue and truth-telling, and treat people as colleagues and collaborators rather than subordinates. This kind of openness scares executives who think they'll run the risk of losing control. But in my experience they gain rational authority and willing followers.[17]

Beyond this, people trust a leader who responds with heart as well as intellect. The leaders we need will develop their Personality Intelligence, which, as we'll see in chapter 10, combines head and heart: knowledge of personality with direct experience of people's emotions. This is what the Bible tells us that King Solomon asked of God: a heart that listens, wisdom and courage, the knowledge of what is the right and the willingness to risk acting on it.

Here is a quick summary of the book's organization:

- In chapter 2, "Revising Leadership Thinking," I give a very abbreviated overview of the important leadership literature that has formed our thinking, highlighting the neglect of the motivation of followers and the underlying assumptions about them that no longer hold. In the new context, leadership theory must include understanding and engaging different kinds of personality.

- Next, in chapter 3, I turn to "Why We Follow: The Power of Transference." People follow the leader for both conscious and unconscious reasons. The most powerful unconscious motivation is what Freud first described as transference of childhood images onto a leader. But Freud viewed transference in the context of the traditional father-dominated family. In this chapter we learn that as a result of the changing social character, the transferential glue that worked in the past no longer holds followers to organizational leaders and has shifted to a more sibling-like, collaborative dynamic as opposed to a parental, autocratic one.

- The leadership implications of this shift are profound. In chapter 4, "From Bureaucratic Followers to Interactive Collaborators," I describe how and why the social character of interactive followers is different from bureaucratic followers, and the far-reaching effects this has on our attitudes toward leadership.

- In the transformed world of interactive leaders and followers, the crucial leadership competence is an ability to *understand* a diverse mix of people in terms of both their sense of identity and personalities. In chapter 5, "Understanding People in the Knowledge Workplace," I explore what would-be leaders should learn about understanding people, and what all of us should learn about understanding would-be leaders.

- The leaders wanted by Interactives are not always the leaders they need. Chapter 6, "Leaders for Knowledge Work," describes the different types of organizational leaders required for knowledge work and shows the role of social character in both facilitating and resisting the changes needed to make organizations more effective and efficient.

- The next few chapters look more deeply at "the leaders we need" in specific, important contexts. In chapter 7, "Leaders for Health Care," I'll show how healthcare organizations are prime examples of knowledge workplaces. The best of these—the Mayo Clinic, Intermountain Health Care, Kaiser-Permanente, Vanderbilt University Medical Center—have benefited from interactive leaders. Both businesses and not-for-profits can learn from their experiences in dealing with resistance to change and creating collaborative learning organizations.

- Education is not just about knowledge; it's also about developing the social character that prepares people to succeed in a culture. In the era of knowledge work, where education makes the difference between success and failure, many children get left behind. In chapter 8, "Leaders for Learning," I describe how the leaders of KIPP (Knowledge Is Power Program), a remarkably successful program of some fifty inner-city charter schools, and Nuestros Pequeños Hermanos (NPH), a home for orphaned and abandoned children I've worked with for forty years, are showing that it's possible to help some of the most disadvantaged children learn and develop the social character needed to succeed in the world of knowledge work. I'll show how the leaders for these disadvantaged kids are in a sense transitional leaders, benevolent despots who provide the strong framework that allows the children to develop the attitudes needed for the knowledge workplace.

• The turbulent and eventful first years of the twenty-first century have made for a fascinating case study in gauging how our president measures up as "a leader we need." In chapter 9, "The President We Need," citing history and using psychological analysis, I describe the qualities of a president who would be able to mobilize Americans to meet the tremendous challenges of our time. We can't always predict how a president will act from past behavior. I list the questions I think we should ask candidates to try and discover whether they have the qualities, and specifically the Personality Intelligence, we need in a president.

• Finally, in chapter 10, "Becoming a Leader We Need," I explore why people become leaders and show how they can develop themselves to engage followers and collaborators. I describe how to develop Personality Intelligence, the ability to both recognize and experience personality patterns and emotions, and to understand organizations as collaborative social systems. These are essential abilities for effective leadership in an interactive world.

I also include an appendix on "Social Character and the Life Cycle," which contrasts the development of bureaucratic and interactive social characters from infancy to old age. By observing this development, we gain a richer understanding of how emotional attitudes have changed and what this means for leaders, followers, and collaborators.

CHAPTER 2

Revising Leadership Thinking

LEADERS HAVE BEEN DESCRIBED throughout history in every way imaginable—as dictators, demagogues, commanders, bosses, benefactors, guardians, coaches, pastors, and trailblazers. But what has been missing is a definition of a leader that covers all these descriptions, and that is, *a leader is someone people follow.* We can expand this definition to state that people follow leaders within a particular context, since being a leader isn't a personal quality, like intelligence. Rather, it's a relationship that exists only as long as people follow the leader.

Missing from the stacks of writings about leadership I've been burrowing through is a theory that fits the cultural context of our time. That's because the kind of leadership needed for past eras doesn't fit the age of knowledge work. Consider differences in modes of production and their leadership needs. In the craft mode of production, effective leaders are master craftsmen with apprentices who want to become just like their masters. In the industrial mode of production, they are managers who design roles and processes, set tasks, and evaluate performance within hierarchical bureaucracies. The most effective are the paternalistic leaders who forge emotional bonds of trust so that employees with bureaucratic social characters want to follow them. The knowledge mode of production is different: the workers typically know more about their work than their managers. The challenge of leadership is to create collaboration among diverse specialists with interactive social characters whose strongest emotional ties are with their colleagues, not their bosses.

I am a knowledge worker, and I'd bet so are most of you who are reading this—in fields like research, health care, education, engineering, law, software, finance, sales and marketing, consulting, government, publishing, the media, entertainment, architecture, and design. Or you may be student knowledge workers who will someday enter one of these fields.

Think of a leader you wanted to follow at work. (I'll leave political leadership for chapter 9.) Why did you want to follow that leader? Because the leader was passionate? Because the leader had strong beliefs? Because the leader had integrity? Yes, these are all good qualities in a leader. But, we can all think of individuals in leadership roles who have had some or all of these qualities and yet we didn't want to follow them. Why not? Because we didn't believe they were taking us to a good place.

Yet passion, belief, and integrity are often cited by CEOs when they make speeches about what it takes to be an effective leader.[1] They aren't lying, but they are avoiding the hard reality that a lot of their employees only follow them because they have to, not because they want to. Of course, people feel better following a person with integrity who seems convinced about a goal or strategy. Even if they don't *want* to follow a leader, they may be more *willing* to follow an upbeat and seemingly honest person. And they may feel juiced up, at least temporarily, by a boss's optimism and enthusiasm. No one wants to follow someone who is unsure, halfhearted, an untrustworthy flip-flopper.

These qualities cited by CEOs belong to the bureaucratic-industrial age, in which the model of effective leadership is the good father, and leaders bind their followers with unconscious transferential ties. But for knowledge workers with an interactive social character, skeptical of father figures, these ties do not bind. Knowledge workers want to collaborate with a leader who makes their lives more meaningful, and that calls for more than the stellar personal qualities cited by the CEOs.

The need for meaning sets us apart from other primates, and it's always made a difference to motivation. But what's meaningful to me may be less or not at all meaningful to you. And what's meaningful to either of us at one time might not be at another time. For example, people working at repetitive jobs in defense factories during World War II were highly motivated to do what they were told because they felt they were helping to win the war. The same job in peacetime might have felt just plain monotonous.

Many workers I interviewed in the 1970s didn't expect to find meaning in their work other than getting a regular paycheck, being able to support a family, and being respected for it. However, in some companies, like AT&T, employees felt pride and found meaning in being part of a great company that provided valuable services. Yet, even then, frontline workers were not enthusiastic about their bosses. And while grudging followership might have been OK for low-level manufacturing and service jobs (although even that's debatable), it won't get great results from knowledge workers whose attitude toward a leader makes a huge difference. That's because they can decide how much of themselves they want to put into their work. Unlike workers performing formatted factory work, knowledge workers can decide whether to just follow or to actively collaborate. So what makes knowledge workers want to follow and collaborate with a leader?

Much of the time those of us in knowledge work don't need a leader; we work as independent professionals or collaborate with colleagues. But when you do join a project you probably have some of the same attitudes I had when I collaborated with Erich Fromm on the village study. I was highly motivated because the project was meaningful, I was learning a lot, and Fromm listened to my ideas and sometimes accepted them. That's essentially the finding from Thomas H. Davenport's studies: "Knowledge workers don't want to work toward a goal because someone else has set it, but rather because they believe that it's right."[2]

In the article "Genentech: The Best Place to Work Now," *Fortune* quotes knowledge workers who joined the company not for the rich stock options, the free cappuccino, the parties, or other great benefits, but because they could do meaningful work. They were continually learning and on the cutting edge of finding cures for different types of cancer. They enthusiastically follow Art Levinson, their CEO, not just because he is passionate and has integrity and strong beliefs, although he has all those qualities, but because he champions science and focuses on "significant unmet needs" in the fields of oncology, immunology, and tissue growth and repair.[3] Clearly, Genetech's workers are Levinson's collaborators, not just followers.

Although we need a new theory for the age of knowledge work, this doesn't mean we can't learn from past thinking about leadership. I find useful nuggets of wisdom about leadership from the Old and New Testaments; ancient Chinese thinking, especially Lao Tzu and Confucius; Machiavelli; Shakespeare; histories of great leaders like George Washington, Abraham Lincoln, Franklin D. Roosevelt, and exceptional military leaders. I also find some of the present-day advice for leaders useful: communicating well and often, listening to people and seeing things from their point of view, giving people proper recognition and recognizing their strengths, accepting responsibility for mistakes, and so on. Some of this advice, like walking the talk and self-control, fits as well in our time as it did when Confucius gave it twenty-five hundred years ago. But much of what I read by leadership gurus would be misleading if I didn't understand it in historical context.

FROM TAYLOR TO MAYO

A great deal of what has been published and taught under the banner of leadership studies during the twentieth and twenty-first centuries turns out to be theories about how to motivate workers in an industrial bureaucracy. We'll see that these theories may fit bureaucracies and the bureaucratic personality at least in part, but not the emerging diverse types of organizations, roles, and followers in the knowledge workplace. What follows is a brief and highly selective review of theories set in their historical context.

Let's go back to the beginning of the twentieth century, when Frederick Winslow Taylor propounded the theory of "scientific management" to make industrial bureaucracies into smoothly running machines. Observing workers shoveling iron ore at Bethlehem Steel, Taylor found that they used a variety of methods. Some workers had long shovels, some short ones. Some bent their knees, others bent their backs. Some lifted five pounds of ore at a time, others ten or fifteen pounds. By studying these different approaches and timing the tasks, Taylor discovered what he claimed was the one best way to shovel ore to increase productivity and minimize backaches. According to Taylorism, the industrial engineer should design jobs, and workers should follow instructions—no deviations from the script. By doing tasks Taylor's way, the one best way, both company and worker would benefit, particularly if the worker shared in productivity gains.

What motivated workers to do such monotonous work? Unless it was a war effort, it was essentially keeping a job and getting paid. But this was a case of having to, not necessarily wanting to, follow a leader who might be either a process designer or a dictatorial foreman who made sure the workers stayed on task.

While many auto and steel workers at the beginning of the century were immigrants from eastern and southern Europe who hardly spoke English or farmers migrating north who were glad to get a steady wage, eager to please the boss, and satisfied to be told the one best way, their children in the 1920s were more educated, less malleable, and more responsive to union organizers. These workers learned how to fool the industrial engineers by slowing their pace when the job was timed and ostracizing those workers, called "rate busters," who worked too fast when the engineers were timing their work.[4]

To go beyond Taylor and make workers into better followers, a new theory of leadership was needed. Starting in 1924, a famous series of studies was carried out at the Western Electric Hawthorne factory in Chicago, led by Elton Mayo and Fritz Roethlisberger of the Harvard Business School. A stated purpose of the studies was to counteract unions by helping managers gain worker loyalty as well as increase productivity—to make managers more effective leaders.[5] Two main findings on how to lead workers emerged from these studies. One was widely adopted, while the other was misinterpreted and generally ignored for some thirty years because it didn't fit the prevailing context.

The first finding was that workers were motivated not only by money, but also by a caring boss. Mayo, a psychologist and anthropologist, believed that first-line supervisors should get human relations training. The idea, which was subsequently taught in business schools and corporate training courses, was that workers would be motivated to do monotonous jobs if they had a boss who could listen to their problems with empathy. In other words, you didn't have to change the Tayloristic theory of one best way. You just had to change the boss's attitudes toward workers.

This idea became widely accepted by managers. In 1978, when I asked Jim Olson, then vice chairman of AT&T, why he thought company surveys showed that workers were unhappy, he repeated Mayo's teachings: first-line supervisors didn't know how to listen and talk to their people. Olson ignored the fact that AT&T managers had been trying human relations techniques for some thirty years and this hadn't solved the problem.[6]

This idea, that a supervisor should be a kind of psychotherapist, was linked in minds of AT&T managers with their belief in the so-called "Hawthorne Effect," an oversimplified interpretation of the study's findings. They often cited this effect to explain a sudden rise in productivity. Supposedly, if you pay attention to workers and experiment with different working conditions, productivity will go up. It hardly matters what you do, you can change their routines, even the lighting in the room, and workers will work harder. Managers at AT&T and many other companies have explained to me that the Hawthorne Effect means that any new workplace experiment will result in short-lived productivity gains that last only until the novelty wears off.

But both of these conclusions were misleading. The workers who were studied at Hawthorne—five women assembling relays—told the researchers that, yes, the supervisor made a difference, but not because he was an empathic kind of psychotherapist. Richard Gillespie, who studied research notes that were left out of the book, found the following comment about the supervisor: "It was he who injected a spirit of play in the group by his comic antics, encouraging them to call everyone by his first name, to take strangers into their facetious conversations, to 'ride' supervisors and fellow operators alike."[7] This isn't psychotherapy, and it's a lot more than paying attention to the workers. It's adding a bit of play to otherwise boring tasks. It's making work fun.

There is also a factor, which neither Mayo nor Gillespie mention, that explains why both the therapeutic and playful managers succeeded in motivating the workers, and that's an unconscious transference to a manager who's idealized, even loved, because he's experienced as a good parent.

However, there was another factor that differentiated the therapeutic and playful manager: with the playful leader, productivity increased even more because workers were allowed to decide among themselves how best to do the job. Pay incentives were also a big motivator; productivity rose when workers were paid for the number of pieces they produced. But to admit the efficacy of participation and pay incentives would have undermined the Tayloristic foundations of prevailing thinking that industrial engineers rather than workers could always determine the best way to do a job. And it would have ruined Mayo's theory that it was just the caring manager that made the difference.

It took more than thirty years for management training to begin to shake off the message that Taylorism plus a caring boss, a combination of hard and soft management, was the best formula for effective industrial-bureaucratic leadership.

THEORY X AND THEORY Y

The human relations approach did not prevent unions from organizing between six hundred thousand and seven hundred thousand of the one million employees of AT&T. How did that happen? Executives like Olson believed that managers had simply failed to develop human relations skills. But workers told me they needed a union to protect them from the rigid rules set by the Tayloristic industrial engineers who didn't understand their resentment at being treated like parts of a machine. Telephone operators even needed a union to demand the right to take a potty break, and the first union victory at the Hawthorne plant was getting doors put on the men's room stalls.

Some managers began to question the combination of Taylor and Mayo. They latched on to new theories, especially Douglas McGregor's Theory Y, based in part on Abraham Maslow's hierarchy of human needs.[8] I find that Theory Y, like so much psychological theorizing, is also poorly understood by many managers. But that's partly because McGregor failed to put it in historical context, so it's incomplete and misleading.

In brief, the theory recognizes that workers are turned off by Taylorism, and adding human relations doesn't motivate them. They're still being treated as though they'd be passive or resistant to change without management control and paternalistic direction. They are still powerless to make changes in their work even when they see ways to improve it. McGregor sees Taylorism as fitting Theory X, that people need to be forced to work. What it misses, he writes, building on Maslow's hierarchy of needs, is that when people satisfy their lower-level needs for sustenance, employment, and security, what emerges are higher-level ego needs for self-esteem, status, and recognition, and beyond that, for self-fulfillment through creative expression. According to McGregor, employees who feel relatively secure get turned off because their work doesn't let them satisfy their higher needs.

Some managers mistakenly think that Theory Y is soft management, another type of human relations. Not at all. McGregor, a psychologist at MIT, was in touch with new management initiatives in technology companies and service industries. He recognized that if jobs requiring initiative or teamwork—what we now call knowledge work—are designed according to Tayloristic methods, workers will be frustrated and productivity will stagnate. For example, salespeople or telemarketing operators should be empowered (a term not used until the 1980s) to explain products and prices to customers, if need be deviating from their scripts. Employees should be allowed to use their brains, even to participate in how they do the job.

However, the importance of context—that Taylorism didn't fit changing business needs—was often ignored by managers. And Maslow, who lacked McGregor's knowledge of business, saw Theory Y only as a way of motivating employees who had higher-order needs, not of managing in a new way to meet the demands of these jobs. Maslow wrote that lower-level people would just take advantage of Theory Y, which he and others misread as soft management. Maslow wrote, "There are many places in the world [he gave Mexico as one example] where only authoritarian management, cracking the whip over fearful people, can work . . . Frequently it turns out that the profoundly authoritative person has to be broken a little before he can assimilate kindness and generosity."[9]

Having worked with Mexican villagers, I find Maslow's view just plain wrong. It isn't based on any research, or even personal experience. This aside, he misses an essential point of McGregor's theory—that knowledge and service jobs call for leadership that empowers workers, not necessarily leadership that treats them with kindness and generosity.

THE MANAGER AS EDUCATOR

Maslow and McGregor missed the point that preparing workers for more complex tasks without a one best way of doing things was not a matter of boosting them up a needs hierarchy, but teaching them to develop new skills and preparing them to take more responsibility. Gratifying ego needs for recognition and status is always a good idea. But more important, to motivate workers to want to follow them, managers had to become teachers and coaches.

I first saw an example of this in the early 1970s. On his own, a foreman began to teach machine operators to share some of his management tasks, like job assignments, inspection, and simple maintenance. During his experiment, which raised productivity, a company vice president cited Maslow to explain why he was skeptical about this initiative. After questioning whether the workers would be responsible enough to take on these tasks, he warned the foreman that he would lose control by being too soft. He said "Aren't you afraid to lose your authority, if everyone can do your job?" The foreman thought about it and said, "Since I started giving it away, I never had so much authority."[10] The workers wanted to follow him not because he was caring, but because he was teaching them new skills and he trusted them to take more responsibility.

By the late 1970s, a number of companies like AT&T, Volvo, Procter & Gamble, and the Cummins Engine Company were forging ahead of what was being taught in business schools, training managers to be coaches so that employees would gain new skills, not new needs. At the Volvo marine engine plant at Vara, Sweden, all the assemblers were coached to work in teams without a supervisor, sharing the management tasks among themselves.[11]

In the 1980s, total quality management (TQM)—sometimes called Six Sigma because the goal was an infinitesimal number of product defects six standard deviations from the original mean number of defects— finally left Taylorism in the dustbin of history. As preached by W. Edwards Deming, first in Japan and then in the United States when Deming was in his eighties, TQM made workers internal consumers in a production process, empowered to reject any defective product handed to them rather than adding value to it and passing it on. The role of management was not to give directions but to design good processes, coach workers, and resolve system problems that caused defects.

But Deming's view of good leadership was more than that. In one of the many conversations I had with him when he was in his nineties, I asked what he considered most important in his work with the Japanese after World War II. He emphasized a context in which the Japanese needed inspirational leadership. "They had lost the war, their products were viewed as inferior, they were depressed," he said. "I made them feel they could be the best in the world." Japanese as well as American managers wanted to follow Deming because, with TQM, he infused new meaning into their work, giving them the conviction that they could surpass themselves, become world-class producers, achieve what they had not thought possible.

But despite his genius, Deming's thinking remained in the context of the industrial age. In our conversations, he brushed aside my attempts to point out that his concept of TQM didn't fit the knowledge workplace. To be sure, TQM is the ultimate method for making products that fit the specs exactly. That's essential if the parts have to fit together, as in a car. But what if there are no specs? What if the worker faced with a customer problem can't refer to a formatted process or solution? A dramatic example of the limitation of TQM is the history of Florida Power and Light (FP&L), which in 1989 won the prestigious Japanese Deming Prize for its quality program. FP&L set up a business to teach TQM to other companies, but its service costs began rising alarmingly, and a few years later a new CEO stopped the whole TQM program. I found out why from an official of the IBEW (International Brotherhood of Electrical Workers), which represented the service technicians. The techs were handed instructions for the exact processes to follow in fixing electrical outages. But in Florida, problems varied and called for different solutions. Based on their experiences, the techs had figured out how to deal with problems in urban areas like Miami, rural areas with thick vegetation, beachfronts, and so on. They had notebooks full of ways to do their work most efficiently and effectively. When told to go by the TQM book, they left their notebooks in their lockers, and the result was less efficient, more costly work.

In knowledge work, productivity depends not just on good processes and getting workers to follow rules, even though that may still be important. But even more important is leadership that succeeds in creating a common sense of purpose and collaboration based on shared operating principles. Once that's achieved, exactly how knowledge workers do their job can be left up to them.

In the 1990s, there was a rise in knowledge work and a change in worker attitudes. The greater the competence required from a knowledge worker, the more likely a basic principle of both craft and industrial work no longer held, namely that the boss knew the job better than the worker. Scott Adams's *Dilbert* cartoons make us laugh at the inept manager of engineers, but the cartoons don't answer the question of how to lead knowledge workers.

And this is not just a matter of leading professionals, as I learned from the union representative at FP&L and directly at an AT&T business service center, where a young service technician named Penny controlled a multimillion-dollar corporate account. She was highly motivated by her relationship with the customer, who wanted to do business with her and her alone. Despite their attempts to connect with the customer, neither the account executive nor Penny's manager were invited to customer meetings. I asked Penny whether she had the skills to satisfy the customer's needs. She answered that she got other technicians to help. For example, she was good at solving voice problems, but she needed help from her friend Annie on data problems. So what was her boss's role? He should keep her informed about business strategy, products, and pricing. He needed to be a teacher. Then, Penny would want to collaborate, not because he was a human relations expert, but because he would be teaching her things she had to know to do the job. He would be adding value for her so she could add value for her customer. He would be treating her as a collaborator, not a follower.

McGregor and Maslow wrote their theories at the very start of the revolution in organization and work resulting from information and communication technology. As I write this, knowledge work has come to dominate the fields of health care, software, telecommunication, much of industrial work/design, engineering, marketing/sales, and financial services. While Penny was a special case at AT&T because she was empowered by the customer, more and more knowledge workers are empowered by their expertise. To be effective, organizations have to modify, even break down, traditional bureaucratic hierarchies into collaborative heterarchies where leadership shifts according to which person has the relevant knowledge.

Anabel Quan-Haase and Barry Wellman at the University of Toronto studied an information services company with two departments, programming and marketing. In the programming department, the programmers have more specialized knowledge than their managers. In a chapter describing the study, Quan-Haase and Wellman explain that "the type of work done by these high-tech employees has reached such complexity that the boss often cannot give much input for dealing with a technical problem. Such circumstances preclude direct hierarchical-bureaucratic supervision . . . management needs to trust and rely on their employees to provide them with the necessary information to make decisions because they are dependent on their expertise."[12]

In software companies like this—Yahoo! and Google are examples—it's not a matter of getting workers to cooperate. Individual workers have to collaborate to do their jobs.

The other department described by Quan-Haase and Wellman was marketing. There, individuals who worked directly with customers were managed in a more traditional hierarchy because hierarchy was more effective. Employees didn't need to collaborate so much with coworkers, but to do their jobs, they did need coaching from their managers.

By viewing the personalities of leaders and followers through the lens of a needs hierarchy, leadership thinking missed what was happening in the workplace. This is not to say that Maslow and his followers were all wrong. It does make sense to think of lower versus higher, more developed needs. But as I'll try to show in chapter 4, these needs should be viewed in the context of social character. The farmers working in a rural factory had a need to leave work early, not because they were on a low level of the needs hierarchy, but because they wanted more time for their independent farming. And the women working on the assembly line who preferred socializing to taking on more complex tasks didn't lack creative needs. They just satisfied them at home, cooking, weaving, and caring for their families.

I've puzzled about why Maslow has had such an appeal both to tough managers and soft liberals. The answer I've come to is that his theory seems to justify the prejudices of both groups. First of all, part of the theory has a certain face validity. Of course, hungry people think of little else other than food. Proponents of economic development can use Maslow to make the compelling argument that starving people won't be productive, that if you don't satisfy basic needs, there will be no economic development.

Furthermore, Maslow's view of human nature—that all people have the potential to be creative if their basic needs are met—has its roots in the humanistic philosophical tradition going back to Aristotle's *Ethics*. This view gives hope that the most downtrodden people can someday build a productive society.

As for the hard-nosed managers using Maslow's theory, they argue that lower-level workers need to be controlled. Because these workers are interested only in making money, there's no point in fussing with more difficult participative management. I heard this argument from a manager in New Delhi in the mid-1980s. He said he'd just become CEO and had tried to engage the workers in Theory Y–type management, but they had resisted, and he believed Maslow's theory explained the reason why. He invited me to a meeting with worker representatives so that I could see for myself. At the meeting, I asked the CEO to describe his idea of employee participation. He did, and I then asked the union leader for his response. "We are not interested," he said, and I asked him why not. "Because we want more money," he said. "You see," said the CEO, "they are low on the needs hierarchy, so they don't need to participate."

I had a hunch and asked the worker, "Have you always felt like this?" "No," he said. "Before this CEO arrived, we did have a scheme to participate, but we were promised a share in the productivity gains. We improved productivity, but we didn't get the money we were promised, so why should we trust management now?"

The CEO might have found this out if he hadn't coded information according to the needs hierarchy. Has Maslow's theory ever been tested? Edward E. Lawler III, a leading expert on motivation at the University of Southern California, reports there is "very little evidence to support the view that a hierarchy exists above the security level."[13] That means that once people have enough to eat you can't predict what will be most meaningful to them by referring to the hierarchy of needs.

I've interviewed hundreds of workers at all levels of companies and given surveys asking about their values to thousands more. Rather than fitting into a single hierarchy, all the needs or values cited by Maslow are shared by all people, as well as other needs that he doesn't include, such as needs for play, dignity or respect, and meaning.[14] Each need or instinctual tendency has its own developmental hierarchy. For example, Jean Piaget, the great Swiss psychologist, describes how the need to play develops from infancy to adolescence.[15] Piaget and Lawrence Kohlberg, the Harvard psychologist, described a hierarchy that's missing from both Maslow and McGregor, namely levels of moral reasoning.

Piaget described how children grow out of egocentrism and authoritarian reasoning only when they start to cooperate with other children and learn to see things from another's point of view. Kohlberg's lowest level is unquestioned obedience to authority. At the next level, people conform to a limited view of what is good for their family or organization. At higher levels, they decide what will benefit others beyond the immediate group.[16]

As knowledge-work organizations become more complex, they require communication among workers and trust that people are acting according to higher-level moral values. This is not just a question of the worker's personality. Leadership makes the difference in the moral level of an organization, whether people are ruled by fear and expected to obey without question or whether they are trusted to do what is best for the organization and its stakeholders, even if this means criticizing the boss. The recent history of corporate corruption has eroded trust in corporate leaders. But creating moral organizations is not only a matter of having leaders who stay out of jail. Autocratic leaders reinforce egocentrism that blocks open communication. That's because everyone tries to please the boss they fear, and other workers become rivals, not collaborative colleagues.

Although the theories of Maslow and McGregor had the value of getting leaders to think beyond Taylorism, they were too flawed to provide a guide for the age of knowledge work. They failed to understand context, both the changing nature of work and the social character.

LEARNING FROM MACHIAVELLI
ABOUT PRINCES AND CEOS

So far, I've focused on organizational leadership below the very top. In thinking about why people follow a CEO, theorists often refer to Machiavelli to justify harsh management. But, while Machiavelli has much to teach us, his lessons are poorly understood because they aren't seen in context.

What can we learn from Machiavelli? If we're not put off by his cynicism; his praise of immoral leaders who succeeded by cruelty, lies, and betrayals; or his amoral advice, we can find bits of wisdom. Hitler, Stalin, and Saddam Hussein, among other despots, used *The Prince* as a guidebook. But Machiavelli is more than a guru for monsters. In a course taught by Leo Strauss, the Machiavelli scholar at the University of Chicago, I learned that Machiavelli not only describes how a leader gets results in different contexts, but also what kind of a leadership personality succeeds with different types of followers.

The Prince was written in a time of continual war.[17] As he reviews the history of his time, Machiavelli concludes that princes need to learn not only the art of war but also how to get people to follow. But most of these followers are frightened and disorganized. Machiavelli advises princes to be ruthless, to make themselves feared rather than loved, because they can control fear. He cautions that unless you're a prince who is totally in charge and already feared, gaining love by being benevolent is always an uncertain venture. That's because your followers will be loyal only as long as they have to follow you out of fear or want to follow you out of greed. Machiavelli writes: "A prudent lord, therefore, cannot observe faith, nor should he . . . And if all men were good, this teaching would not be good, but because they are wicked and do not observe faith with you, you also do not have to observe it with them."[18]

We should view all this is in the context of sixteenth-century Italy, a time when war and betrayal were the norm. But when Machiavelli looks back at ancient Rome, he tells a story about two generals who led a different breed of followers. One, Valerius Corvinus, was kind and considerate. He treated his men, who like him were Roman citizens, as equals. The other, Manlius Torquatus, was harsh and a stickler for the rules, so much so that he had his son publicly beheaded for disobeying his orders. Who was more effective? Both were, says Machiavelli, because they were true to their natures, consistent, and virtuous, so the troops knew what to expect from them. The troops could trust them.[19]

Notably, Machiavelli appears interested only in the effectiveness of the generals—their results. Their troops were willing to follow, in contrast to other generals whose troops deserted or rebelled. Did the troops want to follow these generals? Machiavelli doesn't tell us. Maybe he assumes that the troops would naturally want to follow successful generals for the booty and glory they'd share. What he doesn't consider is that these troops, especially those following Valerius Corvinus, might have projected strong father transferences on to these generals.

Machiavelli concludes, "It does not matter much in what way a general behaves, provided his efficiency be so great that it flavors the way he behaves, whether it be this way or that."[20] Every personality has defects and dangers, he notes, but they can be corrected by outstanding virtue, at least enough to be an effective leader.

However, personality does make a difference for Machiavelli in its fit with the challenges of the times. He writes in *The Prince* that when there is a great deal of turmoil and uncertainty, an impetuous person is more likely to succeed, while in times of relative peace, a cautious, patient person will have the advantage.[21] Can't people change their behavior to fit the moment? That would be the view of some modern proponents of situational management. Machiavelli doesn't think so, because he observes that people can't and don't deviate from their natures. Of course, we can learn new techniques, but how we apply them is always flavored by our personality; and when it comes to the almost instinctual way we approach big decisions, our nature (personality) largely determines how we'll act.

Machiavelli's observations illustrate the difference between situational management and contextual leadership as described in this book. Some management writers contend that personality doesn't matter, that leaders can tailor style to fit any situation. Obviously, this is true to some degree. Almost all leaders can be commanding or consultative. Any leader can learn when to be close and when to increase distance from the troops. But as Heraclitus wrote twenty-five hundred years ago, character is man's fate. There are limits to behavioral plasticity, and when a leader is stressed, personality prevails. A CEO put it neatly when I asked his view of situational leadership: "Most of my interactions are taking place in chaos. I can't stop and think about what my style should be with different people. My style is my personality." Given this, certain leadership personalities fit better in certain contexts.

APPLYING MACHIAVELLI

Leaders still look to Machiavelli for lessons on leadership, but they take away misleading advice, because they read Machiavelli in only one context, the chaotic state of wars and revolutions in sixteenth-century Italy.[22] Regrettably, Machiavelli's advice to the prince, to appear humane and compassionate while grabbing power through lies and betrayals, can still get results, especially when disorganized and frightened people want security and protection, even at the price of their liberty. There are all too many Machiavellian leaders in organizations, psychopaths able to charm their way into power.[23]

But even more benign bosses provoke fear. When I give workshops on leadership to midlevel managers and executives from large companies and government agencies, sometimes I ask them to estimate *how much* fear of the boss exists in their organizations on a scale of 1 (little or no fear) to 4 (high level of fear). Generally, the mean estimate is 2.5–3.0. Then I ask what they think the level should be; the result is almost invariably about 2.0. What comes out in our discussions is that most managers don't trust people to want to follow. They think that without some fear of the boss, the people in their organizations would not always follow. But beyond this, isn't it inevitable that people will always feel some fear of a boss who evaluates them and has the power to reward, punish, and fire them? The only subordinate who feels no fear at all is one who doesn't need the job.

However, if we apply Machiavelli's methodology of analyzing leadership effectiveness to our time, I don't see that we've advanced very much from his thinking. Take the most popular business leadership book of recent years, Jim Collins's *Good to Great*. Like Machiavelli, Collins describes the personality of effective business leaders and gives advice to modern-day commercial princes. Collins's great leaders are described as "disciplined, rigorous, dogged, determined, diligent, precise, fastidious, systematic, methodical, workmanlike, demanding, consistent, focused, accountable, and responsible."[24] They are also described as "humble" and "self-effacing."[25]

To a large extent, these leaders are like Machiavelli's cautious and patient type as contrasted to the impetuous risk takers. But unlike Machiavelli, Collins does not take the intellectual step of describing the context of his findings. Almost all of Collins's CEOs run retail or commodity businesses, where they have succeeded in reviving a mature company by streamlining processes, cutting costs, and getting rid of people who don't add value. None of these businesses have produced innovative products, unless you include marketing innovations like Gillette's Mach 3 razor blades. Collins misses the point that Machiavelli astutely observed: in times of rapid change, as in our time, risk-taking and self-promoting rather than self-effacing CEOs—larger-than-life figures like Bill Gates, Larry Ellison, Steve Jobs, Larry Page, and Sergey Brin—are the ones who exploit new technologies and, with their products, change the way we work and live.

Instead of seeing different personality types in context, as did Machiavelli, Collins's hierarchy of leadership qualities expresses a bureaucratic mind-set that inhibits contextual thinking about leadership. At the bottom of his hierarchy is the capable employee, then comes the competent manager, then the charismatic but egoistic visionary, and at the top of the hierarchy, the self-effacing great executive who puts the good of the organization above his own needs. (There are no women in *Good to Great* because only male CEOs fit the researchers' criteria of exceptional financial results.)

The two types at the top of Collins's hierarchy fit two personality types I've written about, the dogged obsessive and the charismatic productive narcissist.[26] These two types provide a classic contrast that I've found pops up in many different cultural contexts. Narcissists like Napoleon and Hitler in politics, and Henry Ford and John D. Rockefeller in business, boldly grab hold of power in tumultuous times but often overreach themselves, while the obsessives carefully build sustainable institutions in more stable times. *Good to Great* was published right when the narcissistically led dot-com bubble burst and grandiose CEOs like Jean-Marie Messier and Bernie Ebbers crashed. Naturally, the disciplined self-effacing obsessives, with their steady results, seemed not only safe but also appealing.

History aside, what Collins misses is that at the top of organizations today, it's become essential to select managers whose personalities fit the role they play, who want to do what they need to do for success; and the right candidate doesn't always fit Collins's model of greatness. In his book *Winning*, Jack Welch, a great business leader who is not at all humble and self-effacing, shows his acute awareness of personality types when he describes how he picked people for leadership jobs. For a commodity product business he chose a leader who was "in his element with people who sweated the nitty gritty details like he did, talking about ways to squeeze efficiencies out of every process. He was a master of discipline." This is the obsessive type that Collins spotlights. In contrast, the head of an innovative risky business required a visionary, a person who "hated the nuts and bolts of management . . . But he sure did have the guts and vision to place the big bets."[27] Probably also a big ego that gave him the confidence to take these risks.

Like Welch, the best professional football coaches have learned which personalities fit best in which roles. For example, the best offensive linemen typically are conservatives who uphold authority and protect the quarterback, while the best defensive linebackers are rebels who take pleasure in smashing the quarterback—they challenge rules and regulations and are harder for coaches to control.[28] Because personality can make the crucial difference among players with similar skills, these coaches need enough Personality Intelligence to understand followers and collaborators.

However, some coaches and managers have become aware that the attitudes of followers have changed, that the kind of leadership effective in the past no longer gets results. This is not only because the challenges at work have changed, but also because the social character of followers is not the same as it was a generation ago.

In the early 1970s, when I studied leaders and followers in high-tech companies, like IBM, Hewlett-Packard, Intel, and Texas Instruments, most of the craftsmanlike engineers had an obsessive bureaucratic social character. Within the hierarchy, they valued their autonomy. They liked to work at their own pace, and it was hard to get them to communicate and to cooperate among themselves, as well as to inform management about the status of their work. Some were entrepreneurial, but this usually meant trying to sell an idea without any evidence that people would buy the product. This mind-set at AT&T Bell Labs led engineers to try unsuccessfully to sell picture-phones while rejecting cellular telephones.

In my book *The Gamesman,* I described a young manager at one of these companies, then in his early thirties, who seemed to me a prototype for the kind of antibureaucratic leadership needed for companies to innovate and succeed in competition that was just beginning to heat up.[29] In retrospect, this manager seems like a warmer, less self-promoting version of Jack Welch. He eventually reached the top of his company, but rejected the CEO job.

I gave him the name Jack Wakefield, but subsequently, the business press discovered he was Dick Hackborn of HP.[30] Hackborn saw early on that to get results, he had to light a fire under the obsessive engineers, threaten that their slow pace would doom their product, but excite them with the promise of glittering success. He was also a teacher and coach, educating the engineers about the business, the competition, and corporate strategy, loosening them up in a playful way to create teamwork and collaboration.

Hackborn, like Welch, saw himself as not growing people up a hierarchy of needs but developing them to fit the company's needs. Both Welch and Hackborn spent much of their time with their people, answering their questions, responding to their arguments—all the while projecting a vision of success.

Although both Welch and, less so, Hackborn provoked some fear in their followers—because it was clear they wouldn't tolerate anyone who didn't get with the program and perform—for the most part, people were persuaded. Once they wanted to follow, they could be trusted with considerable authority to make decisions on their own.

Hackborn had the foresight to realize a generation ago that the new knowledge workers, a term he found by reading Peter Drucker, would no longer accept paternalistic control, that a leader had to create loyalty not to himself, but to a winning team and a shared purpose.

Leaders can still learn from the way Hackborn and Welch engaged their followers. However, in the thirty years since I wrote about Hackborn, the social character of followers has been changing. There are fewer of the obsessive, uncooperative, bureaucratic types. The emerging interactive social character is naturally more collaborative, but as Hackborn predicted, less responsive to paternalistic control, and with stronger sibling ties (as I'll describe in the next chapter). At one high-tech company, the MITRE Corporation, members of project teams are free to work whatever hours they want at home or at the workplace. The CEO tells me he doesn't worry about performance, because team members won't stand for anyone who isn't getting results.[31] The manager needs to be a leader who communicates purpose as the collaborators manage themselves.

The best professional football coaches have reflected on the shift in the attitudes of players. The tough-talking paternalistic coaches of the past like

Vince Lombardi, who'd berate and shame his team when they lost, would just alienate many of today's players. Coaches like Joe Gibbs of the Washington Redskins, Bill Belichick of the New England Patriots, Andy Reid of the Philadelphia Eagles, Lovie Smith of the Chicago Bears, and Tony Dungy of the Indianapolis Colts model an attitude of collaboration and shared responsibility, older brothers rather than fathers. If there are mistakes, they work together with players to understand and remedy them. Redskins quarterback Mark Brunell said of Gibbs after a Redskin loss in the fall of 2005, "He's always positive. He expects us to work. He's not asking us to do anything he's not committed to doing himself. The best thing about Coach Gibbs is that we're all in this together. And that's the way it should be."[32] To avoid making criticism personal, Dungy and Smith use processes like objective grading systems for game behavior, with consequences for loafing or missing tackles.[33] In contrast, Tiki Barber, the Pro Bowl running back of the New York Giants, blamed his team's postseason losses on his coach's autocratic style. "I think he has to start listening to the players a little bit and come our way—their way—a little bit."[34]

After some losing seasons, Sasho Cirovski, coach of the University of Maryland soccer team, hit on the way to create winning leadership for Interactives. Using a survey with questions such as "Who do you rely upon when your team needs unity and motivation?" he found the team's natural leader and made him captain. In other words, he dropped any attempt to use a father transference to inspire the team and instead engineered unity with a trusted sibling figure, who incidentally wasn't even one of the best players. But with an interactive leader, Maryland went on to a national championship.[35]

I expect some readers of this book will immediately identify with the interactive social character while others will find it harder to do so. I believe this is because we are in a period of transition in which both the bureaucratic and interactive social characters coexist. In the next two chapters, I'll compare them, with a focus on the kind of leader each wants to follow.

CHAPTER 3

Why We Follow

The Power of Transference

I GOT INTO A CONVERSATION with George Raymond (not his real name) on a flight to London on my way to teach a seminar at Oxford on coaching leaders. George is a thirty-four-year-old leader of a technical team in a large media company. He tells me his boss is a bureaucrat who doesn't listen to good ideas, even when they'll save money. The boss wants to be admired, told that his ideas are great, but George just sees the boss as an obstacle, an evil. George describes his own team as a collaborative community where information flows easily, where he leads within the group, not above it. George grew up in a family where both parents were professionals, but his close ties were with friends and brothers, even more than with parents. He loved playing video games, MMORPGs (massively multiplayer online role-playing games) in which he was creating international teams and making quick decisions with no need for a boss. This boss tells him he'd better play by the company rules or else, but George says he is ready to quit if he can find a job with a company that respects what he can do. A few months later he e-mails to tell me he's now joined another company where he's a lot freer, and he gets along well with a boss who is more of a colleague. There will be many more people like George who follow a bureaucratic boss only as long as they have to.

At the end of the twentieth century, historic changes in the experience of life in families and workplaces formed an interactive social character that began to shove aside the bureaucratic personality. But the bureaucratic experience has deeply engraved a powerful model of leadership in our thinking, buttressed by the various schools of psychology. Even Freudian psychoanalysis, with its emphasis on the father transference, reflects the typical attitude of the bureaucratic personality in organizations—the idealizing of paternalistic bosses. In this context, sibling transferences are viewed as rivalrous, like Cain and Abel competing for God's favor, or Jacob outmaneuvering his brother Esau to gain Isaac's blessing. For the interactive personality, in contrast, sibling transferences can strengthen a band of brothers and sisters allied against an irrational boss. It's time that we focus on the psychology of followership that fits the new context.[1]

Let's be clear about the exceptional importance of leadership in a world of individualistic knowledge workers. Leaders are needed not only to drive for results but also to adapt and change organizations and to build bridges and networks to connect people who are diverse in skills, outlook, and identity. In any business, good leadership may be the most essential competitive advantage a company can have. Furthermore, without exceptional leadership, we won't solve our national problems: new sources of clean energy, quality education, and health care for everyone. It's not surprising, then, that management scholars focus relentlessly on the attributes of successful leaders.

But in the effort to grasp and master the skills of great leaders, we tend to lose sight of the fact that there are two parts to the leadership equation. For leaders to lead, they need not only exceptional talent but also the ability to attract followers. And the problem is that followers get short shrift in the management literature, where they are described largely in terms of the leaders' qualities. In other words, they're seen as merely responding to the leader's charisma, passion, integrity, or caring attitude. What most analysis seems to ignore is that followers have their own motives and identity, and they can be as powerfully driven to follow as leaders are to lead.

I've noted that followers' motivations fall into two categories—conscious and unconscious. The conscious ones are well-known. They have to do with our hopes of gaining money, status, power, new skills, or entry into a meaningful enterprise by following a great leader—and our fears that we'll miss out if we don't. What can be even more powerful are the unconscious, sometimes irrational motivations that lie outside our awareness and therefore beyond our ability to control them. In part, these motivations are rooted in emotional attitudes formed early in life, but in large part they also arise from the strong images and emotions in our unconscious that we project onto our relationships with people who have power over us.

THE POWER OF TRANSFERENCE

Sigmund Freud, the founder of psychoanalysis, was the first person to provide some explanation of how a follower's unconscious motivations work. He explained how different characteristics like superneatness, obstinacy, and stinginess fit together in what he called the anal character.[2] This insight into character formation is the foundation of psychoanalytic understanding of personality. However, Freud also discovered a process that explains a lot about why people want to follow leaders. After practicing psychoanalysis for a number of years, Freud was puzzled to find that his patients—who were, in a sense, his followers—kept falling in love with him. Although most of his patients were women, the same thing happened with his male patients. It is a great tribute to Freud that he realized that his patients' idealization of him couldn't be traced to his own personal qualities. Instead, he concluded, people were relating to him as if he were some important person from their past—usually a parent. In undergoing therapy—or in falling in love, for that matter—people were transferring experiences and emotions from past relationships onto the present. Freud thought the phenomenon was universal. He wrote, "There is no love that does not reproduce infantile stereotypes," which, for him, explained why so many of us choose spouses like our parents.[3]

Freud called the dynamic *transference*, and it was one of his most important discoveries. Indeed, for Freud, patients were ready to end therapy when they understood and mastered their transference and no longer idealized the therapist. And even today, identifying and dissolving transferences are the principal goals of psychoanalysis.

But as important as it is, the concept of transference remains little understood outside clinical psychoanalysis. This is unfortunate, because transference is not just the missing link in theories of leadership—it also explains a lot about the everyday behavior of organizations.

Typically, transference is the emotional glue that binds people to a leader, that makes them want to follow even when they are unclear about where the leader is taking them. Employees in the grip of positive transference see their leader as better than she really is—smarter, nicer, more charismatic. They tend to give her the benefit of the doubt and take on more risk at her request than they otherwise would. And as long as the leader's reality is not too far from the followers' idealization—and she doesn't start to believe in their ideal image of her—this can work very well.

The transference dynamic is most likely to get out of control during periods of organizational stress. In such situations, followers tend to be more dominated by irrational feelings—in particular, the need for praise and protection given by all-powerful parents. At the same time, the leader is preoccupied with handling the crisis at hand and, as a consequence, is probably less alert to the likelihood that his followers are just acting out childhood fears. This is what happened to a vice president of AT&T whom I was advising in the mid-1980s, during the breakup of the Bell System. While he was focusing on strategy, his followers felt frustrated that he was not dealing with their anxiety and reassuring them. Even though he was charting a promising new course for his division, employees complained that he wasn't leading them.

Another example of how transference is triggered by doubt and stress is the way people feel better just by going to see a doctor, even before the doctor has done anything for them. In large measure, this phenomenon can be explained by patients' trust, which transfers the childhood experience of being cared for by parents when sick. This type of transference makes it extremely hard for scientists to evaluate certain medications, such as mood-altering drugs. Clinical studies show, for example, that up to 30 percent of people respond as well to placebos—again, trust—as to antidepressants.

People who volunteer for a study in hopes of finding a cure for their ailment may be especially receptive to placebos.

As well as being quite subtle in its workings, transference comes in many guises. It is blind to both age and gender, so stereotyping is very dangerous. A male leader, therefore, should never assume that he is a father figure or a brother figure—nor should a female leader assume she's a mother or a sister. Psychoanalysis has shown that someone can have a paternal transference with a woman in authority and a maternal transference with a man.

Clearly, positive transferences are closely linked to productivity. Suppose an employee believes that her boss will care about her in a parental way. To ensure that this happens, she will make superhuman efforts to please her leader. As long as she perceives that these transferred expectations are being met, she will continue to work hard. Will this benefit the organization as a whole? Yes—she'll want to follow the leader, and this will be fine as long as it's just a matter of following directions. But she's also less likely to think for herself, and this may limit her potential for the kind of creativity needed in a knowledge company.

Transferences can be negative as well as positive. Commenting on my article on transference in the *Harvard Business Review*, Stephen Schneider wrote about his experience consulting to a company with a highly effective COO "unusually committed to her work" and to her boss, the CEO. When, following an acquisition, the CEO became less available for her, the COO, who had been so eager to please, suddenly became distant and aggressive. Schneider found that on a rational level, the COO was clear about her role and content with her status. However, unconsciously, she was angry that the relationship with the CEO was no longer the same. The COO had idealized her boss when he had time to nurture her—he represented all she had never experienced from a distant father. When he turned away to work in the acquisition, the boss became the "bad father" of her childhood, and all her resentment from the past was projected onto him.[4]

Another big risk in transference comes from the fact that it's a two-way street. Just as a follower projects his past experiences onto his leader, the leader responds by projecting her past experiences back onto the follower. Freud called this phenomenon *countertransference* and saw it as one of the most serious obstacles to resolving patients' psychological issues. The danger was that a psychoanalyst would respond to a patient's transferential protestations of love by accepting that love as real. As a result, the analyst might assume the role of a protective parent, furthering the patient's dependency. Or the analysis might end in a love affair rather than a cure. Countertransference is at least as big a problem for business leaders as for psychotherapists. In his novel *Disclosure*, Michael Crichton describes how a ruthless and dishonest woman is promoted above a more qualified man because she reminds the CEO of a favorite daughter who was killed in an auto accident. The CEO does not see her as she is but responds to her as though she were his beloved daughter. It's often the case that a boss will favor a subordinate who shows him filial admiration.

Although strong transferences to a parental figure can hold an organization together, once the leader leaves, rivalries can fracture an organization. That's what happened with Freud himself and with other psychoanalytic organizations founded by charismatic leaders. As long as the competitive, ambitious analysts had to please the parental leader—there were women as well as men in this role—they cooperated with each other and kept sheathed the knives of sharp criticism. Once the parental founder died or left the scene, different training analysts, with their own transferential follower-students, let go of their aggressive inhibition; the result was the splintering off of different schools.[5] Of course, the same thing often happens in family firms after the founder father leaves the scene, but this relationship of children to a parent isn't transference. It's the real thing.

CHANGING TRANSFERENCES

The images we project from childhood are shaped by the family cultures we grew up with, a fact of particular importance today because more people now have family experiences that differ—sometimes quite radically—from what was long considered the norm. For an increasing number of people, the significant person from the past is not a parent but a sibling, a close childhood friend, or even a nanny. As we'll discuss later, the shift from parental to sibling transferences can fit organizations' needs for boundary-crossing project teams and networks. When managers at Boeing sought a leader for a software team that required a lot of collaboration among members, for instance, they joked about finding someone who was the fifth child in a family of nine siblings, someone who was used to mediating among brothers and sisters. In other words, the job called for a different kind of leadership than the traditional hierarchical boss would provide. Sibling leaders have to facilitate problem solving and build consensus. More than parental leaders, they invite collaboration and criticism. As we noted in chapter 2, they are part of the team, not above it.

Another complicating factor is that people can have multiple transferential relationships in an organization. It seems very likely to me that at GE over the past two decades, many employees not only had such relationships with their immediate bosses but also transferred childhood feelings onto Jack Welch, even though they had never met him. In cases of multiple transferences, both the immediate boss and the CEO might unconsciously be seen as father figures. But when this happens, the employee usually experiences the transferences differently. Typically he will relate to his immediate boss from the perspective of a child who is four, five, or even older. But he will regard the CEO as an infant would see an earlier father figure, who is more distant, protective, and all-knowing.

What is shaking things up for would-be leaders is that transferences no longer necessarily work in their favor. In other words, people no longer want to follow leaders because of a positive transference. That's because the changing structure of families—more single-parent homes, dual working parents, and kids growing up with less respect for authority—combined with changes in companies have begun to shape work environments in which people value traditional leadership less. The paternalistic model of leadership that flourished in the large monopolistic firms I worked with from the 1970s to the turn of the century has been frayed beyond recognition. Employees can no longer count on lifetime employment; even promised pensions may be lost as great companies like General Motors flounder and others downsize or restructure. Furthermore, like George Raymond, cited at the start of this chapter, knowledge workers often know more about their jobs than does the boss, whose role thus has to change from

the all-knowing parental figure to someone who clearly adds value for followers. Otherwise, the transference can be negative—the boss experienced
as an interfering, witless parent or the parent who isn't serving them very
well. This is the pattern that more and more describes the interactive social character in the knowledge workplace.

On the one hand, a positive transference can be a facilitator of followership and therefore a source of strength for leaders; on the other hand, it
can be a real threat to leaders because it distorts objectivity. This is why, as
we'll see, the kind of leaders we need will try to understand transference
and will work hard to help executive team members see one another as
they really are. The future of the organization may depend on this ability.
It's worth taking a moment, therefore, to examine the most common
types of transference. In doing so, we'll see more clearly the changing social character and how it can be led.

THE MOTHER TRANSFERENCE

To be sure, there are still many people in the workplace from traditional families, with a bureaucratic social character and traditional transferences to parentlike bosses. But even these people can have trouble with the increasing
diversity of bosses who are so different from their parents and who come in
all genders, races, and national origins. For example, Lydia Thomas, CEO
of Mitretek (now Noblis) in Virginia told me that employees often expect
her to be maternal. How does she respond? She tells them: "I'm not your
mother, but maybe, just maybe, I can be your friend."[6]

Maternal transference differs from paternal transference in that it usually draws on an earlier childhood relationship. Unlike the father, who is
often perceived as distant and detached, and whose approval is dependent
on performance, the mother is often seen both as an authority figure and
as a giver of unconditional love. She is the protective parent who gives us
life and showers us with support, but she is also the first person who says
no. It's the mother who weans us and, for the most part, who toilet trains
us. Later it is she who separates herself from us to go back to work or to
move on to other children. Not surprisingly, she is represented by both the

fairy godmother and the evil stepmother in children's stories. She is both deity and witch, and this deep divide in our psyches can play itself out to dramatic effect in business situations. One only has to look at the public's extreme reactions of love and hate toward Martha Stewart or Hillary Clinton to realize that women leaders stir up some of the most conflicted feelings in our unconscious.

Followers often have a hard time dealing with strong women precisely because they stimulate in subordinates the feelings of awe and fear that the mother once did. Children depend on the help and support of the all-powerful mother. They also want her to be happy and proud of them, and they feel deep guilt if they cause her suffering—a dynamic that some mothers use to control their kids. In my clinical work, I have found that, sometimes, beneath the guilt is the unconscious fear that the mother will cut off her life-giving nurturance.

A negative aspect of maternal transferences in the workplace is that they can generate greater expectations of empathy and tenderness from bosses than can realistically be met. Usually a boss's approval is more contingent, as it should be, on an employee's performance than on warm feelings. A colleague of mine saw this when he coached the forty-year-old vice president of a home-building company, who was told in no uncertain terms by the (male) president that he had handed in a bad proposal. The VP complained that the president should have shown more emotional intelligence in rejecting the proposal. When the president dismissed this complaint as "psychobabble," the VP grew irate. As my colleague immediately realized, the VP was projecting an inappropriate maternal transference. When the company's president didn't respond as the VP wanted, the VP reacted like a rejected child.

On the other hand, positive maternal transferences can give people a powerful sense of support. Think of Ronald Reagan, whose wife, Nancy, was like a protective tigress during and after his presidency; he called her "Mommy." Although his father was a failed shoe salesman, Reagan's own strong mother was a major reason for his self-confidence and success. However, even positive maternal transferences can have bad effects. A close friend of mine taught for eighteen years in a private school where most teachers had a maternal transference with the headmistress, who created a familylike culture. The teachers loved their boss and felt cared for and protected by her, but the warm feelings they had were not a good measure of her ability to perform. As she neared retirement, the school was in the red, and it became clear that the headmistress had done little either to evaluate and develop the teachers or to help them deal with discipline problems. While her successor was less comforting and more demanding, he succeeded in raising money from rich parents, improving teachers' salaries, and establishing rules that were followed.

THE FATHER TRANSFERENCE

The father transference was a powerful glue in an age when male managers brought up in traditional father-led families looked up to bosses in bureaucratic hierarchies. This dynamic was nicely illustrated for me by the top executive who told me his dream of walking into the powerful CEO's office and looking down in horror to see that he was wearing short pants. When I asked his association to the dream, he said, "That's the way I felt when my father was about to scold me for something I did wrong."

Most male CEOs in traditional organizations have consciously or unconsciously encouraged paternal transferences. They tend to show themselves in paternalistic settings—presiding over large meetings or smiling on videotapes—where the message is invariably reassuring, upbeat, hopeful. Even when times are bad, these leaders assure their followers that the downturn is temporary. The message is always the same: "Trust me to steer you through these troubled waters." The claim by CEOs that their success is based on their integrity or their concern for their people, rather than good business thinking, indicates their buy-in to belief in the power of transference.

Some companies go a great distance to promote practices that strengthen paternal transference, although they wouldn't call it that. In the early 1970s, when I worked with managers at IBM, they told me that the company had a strict rule against teams and against shared decision making. The rule had come directly from the legendary CEO, Tom Watson Sr., and it had the effect of forging a direct link between employees and their bosses. Whether he was aware of it or not, Watson was sanctioning paternal transference at IBM. It was further reinforced by the company's paternalistic commitment to employees that good performance ensured lifetime employment.

I saw similar dynamics at work when I was a consultant to the executive team of AT&T Communications during the 1980s. Most of the vice presidents there were uncritically worshipful of their business-unit presidents and the several CEOs who were making disastrous strategy moves—giving up cellular telephony, for instance, and losing billions in an effort to compete in computers. Instead of encouraging healthy debate about the future of the company, bosses expected—and rewarded—transferential veneration. One vice president stuck out because he didn't comply with this company culture. Although his division produced the best results within the long-distance business unit, the executive team didn't appreciate him—not only because his realistic attitude toward his business unit's president implicitly criticized the other vice presidents' transferential overvaluation of the leader, but also because he was an unconventional manager for AT&T at that time. Unlike the others, he delegated responsibility, didn't need to take credit for his division's success, and initiated new businesses. Ultimately, he took early retirement, frustrated by his failure to push his ideas through the bureaucracy.

From a social character point of view, this vice president was a mutant who didn't fit the bureaucratic world. In the new context of a collaborative knowledge workplace his behavior would have been better appreciated.

In my coaching practice, I've helped a number of executives whose careers have floundered because of their father transferences. Fred Wertheim, a brilliant technical manager in his thirties, had reached a level right below the top in two companies before being fired.[7] In each case, he idealized a boss who seemed to treat him like a favored son. However, when the boss didn't support his innovative ideas, Wertheim rebelled, tried to bypass the boss, and was reined in and fired. Once he understood and frustrated his need to attach himself to a father figure, his career took off.

THE SIBLING TRANSFERENCE

The father transference has also made people idealize presidents and ignore their faults. Presidents like Franklin D. Roosevelt and Ronald Reagan stimulated intense father transferences in their followers, but this type of transference has become weaker with subsequent presidents. Sibling transference made its debut in national politics with the first baby boomer U.S. president, Bill Clinton. People didn't relate to Clinton as a father—the kind of transference you might have expected with the nation's commander in chief—but rather as an admired older brother or "buddy" (as Clinton named his dog). Although he had his critics, Clinton was never really expected to be a model of good behavior. Unlike Lyndon Johnson, for whom Americans' positive attitude flipped when their paternal-transferential expectations were shattered by his inability to end the Vietnam War, Clinton was allowed to get away with his womanizing because he was perceived by much of the public as merely a naughty brother.

The growing power of sibling transference is a new phenomenon. I could only find one reference where Freud writes about a sibling transference, and that's based on a woman's experience of a ridiculing brother.[8] But Freud's patients came from traditional patriarchal families in which sibling rivals competed for paternal approval. He had no experience with Interactive families in which it's just as likely that parents compete for the affection of their kids—who are themselves more concerned with being popular with other kids.[9]

At work, the sibling or peer transference can be to someone who is like a helpful older sister or to peers who are like those kids who banded together to escape from authorities. Unlike parental transferences, which make people feel small and idealize authority, sibling transferences forge bonds of affection that allow for critical ribbing as well as mutual aid. Perhaps the huge popularity for this Interactive generation of J. K. Rowling's Harry Potter books owes something to the fact that Harry's parents are dead, his foster parents are abusive to him, and his close relations are siblinglike friends Hermione and Ron.

Transferential feelings about George W. Bush have changed over time. Before 9/11, his popularity was low and, like Clinton, he was seen as a brother or buddy figure, the kind of guy you'd feel comfortable having a beer with (except he didn't drink). His strong leadership response to the 9/11 national trauma triggered infantile paternal transferential feelings in many Americans, the kind of transference toward a protective leader provoked by pervasive anxiety about what might happen next. The Bush team reinforced these feelings politically by emphasizing continued threats by terrorists, ratcheting up the color-coded terror alert at key points in the 2004 reelection campaign, and contrasting the image of a resolute Bush, the nation's protector, to an image of his opponent, John F. Kerry, the unreliable flip-flopper on the invasion of Iraq. Of course, positive transferences can turn negative; the image of protector, forged in the anxiety after 9/11, was shattered by the Iraq fiasco and the inept response to Hurricane Katrina.[10]

DEALING WITH TRANSFERENCES

If all relationships are colored by transference, how can you as a leader ever know if your followers' relationships with you are real? The short answer is that you can't. Even the closest relationships combine objective reality with images and emotions carried over from the past, and there will never be any way around that. However, your followers' motivations for following don't have to be totally grounded in reality in order to work. What's more, there are ways of managing transferences that not only reduce the potential for negative transferences but actually increase the likelihood of positive ones.

A key way that leaders can influence their followers' positive and negative transferences is to become aware of their own transferences. The classic path to self-knowledge is introspection—the approach favored in psychology. But the trouble with introspection is that it can paralyze a leader, especially one with a strong obsessive bent. Endless self-analysis will prevent her from making the quick decisions any CEO must make. Consequently, many of the most effective leaders rely on an outsider to provide an incisive reality check. The "consultant" can be a member of the family—Bill Gates, for instance, routinely uses his wife as a sounding board. Other people turn to a longtime friend or associate; British tycoon Lord James Hanson relied heavily on his U.S.-based business partner Sir Gordon White. Increasingly, leaders also work with executive coaches to get an outside perspective on what is going on and to check their views of subordinates. I've played this role with a number of leaders.

To manage followers' transferences, as well as their own, leaders might even start by raising the level of awareness in the team, bringing the unconscious into awareness—which is what Freud is all about. This effort is especially important when staff members view a leader through different transferential lenses. In such a situation, a leader can deal with his followers' transferences by showing himself as he actually is, thereby demystifying his professional relationships. But to do this, he needs to have a lot of self-confidence. With some executive teams, I've used the personality questionnaire that can be found in my book *Narcissistic Leaders*.[11] When executives share their personality types and discuss how their personalities explain their behavior, this knowledge dilutes transferential projections.

But don't count on these steps to eliminate such projections. So long as they are unconscious, transferences remain strong. What's worse, the positive transference of the follower is likely to become negative before it disappears, as we have seen in public attitudes toward U.S. presidents.

Since subordinates will almost never lose all fear of a leader with power over them, childlike transferences—positive and negative—won't totally disappear. But increased candor and knowledge between leaders and followers can turn a leader from being a projection of hopes and fears into a flesh-and-blood role model that collaborators can emulate. Furthermore, the more people know each other, the harder it is to project, and the more obviously unreal the projections will be.

Leaders will never be able to completely control their followers' unconscious motivations—transference is too deeply ingrained in human nature for that. And no leader can fully understand all followers and collaborators. Yet if the organization is to be protected from itself, followers' projections and motivations must be channeled and managed. The challenge is especially urgent for today's organizations, in which an increasing diversity of people requires us all to move away from stereotyping and really understand differences in personality and ways of thinking and learning.

In this chapter, I've described how a powerful unconscious process, the father transference was the glue that tied followers to leaders in bureaucratic organizations. Leadership was relatively easy because leaders didn't have to understand a diverse bunch of followers. But as family dynamics and the mode of production have changed, leaders can no longer count on paternal transferences. Furthermore, as organizations become global, leaders are faced with a diversity of identities, cultural values, and personalities. To gain followers and collaborators, would-be leaders would be wise to understand their attitudes to work and leadership. In chapter 4, I'll describe the changing social character—the psychological frame that organizes all the other elements of personality so that people are motivated to do what they need to do to succeed in a particular socioeconomic context. Then, in chapter 5, I address the challenge of what we should know to understand people in the global knowledge workplace.

CHAPTER 4

From Bureaucratic Followers
to Interactive Collaborators

IMAGINE THAT YOU'RE a forty-five- or fifty-year-old executive, brought up in a traditional family, now leading knowledge workers in a global company. You think back to how you rose up ranks by helping your boss to succeed. And he in turn showed you the ropes and stuck out his neck to tout you for upper management. You now have some subordinates who want this kind of relationship, but you're not sure they're the best of the bunch. You're impressed by some of the younger men and women who are more entrepreneurial—they don't wait for you to give them objectives; they tell you what needs to be done. But while these go-getters work hard and well together, they don't seem committed to the company; you don't feel the kind of warm tie you felt with your boss. You're not sure they'd be good leaders.

I invite you to put yourself in these three types: the traditional executive and the bureaucratic and interactive subordinates. To create collaboration, as a leader you'll have to understand the strengths and weaknesses of each type of subordinate in order to bring out the best in both.

Social character is an elusive concept, because like individual personality, it refers to both conscious and unconscious aspects of human psychology. We are conscious of our values that give our lives meaning, our talents, and our identities or sense of self. The unconscious aspects have to do with emotionally charged attitudes or motivational systems—experiences from childhood that shape how we relate to others and what most drives us at school and work: what makes us want to do what we need to do in order to prosper in a particular social context.

In well-functioning people, the conscious and unconscious attitudes and values are for the most part connected; the total personality is in tune with the social character, and the social character fits a person's social role. For example, a key element of the bureaucratic social character is the hardworking obsessive personality that has internalized a dominant father figure from early childhood. Someone with this social character will consciously value order and expertise and will want to follow those managers who are like good fathers—demanding but caring mentors. While this person may be aware that he values a fatherlike leader, he's unaware that he's projecting an infantile image onto a manager who may not be very caring and, in doing so, making himself dependent on this manager, imputing knowledge and understanding the manager may not have and undervaluing his own competence.

For people with an interactive social character, the significant person from the past they project onto a leader is often not a parent but a sibling or a close childhood friend who might have brought them into a team or music group or initiated them into a new activity. To be sure, these ties may be weaker than traditional parental transferences. But for Interactives, raised in the new context where the traditional family is breaking down, parental images are not the dominating father or nurturing mother, but rather a more ambivalent figure who couldn't always be counted on to be there when needed.

Furthermore, a defining aspect of the interactive social character is its ability to easily take on new identities, like roles in a video game. That makes some of these people argue they're unique and can't be described in terms of a social character stereotype; they just adapt, whatever the situation. But Interactives are hardly conscious of how they adapt to different situations. It's the need to design themselves according to what sells on the personality market that differentiates the interactive social character from social characters of the past.

Compare the interactive social character to that of the Mexican *campesinos* Erich Fromm and I studied. Their social character wasn't adapted to the industrial world that was fast overtaking them. They were farmers and, with the exception of the hacienda peons who had been liberated by the Mexican Revolution of 1910–1920, their way of life was the same as that of their parents, grandparents, and great-grandparents. Their social character had not changed from that of their ancestors as far back as they could imagine. Their identity or sense of self was rooted in family and place.

Although villagers liked to think of themselves as unique individuals and even had a saying for it—"*Yo soy yo y no me parece a nadie*" (I am myself and I'm not like anyone else)—they had the social character shared with free peasants around the world that I described in chapter 1: cautious, independent, hoarding, patient, fatalistic, dignified, respectful, and egalitarian, but suspicious of anyone outside the family. There were two exceptions to this social character. One was the families of the landless hacienda peons. They had been so damaged by their virtual slavery that they didn't believe they could ever succeed as independent farmers. Even when given land, their passive, fearful, and submissive social character, which was a survival strategy in the hacienda where independence provoked beatings or worse, made them vulnerable to new entrepreneurial bosses. These bosses were the second exception, the productive narcissists who in less turbulent times seem out of sync with society, but who are the first to exploit new opportunities whenever there are dramatic changes in the mode of production.[1]

As noted in chapter 1, free peasants throughout the world share a social character; they are in many ways more alike in their attitudes to work and relationships than they are like city people in their own countries. And if we look back at the United States in the nineteenth century, not including the native Americans and slaves, the large majority of American families also made their living from farming (over 75 percent as late as 1870) as independent land owners. They expressed some of the attitudes of free, liberty-loving peasants throughout the world, but there were important differences, observed by the French visitor Alexis de Tocqueville in his tour of America in the 1830s. Many American farmers combined business with agriculture. They wanted to get rich, and a number of them were speculators, risk takers. Since most had fled oppressive European societies, they were more daring and less fatalistic than peasants whose families have been rooted to the same ground for centuries. Also, as Tocqueville noted, unlike Europeans (and most peasants throughout the world), Americans were educated for public affairs, encouraged to participate in a democracy.[2]

In contrast to the Mexican peasants, who were kept in check by a semifeudal society until the revolution of 1910, American entrepreneurs, some leaving farms for the cities, flourished in the late nineteenth century, exploiting the new technologies in transportation (railroads and cars), metals (steel), energy (oil), and communications (telegraph and telephone).

THE BUREAUCRATIC PERSONALITY

The outcome of these entrepreneurial ventures were great companies organized into bureaucracies with functional departments and specialized roles, regulated and controlled by rules and, increasingly, by professional managers. As Peter Drucker, the outstanding interpreter of management, wrote, bureaucratic management deals with the integration of people into a common venture, and so what managers do in Germany, in the United Kingdom, in Japan, in Brazil, is exactly the same, even though how they do it may be quite different.[3] And one thing they were doing was shaping the bureaucratic social character.

By the start of the twentieth century, many American families were raising their sons not to be independent farmers, but to be managers or government employees in bureaucracies, and their daughters to support their husbands' careers rather than their farms. That meant not only taking care of home and children, but also joining clubs and socializing with the wives of men who could help their husbands' careers.

To be sure, bureaucracies and bureaucrats had been around for a long time. From Mesopotamia, Egypt, and China, bureaucrats have served emperors, pharaohs, and kings. They've been tax collectors, scribes, clerics, or clerks in the court, custom house, or archives. Czar Nicholas I supposedly said, "Not I but ten thousand clerks rule Russia." As far back as we can see, large organizations have been run by bureaucrats.

And bureaucrats have long had a bad reputation, spread by novelists and social scientists as well as politicians. Nineteenth-century novelists pictured bureaucrats as dry, narrow, and heartless. In *Little Dorrit*, Charles Dickens describes Tite Barnacle, who runs the Office of Circumlocution with the mission of making sure that nothing ever happens for the first time. Writes Dickens, "He wound and wound folds of tape and paper round the neck of the country. His wristbands and collar were oppressive, his voice and manner were oppressive."[4] In Herman Melville's "Bartleby the Scrivener" (1853), the American bureaucrat becomes a zombie whose only vestige of humanity is to resist all orders, saying, "I would prefer not to."

And this view expressed the American stereotype. Even before the rise of big business and big government, Americans were especially opposed to bureaucracies and bureaucrats, and this view still distorts popular views of dedicated public servants and industrious managers. The negative attitude goes back to America's Calvinist founders, rebels against all forms of state and church authority—any institution that imposed intermediaries between citizens and elected representatives, between individuals and their God. The ideal for American Protestants was voluntary service to create community. When the new national government was formed in 1789, there was a small public service, with most jobs in finance, record keeping, and copying official documents. But liberty-loving Americans, who feared the kind of controlling bureaucracy that served George III, agreed that if they had to have one, they wanted a bureaucracy that served the people in a society of equals. And to a degree, they succeeded. In 1830, Tocqueville was impressed with the egalitarian behavior of American public servants.[5]

That all changed in the post–Civil War period. The bribe-taking customs official, land agent, and Indian agent soiled the relatively clean image of the American public servant. Reforms, beginning with merit system instituted by the Pendleton Civil Service Reform Act of 1883, somewhat improved the bureaucratic image, and new functions of science and technology increased the prestige of federal employees as the public recognized the civil servant's productive role in agriculture, public health, and education. But the negative stereotype persisted, even though bureaucracies in both government and business have been essential in organizing experts to create and protect our fabulously rich society.

Many social scientists as well as fiction writers have reinforced the negative image of the bureaucrat. Although the German sociologist Max Weber defined bureaucracy as a more just alternative to arbitrary rule and a spoils system, he also wrote that the iron cage of bureaucracy had clamped shut on the free spirit of the Enlightenment. He called bureaucrats "specialists without spirit, sensualists without heart," adding, "This nullity imagines that it has attained a level of civilization never before achieved."[6]

Other social scientists elaborated Weber's stereotype of bureaucrats. John Dewey wrote about their "occupational psychosis," an extreme version of Thorstein Veblen's concept of "trained incapacity"—the loss of ability to reason or think creatively that results from following rigid rules. Daniel Warnotte agreed and described bureaucrats as becoming intellectually and emotionally damaged by their roles, suffering "professional deformation."[7] Erich Fromm put it in psychoanalytic idiom, writing, "Roughly equivalent to the sadomasochistic character, in a social rather than a political sense, is the *bureaucratic character*. In the bureaucratic system every person controls the one below him and is controlled by the one above. Both sadistic and masochistic impulses can be fulfilled in such a system. Those below, the bureaucratic character will hold in contempt, those above he will admire and fear."[8]

Although the sociologist Robert Merton was less harsh in his judgment of the bureaucratic personality, he emphasized that bureaucratic structure reinforces a pecking order.[9] A psychologist might add that it formalizes the hierarchical motivational patterns found in all primates. However, Merton notes that bureaucracy, power, and privilege belong to the role, not the person, and rules can protect people lower down in the system from arbitrary authority.[10]

Merton does affirm that although the bureaucratic personality tends to be precise, reliable, efficient, and prudent, bureaucrats are or become timid and conservative, resisting change. This begs the interesting question of whether certain personalities are attracted to bureaucratic roles or whether the role shapes their personality. I believe it's a mixture of both, but the forging of the bureaucratic personality begins in the traditional family, long before entry into a bureaucracy, and some people develop a personality with strong needs for clarity, precision, and unambiguous authority that fits smoothly into bureaucratic structures.

It's notable that neither the novelists nor social scientists who have stereotyped the bureaucratic personality ever studied these people systematically. Of course, some of them, like Franz Kafka, experienced working in bureaucracies, but most have tended to be radical anarchists who naturally resent bureaucrats who make them conform to rules and regulations in universities and publishing companies.

Having worked as a consultant in government and industrial bureaucracies in twenty countries and in the process interviewed hundreds of managers and employees, I've found variations of the personality type. To be sure, as Drucker stated, managers, almost all of whom share a bureaucratic social character, have done the same kind of thing and have fit in more or less the same kinds of structures everywhere. However, as Drucker went on to state, they may play the role somewhat differently, because of variations in personality type and cultures.[11] Once you view bureaucrats from inside bureaucracies rather than from afar, you will see that while they fit Merton's stereotype in some essential ways—particularly, most find meaning in being respected as experts—there are variations in their intrinsic motivations at work. Some bureaucrats want to help or educate people; others want to defend the public; most take their greatest satisfaction in just doing their job well.[12]

A notable example of public-spirited bureaucrats were AT&T managers and technicians before the breakup of the Bell System. In the late 1970s, what most gave their work meaning was service to the public. And while over time their roles and rules came to be defined in an increasingly rigid way, whenever there was a disaster—hurricane, blizzard, or flood—they ignored the rules and worked together day and night until they had restored telephone service. When people were in need, the hierarchical system was suddenly transformed into a heterarchy where the person with the relevant competence took the lead and others were quick to follow.

Furthermore, even bureaucratic Americans never lose their love of liberty, and they always try to maximize their autonomy at work.[13] Note the popularity of Drucker's management by objectives (MBO) or the cartoonish version, *The One Minute Manager,* the pipe-smoking daddy figure who sits back after giving brief one-minute instructions or feedback and lets subordinate managers do their jobs their own way as long as they reach the agreed-on objectives.[14] But this approach no longer works in the increasingly interactive workplace, where autonomy can get in the way of the collaboration needed to achieve results.

The description of the bureaucratic personality by the novelists and sociologists was a caricature, an extreme example of the type, verging on psychopathology. It would be like describing the interactive personality in terms of Woody Allen's Zelig, a human chameleon, a plastic person without a center who shapes himself to fit whatever sells. Sure, there's truth to this description, but it's the extreme case. As we'll see, the positive potential of the interactive social character supports a more collaborative community at the workplace.

FROM BUREAUCRATIC TO INTERACTIVE
SOCIAL CHARACTER

By caricaturing the bureaucrat, looking with disdain at the conformity and self-importance of the organization man, the critics were distancing themselves from this social character, perhaps even projecting away aspects of themselves that clashed with the ideal of a free, independent people (table 4-1 displays the values associated with the bureaucratic and interactive characters). Who of us in modern industrial society has escaped a socialization process in schools and workplaces where we've had to play a role in bureaucracy, to think and act as bureaucrats?[15] To some extent, the bureaucratic social character fit all middle-class Americans growing up in the age of the manufacturing mode of production, and especially those

TABLE 4-1

From bureaucratic to interactive social character

	Bureaucratic	Interactive
Ideals	• Stability • Hierarchy/autonomy • Organizational loyalty • Producing excellence	• Continual improvement • Networks/independence • Free agency • Creating value
Social character	• Inner-directed • Identification with paternal authority • Precise, methodical, obsessive	• Interactive • Identification with peers, siblings • Experimental, innovative, marketing
Socioeconomic base	• Market-controlling bureaucracies • Slow-changing technology • National markets • Employment security • Traditional family	• Entrepreneurial companies • Internet • New technologies • Global markets • Employment uncertainty • Diverse family structures

who were raised in traditional families. Yet, unlike some of the Asians I've interviewed who are fully satisfied to submit to paternal leaders, many of the Americans I've talked to feel conflicted about their submission to bureaucratic bosses, even though this conflict may not be fully conscious.

I learned about this attitude when studying managers in high-tech companies. In 1969, I was given the opportunity to get a grant from the Harvard Program on Technology and Society to study the people creating new technology—how their personalities influenced their effectiveness and the products they built and in turn how their work shaped the further development of their personalities, especially their values. However, to get the grant, I had to gain entry into companies and permission to interview managers, scientists, and engineers. At that time, I was spending the year as a fellow at the Center for Advanced Study in the Behavioral Sciences at Stanford. While there, I met a first-level manager of a large high-tech company who liked the idea of the study, but he said he was too low in the hierarchy to invite me in. He then introduced me to his manager, who also liked the idea of the study, and who also said he was too low in the hierarchy to invite me in. But he connected me with the human resources vice president, who said that while my project was interesting, only a group vice president could invite me in. He introduced me to one whom he thought might be open to the idea.

The group vice president listened as I described how I'd do the study and offered to share the results with him. Then he said, "I've never met a psychoanalyst before. Tell me something about myself that I don't know and I'll let you come in and do your study." I said, "I'm not a mind reader, but I can tell you something about yourself you may not know if you're willing to take a Rorschach test, to describe what you see in a set of ten inkblots." He agreed and took the test.

Let me note that I had spent many years learning to use the Rorschach both as a diagnostic tool and a research instrument for interpreting emotional attitudes and cognitive style. What I saw in the vice president's responses was deep anger at having to submit to higher-ups and a passionate drive to be free—in other words inner rebellion against his bureaucratic situation. Although this was our first meeting and he had said nothing about himself, I told him what I saw. "OK," he said, "you're in." Obviously, I didn't tell him something that he didn't "know" or else he would not have been so quick to accept my interpretation. Rather, I was affirming feelings that he had never talked about, maybe never even admitted to himself. He decided to let me in because he felt known and thought that he could learn from me about the people he managed and maybe his bosses as well.

The Gamesman, the book that resulted from my study of 250 managers in ten technology companies, was based on interviews lasting from three hours to, in a few cases, more than twenty hours. In it, I described a variation of the bureaucratic personality then rising to leadership positions in these innovative and fast-paced companies.[16] I wrote that the new type—unlike the security-seeking bureaucratic type described by William H. Whyte Jr. in his book *The Organization Man*—was excited by the chance to cut deals and gamble.[17] While the gamesman wasn't a visionary who created new industries, he was skilled at organizing teams and found his greatest satisfaction at work in winning. As the executive who invited me in put it, "Our main ability is that we know how to win at this game of business."[18]

The gamesman became a model for managers in fast-paced competitive companies. Like Jack Welch, who explicitly described business as a game and compared his role to a manager of a professional baseball team, executives in large bureaucratic companies tried to put a new face on their bureaucratic image.[19] After the breakup of the Bell System in 1984, AT&T's motto of universal service was replaced by the goal of winning. However, the attempt by AT&T executives to look different, aided by legions of PR advisers, didn't make them any less bureaucratic in their behavior. The real gamesmen in the Silicon Valley companies that tried to partner with AT&T gave up in frustration with the bureaucrats who over-analyzed everything and then made some disastrous decisions that eventually brought the company close to ruin.[20]

In the 1980s, I first interviewed men and women at work who fit neither the classic bureaucratic type nor the gamesman variation.[21] These people had an instinctual dislike for bureaucracy and bureaucratic bosses. They saw themselves as businessmen and -women, not bureaucrats. They were attracted to work where they were clearly adding value for customers and also developing their own business competence. Unlike the bureaucratic types who sought *autonomy* within the organization, these interactive types strove to maintain *independence* from the company by constantly sharpening their marketable skills.

Unlike the bureaucratic social characters who want a good father–like boss who gives them objectives, leaves them alone to achieve these objectives, and then evaluates them, Interactives typically work in teams where everyone is expected to push each other to get results.

People with the interactive social character fit naturally into projects and teams, but only if they are treated as equals and have a say in how things are done. Unlike bureaucrats who focus on meeting objectives set by the boss, Interactives think business: who are my customers and how can I add measurable value for them? Bosses who don't help to get the job done are just roadblocks or worse.

Like any social character, Interactives have both strengths and weaknesses that make them hard to lead. In *Got Game? How the Gamer Generation Is*

Reshaping Business Forever, John C. Beck and Mitchell Wade report on attitudes to work and leadership of business professionals who've grown up with video games. That included over 80 percent of people age thirty-five and under in 2004, presumably in 2007 a larger percentage of that age group is working in the businesses surveyed by the authors.[22] The gamer attitudes they report fit closely with my own observations of the interactive social character:

- They find meaning at work in adding value for customers.

- They want their rewards based on measurable results, not position or evaluations by bosses.

- They're so confident of their skills that they believe they don't have to work as hard as other people. They think highly of themselves and are quick to label themselves as "experts."

- They see business like a video game in which they can always find a way to win, and they're optimistic they'll succeed. Failure is just a learning experience.[23]

- They see leaders as useless, even evil. Even in MMORPGs (massively multiplayer online role-playing games), everyone can take a turn at leading. It's a matter of coordinating the roles: "The game generation believes in skill, they don't believe in following orders."[24]

- They shift roles and identities easily, depending on what's required in the game. And they agree with the statement "the best way to handle people is to tell them what they want to hear." State the authors, "It's almost as if they see life as a game, and themselves as skillful players . . . A strong majority of the game generation agrees with the statement, 'I can control the way I come across to people, depending on the impression I wish to make.' "[25] This is a good description of the marketing personality.

For Interactives, parents served as enablers and cheerleaders. At work, Interactives want continual feedback from bosses; they want to know how they're doing. But since they don't identify with father figures and distrust parental-type relationships at work, seeing them as stifling independence, they resist the kind of mentoring enjoyed by the bureaucrats. An interactive banking executive told me she didn't want her boss as a mentor or coach, because she didn't want him to know any more than he already did about her doubts or weaknesses. She wanted to be able to hire a coach she could fire if she didn't get the help she wanted. Interactives only accept help from people who don't lay on them a "heavy emotional trip."[26] Also, let's not forget that many Interactives can mentor their elders, particularly when it comes to technology.

Interactive attitudes are spreading throughout the industrialized world. In the 1970s, when I met with a group of bureaucratic Volvo managers, they defined themselves in terms of the company. The company determined their roles and goals, and they didn't question the company's values. They served the company loyally; they were proud to be Volvo men. In contrast, I recently spoke with young Swedish entrepreneurs, both men and women, who demand that companies implement their own values. Otherwise, they're not interested in working for that company. The identity or sense of self of interactive individuals remains separate from the company unless that company becomes an expression of themselves, of their values.

The interactive social character has been formed in a world in which we must adapt to constant change, and we can't count on stable institutions to take care of us. Corporate promises have evaporated with corporate bankruptcy. People succeed and prosper by staying in competitive condition, physically as well as mentally, and by building their own support networks at work and in personal relationships, like the women in the popular HBO program *Sex and the City*.

Despite insecurity at home and at work, the interactive social character has grown up in a richer and more abundant society than has ever existed. Interactive individuals want to enjoy life wherever they are. They want excitement, fun, and adventure even when they're competing, as in TV shows like *The Apprentice* and *Survivor*. But as mentioned in chapter 1, the psychopathology of the interactive social character is the obverse of its strengths; the interactive person can be emotionally detached, unwilling to commit, superficial, disloyal, and centerless. And the question remains of how Interactives will perform in leadership roles when they need to take charge.

In the appendix, I describe what I've learned about the different development patterns of the bureaucratic and interactive social characters from infancy to old age. Clearly, understanding these social character differences is essential for gaining followers and collaborators in the knowledge workplace. But it's not enough. To lead in the global enterprise you'll have to know even more about people. In the next chapter, I'll build on what we've learned about social character and transference to focus in on the most important competence for leaders in the knowledge workplace—understanding people.

CHAPTER 5

Understanding People in the Knowledge Workplace

WHY HAS IT BECOME SO IMPORTANT for leaders to understand the people they lead? Why has it become essential for leaders to develop their Personality Intelligence? I believe the answer has to do with the new context of the leader-follower relationship.

THE LEADER–FOLLOWER RELATIONSHIP

As a framework, I've found it useful to think about this relationship in terms of four categories, which are based on the interaction between essential motivations of the leader and the led (see figure 5-1). A leader may be motivated by a desire for the common good or by a drive for personal power. To be sure, motives may be mixed, and leaders who hunger for personal power over others generally cloak their motives in promises and visions of the common good. But events usually reveal which motive is dominant, especially when they conflict. In turn, followers follow either because they want to follow or because they have to follow the leader. These dichotomies give us four possibilities: One, people want to follow a power-driven leader; two,

FIGURE 5-1

Why and how do people follow the leader?

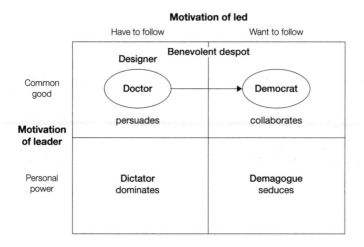

they feel they have to follow a dictator; three, a leader who is working for the common good has resistant followers; and four, people want to follow a leader who is trying to achieve a common good.

Let's focus on each of the four alternatives. Where people want to follow a leader who's out for personal power, they get a seductive demagogue like Napoleon, who appeared at first to be a liberator but ultimately ruined France in his compulsive drive for conquest. Hitler is another example. He gained power with a promise of German glory, but when faced with defeat, he ordered Albert Speer to destroy the country to punish the German people for failing him. In a less drastic way, people can be taken in by political or organizational leaders who promise to protect them, who trigger transferential idealization, but who prove to be just out for themselves. Contrast these power-driven leaders with George Washington, who, like the Roman leader Cincinnatus, could have stayed in power, but gave it up to return to his farm.

Where people *have* to follow a power driven leader, they are oppressed by a dictator whom they follow out of fear. He could be a Machiavellian prince, a Saddam Hussein, or a Stalin. On a smaller scale, these dictators might be bureaucratic or even psychopathic bosses. Who among us hasn't had to suffer a dictator at school or work?

Where a leader who wants the common good has unwilling or luke-warm followers, we find an interesting variety of leadership possibilities. Consider a company that needs to change—to adapt to new markets, face competition, improve results, innovate—but has employees who resist change. One way to deal with this is by engineering change without ever relating directly to followers. Well-meaning managers avoid the challenge of leadership by designing new structures, a slimmed-down workforce, and new processes as well as incentives that force change, as Mark Hurd did at NCR and then at HP. Or they may act more like diplomats who arrange mergers or sell off parts of the company, like Richard Parsons at Time Warner or Howard Stringer at Sony.

A hands-on leader of resistant followers could be a benevolent despot who forces change with both positive and negative incentives, rewarding those who change and threatening to fire those who won't budge. The despot may even trigger a positive infantile transference in bureaucratic followers, and if he produces great results, the resisters may even become willing followers. In some contexts, like traditional Chinese culture, this type of leader may be welcomed.

But in the new context of knowledge work and Interactives, the leader of a resistant workforce is better advised to be more like a kind of doctor who educates and persuades patients to change behavior in their own self-interest; who makes it clear that unless patients follow a new diet and start to exercise, the doctor will stop treating them; and who explains fully the reasons for change, answers all questions, and responds to all doubts. The goal of the doctor is to make patients into collaborators who manage their own conditions. Likewise, the goal of the organizational doctor is to become a more interactive leader, the "democrat" who collaborates with the people who share the same view of the common good. To do that, the doctor-leader both teaches and institutes learning processes. This may be the only way to engage wholeheartedly the new generation of profession-als in a common purpose. We'll find this to be the case in many examples presented in this book.

Ideally, the leaders we need will be democratic, in the sense that they'll have the full support of their follower-collaborators. But to create a positive future, we'll also need many skillful doctors without illusions about what it takes to become a true interactive leader. And in the context of the global economy and knowledge workplace, they'll have to understand potential collaborators, by developing their Personality Intelligence.

This kind of understanding was not so important in the early 1970s, when I was hired by B. O. Evans, the innovative president of IBM's Systems Development Division, to teach six of IBM's highest-potential managers to understand themselves and others. Evans, known for his unique skill in getting difficult people to work together, hoped I could teach these managers to do what he did intuitively. I tried to teach the group in a seminar, but instead they asked me to meet with them individually. That was because they didn't want to expose themselves to people they saw as rivals. Possibly, they might at some future time either manage or report to one of the others, meaning they would either be giving or receiving commands. But they foresaw no need to collaborate with each other.

Evans and a few other executives interested in understanding people were ahead of their time. In the age of industrial bureaucracies and national companies, understanding people wasn't essential. To lead the bureaucratic social character, managers were trained to present themselves as paternal and reassuring, to communicate clearly and to recognize and reward good behavior. And they didn't need training to understand people they thought were just like themselves. To choose successors, executives typically tapped clones. They were all men. At AT&T they wore suits size 42 long; at Ford, they were shorter, just like the Fords.

Many companies remain stuck in a bureaucratic mind-set. But in the late 1980s and early 1990s, some leaders of knowledge companies, especially those in the global arena, decided that to create collaboration, they needed to understand the diverse mix of people in their organizations. It started with executive teams, especially in global companies.

At the end of the 1980s, I was hired by Göran Lindahl, then the hard-charging head of Transmission and Distribution for ABB, the global energy giant, which had just been formed by a merger between Asea, a Swedish company, and Brown Boveri, a Swiss company. There were also large departments in Germany and the United States. Lindahl was concerned because managers from these four countries were complaining about each other, and collaboration was breaking down. What was causing the anger and distrust? Lindahl asked me to find out; as I'll describe later in this chapter, it was due to national variations in the social character, which when understood and discussed by the top managers from these countries, improved trust and collaboration.

In the 1990s and the beginning of the twenty-first century, the corporate leaders who hired me wanted help in understanding themselves, team members, and candidates for top jobs. At first, I used the Myers-Briggs test, an easy nonthreatening way to show differences in the way people think (extrovert versus introvert, sensing versus intuitive, feeling versus thinking, perceiving versus judging).[1] When members of executive teams wanted to understand each other even more, I developed a questionnaire that shows the different personality types based on psychoanalytic theory discussed later in this chapter. Team members shared their profiles and discussed how understanding each other could improve communication and collaboration.[2]

What had changed to increase interest in understanding people? Why did emotional intelligence suddenly become so popular? The answer, I believe, is that in the advanced knowledge workplace, knowledge workers are being forced to collaborate, and it goes a lot better if they understand each other.

The term collaboration has a shady past. In World War II, it meant helping the enemy; a collaborator was a traitor. But now the term has reverted to its Latin root *co-labore*, working together, and, according to a recent IBM global survey of five hundred CEOs collaboration has become the major challenge of the knowledge workplace.[3] Consider the different kinds of collaboration that knowledge leaders need to create: across departments for concurrent engineering and to produce technical solutions for business customers; projects within departments where designers have to interact to develop complex software; partnering between and among companies and governments; and all kinds of collaboration across cultures.[4]

To facilitate collaboration, some companies are trying to shake up bureaucracies with a strong dose of interactive medicine. To move the IBM culture, which was so rooted in clear lines of command and individualism, CEO

Sam Palmisano has organized "jams," online town meetings to get IBMers interacting. The jam on values in 2003 triggered so much criticism of management that some feared a corporate revolution. But by staying the course, Palmisano gained trust that, at least, IBMers wouldn't be punished for candor.[5] In the 2006 jam on innovation, seventy thousand employees of IBM and seventy invited partners offered ideas on four topics: transportation, health, the environment, and finance. These ideas will be organized into projects. IBMers tell me the culture is changing. When they need help, they can call on experts in other areas who respond. Collaboration is reinforced with "thanks awards," symbolic recognition with shirts, umbrellas, backpacks, and the like embossed with the company logo. Any employee can give six of these "thanks" a year.

Interactive jams, even global virtual teams, don't require that people know each other. In fact, there's some evidence that people in virtual global product development teams brainstorm better when they don't see or know each other.[6] The reason may be that when participants are unseen and anonymous, the flow of ideas isn't blocked by quizzical or disapproving looks from the boss. But you can't escape into anonymity or an assumed identity when you're working closely with others face-to-face, especially in a leadership team.

No amount of jam or any other online interactive activity teaches you to understand the people you need to work with. That requires a different kind of learning. Emotional intelligence is part of it, but not enough to understand and predict how others will behave in key roles.

What does it mean to know another person? Ideally, it means describing the person behind the *persona*, the mask of self-presentation, much in the way a good novelist or playwright does. Few people have that valuable skill. For most of us, even recognizing the persona is a step ahead of assuming others are just like us.

You will better understand people in the knowledge workplace if you learn to focus on four conceptual variables that will strengthen your Personality Intelligence. They are:

- Identities

- Social character and its cultural variations

- Personality types

- Intellectual skills

These different concepts are windows on the self—the person—including values, emotional attitudes, characteristic ways of working and relating to others, the identities we give to ourselves, and our ways of acquiring, retaining, and transforming information. Of course, we can't see these aspects of our brains and personality directly, but we can observe patterns of behavior and interpret them in terms of personality type and social character. These concepts are useful only when they equip us to predict and understand attitudes and behavior. We may talk about our sense of identity and, to some extent, our values. But like transferential attitudes, part of personality may not be conscious to us, even though a trained observer can see it in action. Yet we can develop our Personality Intelligence to become more alert to patterns of behavior, and that starts with making use of these concepts.

IDENTITIES—HOW WE ARE DEFINED AND DEFINE OURSELVES

We'd like to be able to define ourselves, to decide how we'll be seen. But from an early age, others define us by how we look and where we're from. For example, despite growing up with a white mother and grandparents, Barack Obama learned that the world defined him as black. Our identity starts at an early age with our physical characteristics: sex, age, size. Later, talents and achievements are added. As we grow older, we internalize the identity given us and start to define ourselves. Our cultures influence how we shape our identity. In the preindustrial era, people identified with family above all, then with place and religion. We've seen that in Iraq, with the breakdown of the state, people have reverted to family and religious identities as their only refuge in the midst of civil war.

In the United States today, we take our national identity as a given. We're Americans, and we feel a sense of identity with other Americans when we meet them abroad. This feeling can get even stronger if they are from the same area or went to the same schools. But historically, our national identity is not so old. After the revolutionary war, many in the former colonies only reluctantly accepted the new American identity, and the Civil War of 1860 showed that Southerners were ready to discard it. But just as national identity was threatened by Civil War, so was it strengthened by World Wars I and II, when all Americans shared a powerful purpose.

Despite creating the EU, people in those European nations resist a common identity. In some European countries—for example, Italy with its North-South differences and Spain with its Basques and Catalans—regional identities still compete strongly with national identity.

It was in the bureaucratic-industrial age that people started to identify with organizations, especially the companies, unions, and professional associations that gave them a sense of security and status. Asked to describe themselves, managers of major companies would invariably mention the company (e.g., "I'm an IBMer"). Of course, family, place, and religion remained part of their identities, and identifications were sometimes expanded further to memberships in fraternities, service organizations, schools, and colleges, especially those that added to the person's sense of importance.

Compared with the interactive social character whose sense of identity can be protean, the bureaucratic social character is strongly attached to its identities. It doesn't bother Interactives to shift identities like roles in video games. Rather than identifying with a company, they identify with a project or mission, a sport, or consumer group. They practice shaping identities that will get them a job or a date on the Internet.

The identities of the bureaucratic social character are essentially individualistic and vertical, like military ranks, buttressed by identifications with parents and authorities. Interactive identities are more fluid and horizontal, moving among and between identifications with siblings and peers, often combining meaning with self-interest, cultural identification with political agenda.

However, in this new age of diverse identities at work, we risk confusing cultural-social character differences with identity interest groups. Kwame Anthony Appiah, a Princeton philosopher, points out that identity groups can include people from very different cultures and a variety of individual values. He argues "that the diversity that preoccupies us is really a matter not so much of cultures as of identities."[7] But identities differ according to how deeply they are rooted in our personalities, and a characteristic of Interactives is their ability to shift identities in different settings. Sometimes, people choose to belong to an identity group at work, mainly because the group promises to gain privileges for them. Unions are prime examples of identity groups that members choose to join, as are professional societies. People may choose to identify themselves with ethnic groups like Hispanics, a name that corresponds to no particular country and that covers people who don't even come from the same culture or even necessarily speak Spanish. In terms of social character, a Mexican villager may be more like a Serbian or Indian villager than like a professional from Mexico City or Havana. But people with a family background from a Latin American country can choose whether or not to take on an Hispanic identity, especially if that gives them some advantage at work.

By satisfying the demands of identity groups, leaders don't necessarily gain willing followers. But if these identities are not respected, leaders will be less willingly followed, possibly resisted. In a democratic society, we enjoy the right to have multiple loyalties, based on multiple identifications, while in an autocratic society, and in some companies that are autocratically led, those in power are threatened by loyalties to any group other than the regime.

Keep in mind that identities can be extremely powerful when attached to deep human needs for respect and support from people we can trust to care about us. Identities can be powerful motivators because they provide meaning for our lives. This is especially true when we feel that an identity determines our friends and enemies. When an identity gives us a feeling of security and pride, any attack on identity is a blow to self-esteem, even a threat to survival. Clearly, clashes between religious, racial, and clan identities continue to ignite bloody conflicts, especially in those societies that have not developed institutions that provide security and strengthen trust. Understanding people must include their identities. Otherwise, as in Iraq, we can blunder into identity wars.

SOCIAL CHARACTER DIFFERENCES—HOW THOSE
OF USE FROM THE SAME CULTURE ARE ALIKE

Once you are aware of the descriptions, it's relatively easy to tell the difference between peasant, bureaucratic, and interactive social characters. However, as in the case of ABB, cultural variations of social character are not so obvious, and they can cause misunderstandings in a global company.

To understand these differences and the reasons why they caused conflict, I asked managers from Sweden, Switzerland, Germany, and the United States to tell me about how they worked together, their relationships with customers, how they made decisions, and how they compared themselves to managers in the other countries. It turned out that while they all had the same formal organizations, each national company had different informal organizations and decision-making practices reflecting cultural variations of the bureaucratic social character. These differences caused misunderstandings and also negative stereotyping. For example, the Germans saw the Swedes as lacking integrity and concern for quality, and the Swedes viewed the Germans as contentious and autocratic.

In fact, the Swedes believed in consensus, and to make sure everyone was singing from the same hymn book, they held frequent off-site meetings. Managers got to know each other well, even called each other "brother," so they were less likely to disagree with each other. Sometimes spouses and children joined these gatherings, tightening the bonds. But the Germans saw all this sociability as a dangerous form of seduction that undermined objectivity and integrity. If you socialized outside of work, you'd be less likely to shoot down faulty arguments; you'd want to please each other. German managers valued objectivity above sociability, and they maintained very formal relations, using the formal *sie* form of address with each other after years of working together; the Swedes, of course, used the intimate *du* as soon as they met. While the Swedes avoided conflict and kept quiet even if not fully convinced the boss was right, the Germans valued tough, sometimes contentious debate, as long as it was based on facts, not position in the hierarchy. However, once the German *meister*—always a respected technical expert—made a decision, everyone marched in step. For them, this was not autocratic, but both reasonable and effective.

Swedish avoidance of conflict sometimes led to decisions made bureaucratically, based on hierarchical position rather than an open clash of fact-based views. Although they appeared more autocratic, the Germans were arguably the more democratic decision makers, since the *meister*'s decision was transparent, based on a clear business logic and all available information.

Swedish and German approaches to product development were also different, owing to their economic histories. Since much of their business went to Middle Eastern, Latin American, and Southeast Asian countries, where the products had to withstand the heat and be easy to repair by local people, the Swedes were used to producing robust, easy-to-service electrical-energy products that could withstand rough climates. Furthermore, since the Swedish engineers knew a lot more about the products than did their customers, they decided what the customer needed. They joked that if the customer is king in the industrialized world, the king is the customer in some of the Middle Eastern countries they served.

The Germans produced more complex products for domestic use, and their customers were typically electrical engineers with advanced degrees who knew as much as they did about the products. They were producing for a highly developed industrial infrastructure rather than a developing country, and the keys to success were zero outages and continual quality improvement, which is a strong German value.

No wonder Swedes and Germans misunderstood each other. And both distrusted the Swiss, complaining that the Swiss would make agreements and then renege on them. Furthermore, Swiss costs were out of control. It turned out that the reason Swiss managers sometimes asked to change an agreement stemmed from the fact that they were all in the army reserve, and a subordinate at work might be a superior at the military summer camp. It was best to get agreement from everyone to avoid making powerful enemies, and sometimes after an agreement had been made by one manager, another found out and disagreed, and they reconsidered the issue. As for costs, the

Swiss were used to customizing expensive energy solutions for different cantons, and as with Swiss banks and hotels, Swiss quality is expensive.

The Americans were different from the others. They had factories that mass produced products for very competitive markets. Their margins were thin, and they focused on cost control. Organized in traditional industrial bureaucratic hierarchies with much less job security than the Europeans, the Americans were politically acute about who they needed to follow. And in this Swedish-controlled company, they did not make waves. They were nobody's problem.

By describing and discussing these differences, ABB management cleared up a lot of distrust and miscommunication. They clarified how decisions should be made, and they encouraged more of the German style of open debate, which moved them toward an interactive style of collaboration.

European managers, especially those at the top who still have the bureaucratic social character, continue to struggle with cultural differences. A *Financial Times* survey of two hundred CEOs in France, Germany, and the United Kingdom reported that German managers, just like the ones at ABB, supported constructive conflict. French CEOs boasted of making decisions without having to listen to subordinate views.[8] This is in the tradition of French graduates of *grandes écoles,* especially École Nationale d'Administration, who move between the public and private sectors with an attitude of superiority and entitlement. Another group of French CEOs ran family firms, in which they didn't even have to answer to outside directors. However, even if French CEOs wanted to be more collaborative, they'd have a hard time getting subordinates to play along. One of my students at the executive program run by the Säid Business School at Oxford moved from IBM, where he led a collaborative team, to become CEO of a French company. Even though he asked his direct reports to call him by his first name, they insisted on "*Monsieur le président.*"

The U.K. CEOs cited in the survey claimed they liked to be challenged. In my experience in the United Kingdom, however, this depends on how secure they feel. Certainly, unlike the French, they don't want to look like autocrats; and like the Dutch, the Brits enjoy making fun of puffed-up leaders.

Lindahl later sent me to nine Asian countries to find out how local managers and expatriates viewed strategy, organization, and one another.[9] Besides asking about these factors, I asked two other questions: "What is your view of a good manager?" and "What is your view of a good father?" The answers were always related—a good manager was similar to a good father. But there was a sharp divide between the responses of Westerners and those of many Asians.

The Westerners, Americans and Scandinavians in particular, viewed good fathers and good managers as people who were helpful when needed but who generally allowed their followers autonomy. By contrast, the Asians— especially the ethnic Chinese in Taiwan, Singapore, and Indonesia—wanted a father-manager who protected them and taught them: a benevolent despot. In return, they would give the leader complete loyalty and obedience. Not surprisingly, these Asians also experienced Western leaders as bad parents who woefully neglected their children. However, young managers from Beijing, where the Cultural Revolution broke traditional family patterns, responded more like Interactives. They described the ideal leader as a good basketball coach who put people into the right roles, promoted teamwork, and knew how to adapt strategy to changing competition.[10]

Differences between the West and much of the East are further amplified by the relative decline of parental authority in the United States and Western Europe. Managers from many Asian and Eastern European companies still come from traditional families, and thus tend to develop paternal transferences—so they often find it difficult to deal with American organizations increasingly motivated by maternal and sibling transferences. And Westerners often fail to appreciate Asian and East European organizations' need for leaders who reward loyalty with paternal interest.

A huge challenge for global managers is leading people you don't see operating in different time zones, many speaking broken English and with different cultural values. The Interactives who from age ten or eleven have been in touch with global correspondents will, I believe, be a lot more comfortable with global management. Furthermore, global business, the Internet, and video games are creating common values at work and are shaping the interactive social character. One Interactive software expert remarked in a seminar I attended that leaders should forget trying to deal with different values and instead get everyone to sign on to a common purpose. That's good advice.

Meanwhile, researchers try to provide global managers with guidebooks on cultural differences. The pioneer in this field is Geert Hofstede, who in the 1970s surveyed employees of IBM in sixty-four countries. While Hofstede reported suggestive differences on four (later increased to five) dimensions, he advised that "to understand management in a country, one should have both knowledge of and empathy with the entire local scene." Hofstede cites history and novels to describe the context of the dimensions he used, a good practice.[11]

When I consulted in Finland to Nokia, Cultor, and Ahlstrom, I was advised to read *The Unknown Soldier,* a novel by Väinö Linna, about two officers in the Finnish war with Russia. One is distant and arrogant, hated by the soldiers who only grudgingly follow him. The other is modest and brave, lives just like the troops, leads them into battle, and is unquestionably followed. This is the ideal for a Finnish CEO, to be a role model not a father figure, but it presents problems when an admired leader is followed without question and followers don't disagree with the boss, even when they think he's wrong.

Hofstede recognizes the limitations of findings based on responses to surveys. By themselves, they lack context, and none of the studies I've seen takes account of identity differences or social character differences among subcultures within countries. Furthermore, a statistically significant correlation may explain only a small percentage of the variance in the responses to survey questions. (These studies report product-moment correlations that when squared show the percentage of the variance explained. For example, a correlation of 0.5 may be highly significant, meaning it could occur by chance alone less than once in one hundred samples or more, but only accounts for 25 percent of the variance, leaving 75 percent unaccounted for). If this seems too academic, we can just say that these correlations are suggestive about cultural differences but leave much unexplained. And it bears repeating that correlations don't prove causality.

PERSONALITY TYPES—HOW WE ARE LIKE MANY OTHER PEOPLE

Social character is that part of learned personality shared by people in a culture or social class. To understand the people you work with and determine which roles they'll best fit, you'll have to focus in on individual personality.

Companies typically seek employees who demonstrate behavioral strengths, positive patterns of behavior. The Gallup organization offers a useful inventory of strengths that combine elements of genetic and learned traits and talents.[12] But these behavioral traits, like "achiever," "command," creating "harmony," "woo" (win others over), or being "strategic" can be performed in different ways with different motivations. For example, an achiever can be an obsessive perfectionist aiming to be the best at his game, like Tiger Woods, or someone driven to change the world with his products, to create a new game, like Steve Jobs. And a skillful wooer may be either caring, seductive, or inspirational. It's good to focus on strengths, but we increase our Personality Intelligence by understanding the anatomy of these strengths.

There is little agreement among psychologists about how best to describe individual personality. Each psychological theory views personality from a somewhat different angle. That's understandable, since we are dealing with interpretations of complex behavior patterns, emotional attitudes, and experience. However, psychologists do agree about five genetically influenced personality traits that can be observed from infancy on. These traits of temperament, called the Big Five, are:

- Openness to experience, curiosity, interest in variety versus sameness

- Agreeableness versus suspiciousness

- Emotional stability versus emotional instability or neuroticism

- Conscientiousness, self-discipline, sticking with a task versus being easily distracted

- Extraversion, sociability versus introversion[13]

Another approach to personality based on C. G. Jung's theories describes "archetypes" that leaders can take on, such as "wise king," "magician," "nurturer," or "warrior."[14] (Franklin Delano Roosevelt thought of himself at different times as a magician, a warrior, and a quarterback.) Some of these archetypes are similar to roles in the MMORPGs like *World of Warcraft* so popular with Interactives. These roles appeal more or less to the different personality types observed by Sigmund Freud and Erich Fromm that I describe in my book on narcissistic leaders. So far, I've referred to them in passing, but I'll briefly review the four types here.[15] They are: *erotic, obsessive, narcissistic,* and *marketing.* Keep in mind that no one is a pure type, but while we are all mixes, one type usually dominates a personality. Also, each type has positive or productive potentials as well as the negative or unproductive potentials that can result in personality disorders. Each type can be either good or bad.[16]

The productive erotic type is a helper: caring, cooperative, idealistic, communicative—the kind of person who stimulates love and supports others. The unproductive erotics are dependent, needy for love, and gossipy. They tend to avoid conflict and to exaggerate their emotional reactions. Freud writes that erotics "are dominated by the fear of loss of love and are therefore especially dependent on others who may withhold their love from them."[17] You are especially likely to find professionals of this type in health care, education, and the arts. I've also found them in staff roles in companies, where they often attach themselves as helpers to top executives.

The productive obsessive is the systematic type: inner-directed with a strong sense of responsibility and high standards, conscientious and reliable. The unproductive obsessives are nit-picking, overcontrolling, stubborn, and stingy, the elements of what Freud termed the anal character. This type can be effective in leadership roles in the professions and industry, especially when the challenge is cost cutting, but less so when there is a need for innovation.

Freud drew a distinction between narcissism, which we all have, and the narcissistic personality. Narcissism is essential for survival, since without a dose of it, we wouldn't value ourselves any more than anyone else. Although any personality type can have an excess of narcissism in the form of egoism, or hubris, with success, the narcissistic personality is more vulnerable than other types to getting puffed up. That's because narcissists care less than the other types about what others think of them. They answer mainly to their own internal ideal self.

Freud describes the narcissistic personality as "independent and not open to intimidation. The ego has a large amount of aggressiveness at its disposal, which also manifests itself in a readiness for activity . . . People belonging to this type impress others as being 'personalities', they are especially suited to act as a support for others, to take on the role of leaders and to give a fresh stimulus to cultural development or to damage the established state of affairs."[18]

Narcissists, and Freud saw himself as one, have not internalized parental models, so—lacking a strong superego that programs a moral code—they are free to write their own. The gifted and productive ones are innovators, independent thinkers who want to project their vision onto the world and are the type best able to inspire followers with their passionate conviction.

Unproductive narcissistic traits are arrogance, grandiosity, not listening to others, paranoid sensitivity to threats, extreme competitiveness, and unbridled ambition and aggressiveness. These traits have undermined narcissistic leaders, even those who have gone from great success to disaster, like Napoleon and Henry Ford.

When Freud observed personalities in the early twentieth century, obsessives were the dominant type, the model for character development. This was because their personality type fit hand in glove with the social character formed in the era of craft and bureaucratic-industrial production. But as the mode of production and its cultural frame shifted to service and knowledge work, a new personality type emerged to fit its demands. Fromm termed this chameleonlike type the marketing personality. It has become the dominant personality type of the interactive social character.

The productive marketing type combines independence with interactivity. Flexible to the point of being protean, marketing types are decisive when adapting to changing situations. I've described negative traits in chapter 4: lack of a center, insincerity, disloyalty, and superficiality. Like narcissists, marketing types lack a strong superego, because they don't identify strongly with parental figures, but their moral code is continually programmed and reprogrammed by groups they consider essential for their success. The effectiveness of a leader with a marketing personality depends greatly on the quality of the leader's close colleagues, since marketing types tend to form their views interactively, shaping them to what they think leads to success.

Why do I suggest using these psychoanalytic types rather than simpler behavioral types? There are two reasons. One, although typologies like introvert versus extrovert describe observable traits, these are inborn elements of temperament, neither learned nor learnable. And behavioral patterns like the Gallup strengths don't always predict how these strengths will be expressed. The psychoanalytic types may be influenced by inborn personality traits, but they are mainly formed in the socialization process. Each type expresses a particular constellation of universal human needs or emotionally energized values: motivational systems shaped in the stages of development described in the appendix. The genius of Freud included the ability to think systemically, to connect dynamic behavioral traits into types. Each psychological type describes the interaction of universal motivational patterns—fight-flight, attachment, play-mastery, pleasure-pain, exploration— but each type shuffles these differently, with one or another element as dominant. Furthermore, Freud worked at describing how these types develop in childhood, and although some of his descriptions are partial or unconvincing, they open up an area for further research of the sort Fromm and I reported in our study of child development in the Mexican village.

Clearly, personality types should be viewed through the lens of social character. For example, the obsessive personality takes on a different coloration in the peasant, craftsman, bureaucratic, and interactive social character frames. The cautious and frugal farmer, the precise and hierarchical professional, and the expert and precise interactive knowledge worker all share obsessive values of mastery, autonomy, and hard work. All have tendencies to be overcontrolling, compulsively clean, and hoarding. But they use different tools and master different modes of production with different roles, rules, and relationships. They have internalized different cultural values. The marketing personality isn't found in traditional peasant villages where identities are firmly rooted in family and place. It was formed in the postindustrial culture, where all types take on its elements of flexibility and interactivity. Given this relationship between individual personality and social character, the social character might also be called the cultural personality, a macro personality that both frames and colors all the micro personality types within a culture.

The second reason I suggest using these psychoanalytic types is that I've observed these types in my clinical work as a psychoanalyst and supervising other therapists. The types were useful both in my research on Mexican villagers and study of corporate managers. Furthermore, in applying the questionnaire based on these types in leadership workshops, my students, colleagues, and I have been able to understand and predict styles of leadership. Not surprisingly, we've found that high-tech entrepreneurs who take the big risks are narcissistic visionaries, the executives who squeeze efficiencies out of every process in production companies are obsessives, and professionals who customize their services and sell their personalities are marketing types.[19] Furthermore, these types are consistent with the observations of such diverse analysts as Machiavelli and Jack Welch about fitting personalities to leadership roles.

When I've used the personality questionnaire with executive teams, the result has been a more open conversation. For example, vice presidents of one executive team complained that the CFO didn't respond to their queries. The CFO's questionnaire showed he was a (erotic) helper, but his interest in helping was directed solely to the CEO who he saw as a father figure. As a result of this discussion, which brought to light an attitude the CFO had not been aware of, stronger links were forged between the CFO and vice presidents. Furthermore, the CFO understood why he so often felt insufficiently appreciated by his boss who he'd unconsciously experienced as the uncaring father he was desperately trying to please.

In these conversations about personality, team members have become more interactive with fewer examples of serial monologues. I asked Tony Barclay, CEO of DAI, a global development consultancy, what difference it made after his team had shared the results of the personality questionnaire.

He said, "We began to talk to each other in a different way and ultimately to be more direct with each other. It saved time." Barclay added that this process of discovery also sensitized executives to differences in cognitive style. For example, "Some people respond to new proposals right away. Others need time to digest them. If you respect that and don't judge it as stubbornness, you sometimes get better results by waiting a while until they come back with their views."[20]

INTELLECTUAL SKILLS—HOW WE THINK

In traditional bureaucracies, not much attention was paid to styles of thinking. Some people were considered brighter than others, quicker at solving puzzles and citing facts. Recruiters judged job applicants' intelligence mainly on the basis of their grades. In the knowledge workplace, analytic intelligence, the kind tested as IQ, is still necessary, but not sufficient. We'll see in chapter 10 that effective leaders also express different types of intelligence, such as emotional intelligence; strategic intelligence, including systems thinking; and street smarts.

How can you learn to understand the people you want to follow or collaborate with you? This chapter is meant to take the reader a step toward developing Personality Intelligence. However, while concepts like identities, social character, and personality can sensitize us about people's values and patterns of relatedness, unless we are also fully present with them, listening with our hearts, we can't really know other people, we can't experience them directly. Even when they smile and nod their heads, we won't know whether their enthusiasm is real or their feelings are really positive. Even when they cry, we won't know whether they are sad or furious. To understand others, we have to listen actively, using the conceptual framework presented in this chapter as a context to understand what we see, hear, and experience.

Clearly, the diversity of identities and personalities complicates leadership for the knowledge workplace, particularly since leaders can no longer count on the bureaucratic character's paternal transferences. Interactives seem to grasp this better and to recognize that the capability to understand differences in culture and personality is essential for effective collaboration in knowledge work. However, they will become more effective leaders by developing their Personality Intelligence.

In the next three chapters, I'll describe the kinds of leaders we need in knowledge organizations, making use of my experience and research in business, health care, and education. Then, in chapter 9, I'll speculate on the kind of president we need in this historic age of transformation.

In chapter 10, I'll describe in more detail what it takes to develop Personality Intelligence. Leadership development in the age of knowledge work requires continual learning, especially learning about people.

CHAPTER 6

Leaders for Knowledge Work

THE LEADERS WE WANT are not always the leaders we need. This has been true throughout history, and the result of getting the leaders people want has sometimes been the fall of nations and collapse of companies. Remember that, despite warnings from the biblical judge Samuel, the Israelites wanted a king, got one, and were sorry later. And in our time, boards of directors have hired dominating, charismatic CEOs who turned out to be costly busts. People continue to elect inept and corrupt leaders. Some of these leaders have satisfied unconscious and irrational transferential needs. The bureaucratic social character has been drawn to father-figure leaders—tall, commanding, and confident. But Interactives want to be collaborators, not followers. They'd most like to join a band of brothers and sisters, and if they want a leader at all, it will be someone who'll stay around only to provide a service for them. But just because they know what they want doesn't guarantee they'll get the leaders they need.

In this age of turmoil and transformation, we demand more of our organizations than ever before. We want companies to continually innovate, producing ever better products at lower costs. We want to travel farther and faster. We want more energy for light, heat, and air-conditioning, but, shocked by the suddenly limited supply of fossil fuels and the huge threat of global warming, we want companies and government to give us clean, cheap solutions. As brilliant technicians automate away jobs and companies send work overseas, we want our schools to educate the young—not just the elite, but everyone—to fill the roles in these organizations. And as our aspirations to live longer and healthier lives grow, we want healthcare organizations to perform what in the past would have been thought miraculous.

This chapter and the two that follow describe the kind of leadership required to organize knowledge workers to meet these new demands.

The challenge for leaders in these organizations is to transform bureaucracies in which individuals comfortably played autonomous roles into collaborative communities. And to meet this challenge they need to understand the people who will be the leaders and collaborators, and develop their Personality Intelligence so that they're not misled by transferential distortion. For just as the bureaucrats got in trouble by seeking a daddy figure, the Interactives risk disillusionment in their quest for leaders who make no demands on them.

Rowena Davis, an undergraduate at Balliol College, Oxford University, won the Templeton Prize in 2005 by describing as the ideal leader the kind who appeals to Interactives.[1] Jonathan (she doesn't tell us her subjects' last names) connects people who want to collaborate and then gets out of their way; Nita, another admired leader, builds networks for change. Davis says that these leaders "create space and opportunity for action." And they listen to the people they serve. They aren't full of themselves, they avoid acting superior, and they don't cause inequality. One admired business leader of this sort is Dee Hock who built the nonhierarchical Visa network.[2] Pierre M. Omidyar, founder of eBay, is another example. But these leaders didn't just create space. They had a business strategy and built the processes that businesses and customers could use.

They are in fact more like the executive type of leader described by Bryan Huang, a thirty-two-year-old interactive entrepreneur from Beijing who has organized an Internet conversation about leadership in China. He tells me, "There are two kinds of good leaders. One is the emergent leader who facilitates the flow."[3] Examples would include Rowena Davis's ideal leader and the network leaders who are needed to gain collaboration across organizational boundaries. The other, says Huang, is the executive leader "who has a vision people want to follow and can show how to make it happen."[4]

A danger for Interactives is insisting on filling leadership roles with non-leaders, people no one follows. Years ago, the sociologist David Riesman pointed out this problem in his study of how university presidents were being selected. He observed that increasingly the selection process resulted in choosing someone who satisfied all constituencies: faculty, alumni (for fund-raising), football boosters, diversity groups. Such an individual might be a good facilitator or mediator, even a network leader, but not a visionary with strong views.[5] And recently, some visionaries who have made it through the selection process, such as Larry Summers at Harvard and Ed Hundert at Case Western Reserve, have provoked faculty censure and haven't lasted long in their jobs.

But in this time of historical change, even the most effective network leaders are not the only kind we need. They won't stretch us out of our comfort zones, they won't inspire us to tackle the big problems facing our country, they won't transform bureaucratic organizations for the knowledge age, and they won't make the tough decisions that have to be made when there's no consensus. For that, we need different types of leaders who collaborate. Knowledge-age organizations need a leadership system rather than a set of individual leaders.

In the age of knowledge work, leadership has become more essential as well as more complex than in earlier times. We saw that farmers and craftsmen work alone or in a relationship of master and apprentices, and that the bureaucratic manager controls a hierarchy of people with autonomous objectives and formatted tasks. In both these modes of production, the social character supported strong parental transferences that bound followers to leaders. In both, leaders knew their followers' work better than the followers themselves did. But knowledge workers are specialists challenged to collaborate across boundaries. They usually know their work better than their bosses, and their closest ties may be to colleagues.

We saw in chapter 2 that these Interactives don't want to follow bureaucratic bosses and may even rebel against them. Paul Adler, a professor at the University of Southern California business school, describes a group of interactive software developers who flat-out refused to follow a bureaucratic manager, even though they recognized his technical expertise. They thought they'd function better as a collaborative heterarchy, in which leadership would shift according to which specialist had the relevant knowledge for the task at hand.[6] Teams like these need leaders, not managers, to set and interactively communicate a meaningful purpose, and then make sure things happen as planned. The team can pretty much manage itself.

This chapter and the next cover the spectrum of knowledge work and describe the kinds of leaders needed in the knowledge organizations I've worked with, studied, or learned about from other researchers. Clearly, business leads government and not-for-profits in designing organizations, strategies, and styles of leadership for knowledge work. That's because business must continually compete to survive. Those leaders who make use of the best ideas succeed, so they constantly scan the business world to find out what works. But business by itself can't solve the needs we have for health care, education, a sustainable environment, energy independence, and national security. That takes a combination of policy, programs, and organizations in both the public and private sectors, working together.

THE KNOWLEDGE WORKPLACE

To understand the kinds of leaders needed for knowledge work, consider the existing jobs in the United States. About 80 percent of them are labeled service work by the Department of Labor, but we can view these jobs in terms of a national employment space bordered by a horizontal axis of service work and a vertical axis of knowledge work (see figure 6-1). Each axis goes from low- to high-paid jobs. Low-paid service jobs include janitors, hotel workers, waiters, maids, security guards, and cleaners. High-paid service would be international fashion models and professional athletes, jobs that of course demand some knowledge. Low-paid knowledge work describes lab technicians, accountants, translators, and simple programmers; high-paid knowledge work includes editors, marketing experts, scientists, mathematicians, economists, financial analysts, product developers, and inventors. Bisecting this knowledge-service space is a vector of solutions—

FIGURE 6-1

The need for leaders

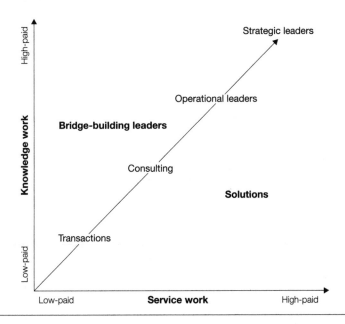

the application of knowledge so that it becomes a service. This vector rises from simple transactions like sales to teaching, medical, legal and financial consulting to the kinds of leaders needed to give purpose to, integrate, and operationalize the knowledge work. This is a dynamic space, constantly changing as inventors and programmers on the vertical axis automate transactional and, increasingly, professional and consulting work. Telephone operators disappear, ATMs replace transactional bank tellers, buyers and sellers use the Internet and displace middlemen. However, these knowledge workers don't just destroy jobs. They can also create new jobs in renewable energy, health care, nanotechnology, and so on. But that requires leaders.

In knowledge-creating companies, we find three kinds of leaders who have to work together. They are:

1. *Strategic visionaries:* The leaders who, envisaging the need for a new strategy and organizational transformation, prod, push, and persuade others to follow. They are often productive narcissists,

bold innovators, like Steve Jobs, Larry Ellison, and Bill Gates. But they can also be more collaborative marketing types like Bob Iger of Disney who was smart enough to buy Pixar, thus getting John Lasseter's creativity, as well as Steve Jobs as a board member. The collaborative strategist seeks to build the vision through discussion with collaborators rather than authoritative pronouncements from on high. The history of IBM shows the contrast between the industrial and knowledge modes in sharp terms. When Thomas Watson Sr., the productive narcissist, wanted to establish the values for IBM to live by, he wrote them down, published them, and continually repeated them. But we saw that when Sam Palmisano, a more interactive marketing type, wanted to transform IBM for the knowledge age, he opened the company's intranet to all employees for frank, freewheeling "jams" in which he participated as an equal, and from which new values and ideas emerged.

2. *Operational implementers:* These are systematic obsessive types, also usually needed in organizations. They make sure the strategy is implemented; they turn shared purpose into results. There are a number of well-known examples of successful partnerships between obsessive operational leaders and narcissistic visionaries, including Herb Kelleher and Colleen Barrett of Southwest Airlines, Andy Grove and Craig Barrett of Intel, and Bill Gates and Steve Ballmer of Microsoft. Indeed, many narcissistic visionaries, like Don Quixote, would survive only if partnered with a down-to-earth obsessive Sancho Panza. The operational types sometimes architect the processes that sustain a system, but in a collaborative knowledge mode, they work less through tight controls and organization charts and more through process alignment and cross-boundary conversation. To transform resisters into collaborators, they need to learn to be interactive "doctors" rather than dictators.

3. *Bridge-builders:* Advanced solutions companies need network leaders with the ability to develop trusting relationships across

organizational boundaries. These leaders, usually a combination
of helping and marketing types, but sometimes with a strong
dose of narcissistic ambition to transform, may do more than sustain networks; they may build bridges, not only across corporate
departments, but also between companies and different national
cultures. Lynda Applegate, a professor at Harvard Business School
facilitated the Global Healthcare Exchange, combining companies to cut transaction costs and gain stronger bargaining power
with suppliers. DAI, an international development consulting
firm, used the bridge-building leadership of Joan Parker to bring
together pharmaceutical companies with development consultants and national governments to address the problem of
HIV/AIDS in African communities. Navy captain Linda
Lewandowski was put in charge of the Sense and Respond Lo-
gistics (SARL) project in the Pentagon's Office of Force Transformation to facilitate the rapid delivery of weapons and
ammunition to battlefield units. She had to enlist different U.S.
and allied services to participate in a network of communication
and response, a dramatic change from the old way of negotiation
between the bureaucratic service hierarchies.

Of course, this role is better filled by the interactive social
character who is used to bringing people together to solve problems than by a bureaucratic expert who is used to directing people to follow instructions. Bridge-builders may have little formal
power—their power comes from their skill in creating consensus.
An interactive bridge-builder tells me that she sees her role as
getting people to understand each other. "People allow me to
take this role," she says, and she agrees that she has authority because it's freely given to her, more than if she had a formal
bridge-building role. Having had this role myself at AT&T
where the goal was to transform a rigid bureaucracy into a learning organization, I can testify that bridge-builders don't need a
formal managerial role, but they do need support from the top.
And in fact, having a formal role could limit effectiveness by

identifying the bridge-builder with the interests of one or another unit.

It takes these three kinds of leaders working together to achieve a common purpose, especially in complex knowledge companies. And of course, whatever their style, effective leaders infuse energy into an organization with their passion and conviction; they stretch people to perform beyond their comfort zone, and they insist on results.

LEADERS FOR SOLUTIONS

While traditional leaders view Interactives as hard to lead and as having an anarchic ideal of leadership, Interactives better fit the needs of many companies moving away from product-based business models to knowledge work and particularly solution strategies. To avoid narrowing profit margins for products that are becoming commodities, companies like GE have been wrapping products in services that require employees to work collaboratively with customers.

In the late 1990s, I was a consultant to ABB (Asea Brown Boveri) in Canada at a time when the company's electrical products were becoming commodities and margins were disappearing. To boost profits, we explored the potential of doing business with large customers like the zinc-mining and -smelting company Cominco, which proposed partnering with ABB (rather than merely buying equipment) to increase energy efficiency and decrease environmental pollution.[7] To pursue this opportunity, ABB had to pull technical people together from its different business units to collaborate with Cominco's engineers, and this called for network leadership. ABB had it in Borje Fredriksson, a productive marketing type with an interactive social character.

Fredriksson had to persuade traditional bureaucratic ABB managers that other large customers from paper and pulp companies and utilities really wanted to buy solutions rather than products. He did this by bringing the customers to management meetings and letting ABB's managers question them directly. Fredriksson and I then interviewed managers about what organizational changes would be needed to realize the new solutions strategy. We again brought the key managers together in an interactive process to design the new system. Recognizing that they would have to communicate the results to their own teams, these managers decided they would continue the interactive process, and they defined it as follows:

- Dialogue—meeting of the minds

- Constructive engagement

- Seeking logic

- Full trust—openness

- Understanding each other

- Common language

- Openness to different perspectives

They also defined what it is *not*:

- Telling people

- Explaining to your staff

- Just listening

After using an interactive process to design the structure, processes, and measurements needed to implement a solutions strategy, they answered their own question: Why use the interactivity process?

- Interactivity is the glue that makes the whole bigger than the sum of its parts

- Otherwise the strategy will not be fully understood

- Interactivity will continuously develop and improve the strategy itself

Regrettably, Fredriksson's initiatives and efforts to develop the solutions strategy were undermined by ABB's bureaucratic top management, which kept in place a business unit (BU) structure and incentives tailored for delivery of products, not collaborative solutions. BU managers could reach their targets and win bonuses by selling lots of products, but they weren't paid to spend a lot of time developing relationships with people from other organizations within ABB and with customers, even though that would have benefited the company as a whole. So ABB had the creative network leader in Canada but not the visionary needed at the top in Zurich.

Many companies are like ABB, where employees with the bureaucratic social character are much more comfortable with a clear line of authority than with collaboration. But those companies that are shifting from selling products to coproducing solutions with their customers recognize they need to move away from traditional hierarchical bureaucracies. They need to redesign processes and change measurements and incentives, and they need bridge-building network leaders like Fredriksson. Jay Galbraith, another professor at the University of Southern California, has written about efforts to make this sort of shift and about the network leadership sought at companies such as Nestlé, Nokia, and Citibank. He describes the shift in terms of forming cross-boundary networks that require leaders who can build trusting relationships to facilitate consensus-based decision making. He reinforces the point that the best bridge-builders don't need formal authority and adds that formal authority without talent, which includes Personality Intelligence, won't succeed.[8] Bridge-builders succeed only when the operational collaborators grant them authority and the visionaries at the top empower them.

This kind of leadership system is needed not only in solutions-creating technology companies, but also in healthcare organizations, which need to produce solutions for health problems. The next chapter describes the best of these organizations and the leaders they need.

CHAPTER 7

Leaders for Health Care

THE HEALTHCARE INDUSTRY is huge, making up from 13 to 16 percent of the U.S. economy. It's a knowledge industry that should provide solutions rather than just products and services, but its mode of production and the social character of many of its key professionals lag behind the times. Health care is an industry desperately in need of visionary leaders who partner with operational and network leaders to transform organizations and even influence the social character of physicians.

The troubling issues concerning health care in the United States are becoming better known: zooming costs; the increasing numbers of uninsured as companies drop coverage of employees; significant variability in diagnosis and treatment as complexity of new knowledge and technology outraces the learning abilities of doctors; hundreds of thousands of life-threatening, avoidable mistakes in hospitals. Although other industrialized countries provide health insurance for all their citizens, they suffer the same problems of cost, complexity, and quality of care. The United States boasts some of the best doctors and hospitals in the world, yet, while we spend twice the amount per person than does the United Kingdom, we don't see corresponding benefits in terms of health. Rather, the evidence indicates we're worse off.[1]

To improve health care and make it available to all Americans, crafting a new national policy is essential, but it's not enough. Effective organizations are needed to deliver health care, and, as the chapter will show, there are different excellent models. As with all knowledge work, there's no one best way to organize health care. We'll see that while even the best of health-care organizations can't copy each other, they can learn from each other.

Since the late 1980s, I've worked with executives from medical groups, businesses, government, unions, and religious organizations to help craft national policy on health care. I've also studied and consulted to some of the best healthcare organizations in the United States, and shared observations and ideas with researchers from the United Kingdom, France, Italy, and Sweden.[2]

I was first recruited to this field by Dr. Henry Simmons, a visionary leader who put together a high-level group from business, government, academia, and medicine to explore the issues, digest knowledge from the experts, and shape policy. Simmons asked me to facilitate the process, and so began my learning journey.

Simmons was trained as an internist at the University of Pittsburgh Medical School, but practicing medicine didn't satisfy his ambition. Like many visionary leaders, he felt he should be doing more to make a difference, to change the world for the better. While still practicing in Boston, he got a degree in public health from Harvard. He looked for experts he could learn from and one of them, impressed by his idealism and energy, offered him a job as deputy assistant secretary for health in the Nixon administration. He stayed in government through the Ford administration, serving as director of the Office of Professional Standards where he instituted the first national standards review, and director of the Bureau of Drugs at the Food and Drug Administration (FDA). In these jobs, he was shocked to see the quality problems in medicine and wanted to find out how to solve them. After leaving government, he took a job at Booz Allen Hamilton, studying how to improve hospitals, and had a stint as CEO of Hunterdon Medical Center in New Jersey, where he got a taste of how hard it is to lead doctors. During the Reagan administration, he was a member of the Grace Commission to streamline government, where he got to know CEOs of big companies. When that service ended, he turned down a deanship and professorship because he wanted to create his own commission as a start to transforming American health care, and he persuaded the Pew Foundation to fund it. You have to be a productive narcissist to believe that without any formal power you can change the healthcare system of the United States.

The National Leadership Commission Simmons organized learned that the problems of health care in America were systemic, meaning interrelated. For example, costs can be cut significantly if the quality and variability of treatments are controlled. And with universal coverage, care for the uninsured in emergency rooms would no longer be funded by higher insurance premiums for the insured. Also, a universal system would cut the time and cost doctors and hospitals spent filling out myriad insurance forms. Once the commission understood the need for a comprehensive solution, Simmons and his staff produced a policy proposal.

At that time, the leaders of the Senate, Republican Bob Dole and Democrat George Mitchell, spoke before the commission and appeared ready to jointly back legislation making use of the commission's work. But before they acted, Bill Clinton became President and Hillary Rodham Clinton was charged with overseeing healthcare policy. Incorporating some of the commission's main ideas, she set up her own project to provide insurance for all Americans. The failure of her attempt is well-known. Strong lobbying and the "Harry and Louise" TV ads—paid for by the pharmaceutical industry—argued that with the Clinton plan, government would dictate our medical choices. This turned the public and Congress against what was already an overly complicated proposal.[3] Furthermore, by not engaging key stakeholders—the hospital industry, healthcare professions organizations, the pharmaceutical industry, state governments, and of course, Congress—in crafting the plan, the Clintons lacked allies who had any commitment to it. I believe a major cause of their failure was that the Clintons didn't want to share credit. Unless one party has a huge majority, as was the case during the Roosevelt years when the Democrats passed social security legislation, a national plan that increases the government's role in providing coverage, controlling costs, and setting standards will pass Congress only if both parties share the credit.

Once the Clinton plan was history, Simmons determined to build a bipartisan coalition, including organizations representing all stakeholders, to shape and support a comprehensive policy based on five principles:

- Healthcare coverage for all

- Cost management

- Improvement of healthcare quality and safety

- Equitable financing

- Simplified administration

Simmons has had a remarkable ability to persuade others to join his ambitious project. Recognizing that success was much more likely if support was bipartisan, he recruited as cochairmen of the commission and coalition Democrat Paul G. Rogers, a highly respected former chairman of the Congressional committee on health at the time Simmons testified for the FDA, and Republican Robert D. Ray, a greatly admired former governor of Iowa. They in turn persuaded former presidents George H. W. Bush, Jimmy Carter, and Gerald Ford to become honorary cochairmen. Simmons, together with Rogers and Ray, then signed up almost one hundred dues-paying organizational members representing business, unions, providers, pension funds, religious, and interest groups like AARP.[4]

In the early years of the coalition, I attended some of the bimonthly meetings, in which coalition members were brought up to date on the many policy studies and initiatives coming from the Institute of Medicine, think tanks, and universities. But the coalition wasn't able to agree on a new version of a comprehensive plan. The religious representatives, like those from the United States Conference of Catholic Bishops, were mainly concerned with coverage for all. Unionized companies, like Safeway, which provided expensive benefits to workers, wanted a level competitive playing field—and that meant getting Wal-Mart to bear the same costs. The businesses on the coalition called for cost control, but some of the medical groups, hospitals, and drug companies resisted any policy that threatened their revenues. GE had a schizophrenic attitude. The company liked the idea of paying less for employee benefits, but its healthcare division was a major engine of corporate growth, and cost control could hurt sales.

In 2003, Simmons asked me to come back and facilitate a process to gain consensus on a set of interconnected specifications for reform. Meeting monthly with the coalition members, with many subgroup discussions in between, we were able to agree on a linked series of targets, criteria, and options. The process I used in facilitating the agreement was:

- Get agreement on the problems and the state of knowledge.

- List the solutions offered by experts and coalition members.

- Get agreement on acceptable alternative specifications.

It wasn't easy to come to this agreement, but coalition members were willing to go along when there was two-thirds support for an alternative. However, if a member strongly objected to an alternative, that objection was fully discussed and we attempted to tailor the alternative, as long as it did not contradict the agreed-on five principles. In the end, almost all coalition members signed on to the specifications. Ideally, these should be adopted concurrently, but at the least, any steps taken to improve healthcare by national or state governments should be evaluated in terms of whether or not they advance the country toward these interrelated specifications.

The report makes an important point that is not sufficiently understood by policy makers, particularly those who lack systems thinking:

Partial or piecemeal reforms, even those conceived and implemented with the best of intentions, can produce unanticipated adverse consequences. For example, a dramatic expansion of access, implemented without accompanying measures to improve quality and manage costs, could produce an overloaded healthcare system that delivers worse care (albeit to more people) at higher costs. Similarly, constraints on costs (and reimbursements for care), pursued in isolation, could compromise both access and quality.

We believe that a systemic approach can increase not only the substantive coherence of reform, but also its political feasibility. Thus, if constraints on healthcare cost increases were proposed in isolation, providers might understandably anticipate that their revenues going forward would be diminished. By contrast, if those same constraints were conjoined in a systemic strategy with an assurance of coverage for all Americans and financing for their care, providers would receive payment for care that they now provide, with little or no compensation, to uninsured patients.[5]

After the report was published, Simmons contracted with economist Kenneth Thorpe, Robert W. Woodruff Professor at Emory University, to project the costs and savings of four scenarios consistent with the specifications: (1) employer and individual mandates, (2) expansion of existing public programs to cover the uninsured, (3) creation of new programs targeted at subsets of the uninsured, and (4) establishment of publicly financed universal coverage like the Canadian system. Taking into account cost management, improvement of quality and safety, and simplified administration, Thorpe estimated annual systemwide savings of $182 billion in the tenth year of implementing reform. Cumulative savings for that same ten-year period would range, across scenarios, from $320 billion to $1.1 trillion.[6]

What will it take for Congress to pass a comprehensive program? Clearly, advocacy by the experts, churches, medical groups, unions, and a number of businesses hasn't been enough to counteract a combination of free market antigovernment ideology and the self-interest of groups that fear losing profits.[7] Maybe we need to wait until more people lose their coverage and start electing representatives committed to taking action. Clearly, it won't happen without leaders in the White House and Congress who can educate the public and galvanize a response. Furthermore, public policy alone won't improve the quality of care. That calls for great healthcare organizations with exceptional leaders. We'll see that some do exist.

LEADERS FOR HEALTHCARE ORGANIZATIONS

Policy makers function in a rarified atmosphere, far from the organizations that have to implement their policies. Listening to the reports about the poor quality of health care, I asked myself whether some healthcare organizations were doing things right, especially improving quality and controlling costs. In the healthcare business, where there's a huge variation in management approaches, someone somewhere is usually ahead of the curve, and you can always learn from the best cases. In 1998, Dr. Paul Griner, an old friend and Harvard classmate had just retired as CEO of Strong Memorial Hospital in Rochester, New York, and moved to Washington, D.C., where he was a vice president of the Association of American Medical Colleges (AAMC).[8] He had been visiting academic health centers and had reported the problems of leaders in developing a vision.[9] It was Griner who encouraged me to study the organizational practices and leadership of the best health organizations in the country to see if there was a good model for others to follow. Dr. Roger Bulger, then president of the Association of Academic Health Centers, also supported the idea, as did Henry Simmons. They recommended the project to the Robert Wood Johnson Foundation, which was at first skeptical about whether the healthcare organizations would let me in, but they were persuaded because Griner, Bulger, Simmons, and the other medical luminaries on the project's advisory committee offered to pave the way.[10]

A project team—myself and research associates Richard Margolies, Barbara Lenkerd, Doug Wilson, and George Casey—made study trips to the University of Rochester Medical Center; Intermountain Health Care in Salt Lake City; Aetna Healthcare; the University of Michigan Medical Center; Penn State Milton S. Hershey Medical Center; the Geisinger Clinic; Shands HealthCare ("Shands-University of Florida"); the Mayo Clinic (in Rochester, Minnesota, and Scottsdale, Arizona); Scripps Health (in San Diego and La Jolla, California); Vanderbilt University Medical Center; and Kaiser-Permanente Medical Center in Oakland, California.[11]

We found that leadership is essential to improve the quality of patient care and cut unnecessary costs. In some of the most prestigious healthcare organizations, we found an angry clash between doctors practicing an obsolete craft-based mode of production, and hospitals, organized like industrial bureaucracies, whose administrators were attempting to force the physicians into the iron cage.

The result was a cold war in which all the parties—doctors, hospitals, patients—were losers. In contrast, we met visionary leaders who were transforming both the medical mode of production and hospital bureaucracies into learning organizations, self-organizing and adaptive to the changing technology and markets.

To fully grasp the leadership challenge, we need to understand the social character of doctors. Traditionally, medicine has been much like a craft, organized like a cottage industry with sole proprietors and small partnerships, based on the physician's reputation and personal relationships with colleagues and patients. Doctors reinforce their professional identity within a guildlike structure that determines membership and monopolizes functions. There are, to be sure, some important differences: unlike artisan crafts, medicine depends on a widely shared, relatively open scientific knowledge base. Yet the parallels are striking. Although the doctor's education begins with formal training, specialization is gained through apprenticeship.[12] The ideal leadership model, as with other crafts, is the most accomplished practitioner, the master craftsman who represents the interests of his peers. If he does that effectively, he creates a strong transferential followership. The physician-patient relationship has depended on the patient's trust of the doctor's expertise and caring attitude. For centuries, the technology has been hand tools—stethoscope, scalpel, needles, etc.—and a limited number of useful medicines. The model of care has been biomedical, with a strong dose of positive transference to the doctor as a parental figure to cement trust and strengthen a placebo effect that aids natural self-healing.[13]

Historical studies have shown that the model of the autonomous professional physician in America has been institutionalized through a long process starting in the nineteenth century, driven in part by the need for doctors to establish a solid basis of prestige to replace the image of unregulated quackery of the time. The establishment of medical education and licensing was crucial to creating a sense both among the public and among physicians themselves that their use of up-to-date scientific knowledge and their professional ethics warranted respect and financial reward. During the twentieth century the AMA (American Medical Association) worked for this professional autonomy, repeatedly fighting off regulators.[14] Although physicians now use more complex tools, many remain in a kind of cottage industry type of organization. Even when specialists are professors in academic health centers, these centers become like feudal kingdoms, where the vice president for health affairs is king, the dean of the medical school is lord of the manor, department chairs are the barons, and the local practitioners (LMDs)—who send their patients to the specialists in the castle—feel they are treated like lowly serfs.

The explosion of medical knowledge, new drugs, and new technologies calls for standardization and collaboration among experts. But the craft mode of production resists standardization. Each craftsman does things his own way, which is why there is so much variability in medical care, and so much misdiagnosis and needless cost.

Inevitably, this craft mode has been attacked by bureaucracies. As the doctors have held on to their traditional model, cost-control efforts such as health maintenance organizations (HMOs) and medical protocols imposed by insurance companies have weakened their autonomy and pushed many into joining group practices or becoming employees of healthcare organizations. Furthermore, both the changing social character of patients and the information revolution have also undermined the doctor's unchallenged authority. Interactives, used to parents who served them, are less likely to project an uncritical, idealized transference on to the doctor. Interactives are also more likely to surf the Net for the rich lode of medical information and question a doctor's diagnosis. These assertive patients are aware that what the doctor learned in medical school may now be out of date. If this were not enough to ruin the doctor's image of what practicing medicine should be like, lawyers lie in wait, ready to file for malpractice if the doctor makes a mistake.

So doctors are being forced to follow rules laid down by insurance companies to guarantee reimbursement and avoid malpractice suits. Given the complex regulations and paperwork, the risks to practice, and rising costs of malpractice insurance, they've been drawn to the protection of large groups and hospitals and pushed into an industrial-bureaucratic mode of production.

But physicians become unhappy employees in bureaucracies or in "focused factories" that specialize in a particular type of treatment. Instead of being independent physicians, they become "providers" or else managers more engaged in monitoring than in mentoring colleagues who will themselves be measured on business profitability.

To be sure, useful learnings from industry, particularly total quality management, have been used to achieve dramatic results in hospitals, reducing variability in practice and supply management and improving quality of care. Notable examples are SSM Health Care, with twenty-three Midwest facilities, led by Sister Mary Jean Ryan; and the Pittsburgh Regional Healthcare Initiative led by Paul O'Neill, the former treasury secretary and Alcoa CEO.[15] Dr. Kenneth W. Kizer, led a remarkable transformation of the Veterans Administration (VA) healthcare system—comprising 172 hospitals, 600 ambulatory care and community-based outpatient clinics, 131 nursing homes, 40 residential care facilities, and 206 counseling centers. In all these cases, it was great leadership, not government laws or regulation, that produced the results.[16] The methods have been proven, but lots more leadership is needed to get physicians to collaborate with nurses and administrators.[17]

Statistical process control and informatics have proved powerful tools to improve outcomes by constructing clinical pathways of best practice. When these are used by physicians at hospitals like LDS in Salt Lake City and Rady Children's Hospital in San Diego, the cost of treating certain conditions can be cut in half. But within these hospital bureaucracies, many physicians resist any further limitation of their freedom to make medical decisions on their own.

THE IDENTITY OF DOCTORS

Resistance to change is rooted in the typical physician personality type and the professional socialization that molds this personality to fit the traditional medical mode of production. Based on interviews and questionnaires we gave to senior physicians and medical school graduates, we found that most had a particular professional variation of the bureaucratic social character. The most common personality type was a productive obsessive-erotic personality—systematic, careful, and caring. Doctors saw themselves as expert-helpers who are supposed to have all the answers to a patient's complaint. A few doctors, particularly orthopedic and cardiac surgeons, were narcissistic-obsessives.

As defined by the *Oxford English Dictionary*, an *expert* is "a person with the status of an authority by reason of special skill, training or knowledge." The root of expert is the Latin *expertus*, meaning tried or experienced. For experts in any profession, both self-esteem and employment security are gained by status and respect, recognition by peers and superiors. The physicians we interviewed typically display their awards and diplomas on their office walls to testify to their achievements and impress their patients. Experts have a strong need for autonomy. At their best, they stand for high standards of service and knowledge. The physician's view of professionalism fits the Calvinistic concept of professing a calling to serve others—the meaning of their work is not just exercising expertise, but also helping suffering people.

However, at their worst, their obsessive qualities make these experts inflexible know-it-alls. Rooted in a craft system of master and apprentice, where knowledge is based on experience, at a time when medical knowledge quickly becomes out-of-date and competence calls for continual learning, the physician's personality can be a major roadblock to change. Physician experts prize control and resist empowering others, which they see as loss of control. This is a complaint we heard repeatedly from nurses and administrators. Physicians, like many other experts—for example, university faculty—don't appreciate the added value of the organization over what they do as individuals. They relate best with peers, mentors, or younger high-potential apprentices, all of whom share their values. Many of the faculty members we interviewed at academic health centers maintain their autonomy through research grants that fund their own shops. They justify being part of an academic organization for the prestige of being a professor and the opportunity to gain acolytes. But since their independence, prestige, and promotions depend on research grants and publications, serving patients is not their first priority.

In most of the leading academic health centers, we found a corrosive hierarchy of status. Full-time clinicians feel slighted, and they believe that many celebrated researchers who are known as great specialists don't spend enough time with patients to keep up their skills as clinicians. While they recognize exceptions, most of the full-time clinicians think that the triple-threat ideal of the teacher-researcher-clinician can't be sustained. And of course, nurses, technicians, and administrators feel that doctors treat them like second- or third-class citizens.

The clash of cultures between physicians and hospital administrators is a conflict between the craft mode of individual authority, self-generated revenue, personal style of care, and patient advocacy as opposed to the industrial bureaucratic mode of centralized management, financial controls, standardized procedures, and rules based on fairness.

TOWARD A KNOWLEDGE MODE OF PRODUCTION

Can health care be reorganized as a knowledge mode of production that tackles variability of practice, improves outcomes, and controls cost, yet allows physicians to be creative and maintain a healing relationship with patients while retaining the best values of the craft tradition? Unless this question can be answered in the affirmative, many of the policy proposals offered by the National Coalition on Health Care won't connect with the real world of health care.

Together with Drs. Bulger and Griner, I began to sketch out a model of health care as a knowledge mode of production. We contrasted the logic of productivity in the industrial and knowledge modes as it applied to health care. In manufacturing, productivity depends on the producer's processes and practices. In professional knowledge work—law, medicine, consulting, teaching—and in any solutions work, it depends on both producer and client, on coproduction. The lawyer or accountant's productivity rises when the client keeps good records, the teacher's when the student studies, the consultant's when the client can use advice.

This is especially the case for health care in regard to chronic conditions like diabetes, asthma, and congestive heart failure. When patients manage these conditions, not only in terms of diet and exercise, but also record keeping and self-medication, their health improves and so do medical costs. At Intermountain Health Care, an average of $30,000 annually was saved over a period of fifteen years for those diabetes patients who managed their own care. This was because these patients didn't end up in emergency rooms, in desperate shape with kidney failure, blindness, or the need for an amputation. At present, 225,000 Americans die of diabetes each year.[18] If diabetics were educated to manage their own care, lives would be saved. Intermountain estimates such education takes over a year, and until recently, insurance paid for treatment but not education. (The incentives are all wrong—the doctor makes more by doing for patients what they would be better off doing for themselves.) Intermountain also helps to connect patients through the Internet, so that doctors can monitor the patient's self-treatment. But again, doctors need to be paid to do this, or patients need long-term membership in HMOs like Intermountain and Kaiser-Permanente, so that it's in the interest of the insurer to educate patients to treat themselves.

Bulger also tackled another persistent problem—errors in medication. These often result from incomprehensible physician handwriting. Bulger demonstrated this to a group of doctors by writing a number on a blackboard. Half of them thought it was a 0 and half a 6. In a knowledge mode of practice, doctors use IT in making decisions and ordering treatment. Bulger argued persuasively that using IT and advanced informatics in prescribing can also increase safety as well as quality of care.

The ideal health system will challenge physicians and all healthcare professionals—nurses, administrators, technicians—to work together to improve productivity and also the patient's experience. In most systems today, patients with complex problems have to trudge from one specialist to another, making their own appointments, carrying their records from office to office, repeating their medical histories, filling out similar medical history and insurance forms over and over again. It's a hassle that can only be solved by transforming the medical mode of production.

The ideal moves from what is essentially a sick care system to a true health maintenance system. It expands the care model from a purely biomedical and craft mode to a biopsychosocial and epidemiological knowledge mode of production. This move requires collaboration between healthcare professionals and everyone in a community.

The ideal also calls for a new kind of medical education that was pioneered by Dr. Ed Hundert when he was dean at the University of Rochester medical school. Students learned the *business* of medicine as well as science and the clinical arts. They learned to collaborate with patients and other healthcare professionals. The ideal calls for organizations in which all the professionals collaborate to further their common purpose, not in response to the command-and-control systems of the industrial mode of production, but because they understand and support the purpose and practices (see table 7-1). Then there won't be any conflict between

TABLE 7-1

The transformation of health care

	Craft	Industrial	Knowledge
Structure/roles			
Organization	• Cottage industry	• Bureaucracy • Focused factories	• Collaborative learning organization
Role of physician	• Sole proprietor • Small partnerships	• Employee • Entrepreneur	• System stakeholder • Leader
Relationship: physician with patient	• Authority • Submissive-trusting	• Provider • Customer	• Partner-teacher • Coproducer-learner
Business model			
	• Personal relationships • Reputation	• Price • Scale • Service	• Community needs • Prevention • Health improvement
Operating systems			
Technology	• Hand tools	• Electromechanical • Chemical	• Information • Biogenetic
Quality and cost control	• Peer review	• Statistical process control • Utilization management • Outcome measures • Clinical pathways	• Continuous improvement • Shared responsibility
Learning	• Individual	• Organizational	• Community
Model of care			
	• Biomedical	• Biomedical	• Biopsychosocial • Epidemiological
Physician skills			
	• Clinical	• Managerial	• Business • Partnering
Style			
Leadership model	• Master-apprentice • Mentoring • Ombudsman	• Manager • Monitoring	• Visionary • Dialogue • Motivating
Values			
	• Caring • Personal trust • Expertise	• Profitability • Service	• Teamwork • Innovation

physicians' autonomy and the organizational goals. For example, physicians will be fully convinced that by tackling variability of practice they'll benefit their patients as well as their organizations.

Transforming the healthcare mode of production to a knowledge mode of production resolves the conflict between physicians and hospitals in a way that preserves the best values of both (see figure 7-1). And this transformation is essential to improving the healthcare system, not only in the United States, but in all countries where physicians are wrestling with the explosion of medical knowledge and technology. But this system needs leaders with skills that are different from either the craft or industrial modes. We'll come back to that after we visit some of the organizations that are trying to transform themselves toward this ideal.

I first proposed the model shown in figure 7-1 in 1998 at a meeting of heads of academic health centers, where it was well received and became the leading chapter in the Association of Academic Health Centers (AAHC) book *Creating the Future*.[19] More recently, it was featured in a

FIGURE 7-1

Hospital versus physician mode of production

Hospitals Bureaucratic mode	Physicians Craft mode
• Centralized administration • Controls by budget and information • Standardized procedures • Rules and regulations	• Individual authority • Self-generated revenue • Personal style of care • Advocate for patient

Hospital-physician partnership Knowledge mode
• Cross-functional clinical programs, product lines • IT systems for order entry, records, scheduling, decision making • Evidence-based practice, processes, pathways, protocols • Control of suppliers • Transparent measurement system • Interactive leadership • Partnerships with providers, payers, and companies

book based on a project headed by Richard Normann, as a model for European healthcare systems.[20]

How close are our best healthcare organizations to this model? In 1999, at an AAHC workshop, leaders of academic healthcare organizations filled in a survey on the elements of the knowledge mode. These leaders indicated that there's a large gap between ideal and practice in making service to patients the highest priority. (A notable exception is the Mayo Clinic.) They reported major gaps in adopting the information systems needed for order entry, antibiotic safety, electronic records, and, beyond these, the informatics that facilitate doctor-patient collaboration on managing chronic conditions. Vanderbilt University Medical Center proved to be an exception, and we later found that Kaiser-Permanente and Intermountain Health Care, not academic organizations, have also made significant strides in IT development, as have others, like the VA system and Partners HealthCare in Boston.

Consistent with the craft mode, there was also a large gap in addressing practice variability, as well as in evaluating physician results. These executives reported that the specialists in their faculties resist attempts to limit their autonomy or to judge each other's work.

Finally, these academic leaders were frank in admitting that they had not forged relationships of trust with the doctors they managed, and they were failing to communicate a vision of transformation. When they held off-site planning meetings, typically facilitators boarded the wish lists of the department chairs. Then the group prioritized the areas they wanted to support. Inevitably, these were the areas that would attract the most research money: cancer, heart disease, the brain. Usually at the end of the offsite, the doctors signed on to a value statement. The top of the list was patient service, even though everyone knew this wasn't really their organizations' highest priority.

Few of these leaders aspired to be transformational leaders. They were more like ombudsmen, representing and defending their medical faculties. By protecting members of their guild they gained loyalty as the feudal lords of the academic castles. The leadership consultants they hired advised them to sharpen their emotional intelligence, storytelling ability, and mentoring competence to tighten their transferential hold over their vassals.[21]

But those are not the essential qualities of the leaders we need to transform organizations in the age of knowledge work.

THE BEST OF THE BEST

Which of the healthcare organizations we visited came closest to the
ideal? There were four, each somewhat different from the others. According to our findings, these were the Mayo Clinic, Intermountain Health
Care (IHC), Kaiser-Permanente (KP), and Vanderbilt University Medical
Center (VUMC). (Our method was to interview organizational leaders—
executives, chairs, head nurses—based on their responses to a gap survey
that described the qualities of an ideal knowledge model. The survey can be
found at the end of this chapter.)

Mayo Clinic

The most collaborative organization we visited is the Mayo Clinic,
founded a century ago by two brothers, William and Charles Mayo. The
visionary leader was William, who challenged the growing trend of individual professionalism in American medicine. He wrote: "It [has become]
necessary to develop medicine as a cooperative science; the clinician, the
specialist, and the laboratory workers uniting for the good of the patient.
Individualism in medicine can no longer exist."[22] Long before current efforts to develop integrated information systems, Mayo pioneered a medical records system for sharing information. The clinic was among the first
to offer organized medical specialties like orthopedics and pediatrics, and
the first to organize those specialties in patient-focused teams. William
Mayo also built a learning organization to continuously improve patient
care. Whenever he heard of a new surgical treatment, he went to study it.

Recently restating their "core principles," Mayo physicians write: "Practice medicine as an integrated team of compassionate, multi-disciplinary
physicians, scientists and allied health professionals who are focused on the
needs of patients from our communities, regions, the nation and the world."[23]

And they mean it! We observed in our visits to Mayo clinics in Rochester, Minnesota, and Scottsdale, Arizona, that the patient really does come

first; research and teaching are important but secondary, and research is aimed at clinical utility. Furthermore, specialists cooperate across disciplines in ways seldom seen in other academic health centers. Mayo doctors are salaried, and all departments are treated as cost centers, so physicians can take as much time with patients as they consider necessary. On the wall is this quote from William Mayo: "The best interest of the patient is the only interest to be considered." And administrators at Mayo see their role as serving doctors rather than struggling with them about costs. Of all the organizations we surveyed, Mayo was the only one in which most gaps between ideal and practice were small; whereas others said that they espoused but did not practice "patient service as the highest priority," Mayo doctors saw themselves as constantly striving towards this ideal with the full support of the institution.

Mayo offers a glimpse into a resolution of the clash between the bureaucratic-hospital mode of production and the craft-physician mode: one that sustains a knowledge mode, a transparent learning culture where physicians become persuaded that principles and processes are good for all stakeholders. In Rochester, we found a harmonious relationship between the Clinic and St. Marys Hospital, founded and run by Franciscan sisters. The partnership, created by William Mayo, still thrives.

Although Mayo is clearly physician led, nurses sit as equals on major committees. Each clinical department has both a clinical manager and a nurse manager, and they are both involved in research. There is a career development program for nursing. Unlike in most other healthcare organizations, nurses feel they have the authority to criticize doctors who haven't done things properly, and there are protections for those who speak up. A nurse manager told us, "We accept the doctors as leaders, but not as bosses."

Openness, self-criticism, and self-renewal are Mayo strengths. By constantly reinforcing a culture focused on the customer-patient and encouraging criticism among professionals according to what is best for the patient, Mayo raises the level of collaboration. Contrast this with most healthcare organizations (and most corporations), where professionals keep quiet about their colleagues' errors and whistle-blowers are punished. Mayo is a model for professional knowledge companies of all kinds that are trying to create collaboration among specialists.

Mayo is inspiring. If I had a complicated illness with the probable need for specialists in more than one field, I'd take a plane to Rochester. But no one is perfect, and the Mayo doctors did check some gaps.

As in many of the best companies I've worked with, there's an attitude of rejecting ideas from the outside, the not-invented-here syndrome, a distinct contrast to the Mayo brothers, who traveled great distances to learn the newest surgical techniques. While some department leaders have persuaded physicians to adopt evidence-based medicine, others have lagged behind. One Mayo chair said: "Many physicians are still in a cottage industry and resist evidence-based medicine. And it can still take too much time to negotiate between departments, which results in patients having long waits." A nurse suggested that patients bring along a Russian novel to occupy themselves during these waits.

At the time of our visit, Mayo was just starting to expand an advanced IT system including checks for harmful interactions of medications, order entry, improving communication among physicians, and gaining knowledge about outcomes so that the doctors could make better clinical decisions by designing guidelines and protocols. And even though mutual respect is a core Mayo value, some administrators feel like second-class citizens. Said one, "MDs act like they know everything. They act like everyone else is a dummy." But others thought only some doctors acted this way and that some administrators invited this attitude. Overawed by the physicians, they were passive when they needed to push back. But all of this seems to me par for the course. Even in the best of organizations, there are complaints, especially about status and bruised egos.

The strengths and weaknesses of Mayo are intertwined, but overall, this is an excellent example of a collaborative craft model moving slowly to a knowledge mode. But it's doing so without transformational leadership. William Mayo, the visionary leader created such a great organization that it would be hard for a new visionary leader to boost the clinic to another level. It will happen because the Mayo chairs have become convinced of the need for change.

Can Mayo be the model for other healthcare organizations?

Effective though it is, some of its limitations have resulted in its so far remaining unique and, furthermore, confined to particular niches. The most important limitation is that it remains grounded in academic health centers; it has not fully entered the bare-knuckle world of large-scale business competition. Attempts to expand into primary care centers have had mixed success and were abandoned in Arizona. Mayo is most effective where patient problems require complex customized solutions. Although physician interactions go beyond the individual-craft model, they remain quite personal and small-scale. Thus it seems likely that some of the lessons from the industrial model will need to be incorporated into the collaborative Mayo approach.

This fusion, however, is not a simple matter, as we'll see in the section describing Mayo attempts to learn from Intermountain Health Care.

Intermountain Health Care

IHC, headquartered in Salt Lake City, has been repeatedly rated number one in the nation by independent rating agencies.[24] IHC was formed in 1974–1975, when the Mormon Church decided to divest itself of its 14 hospitals. After buying 10 more hospitals and a number of physician practices, IHC comprised 24 hospitals, 26 health centers or neighborhood clinics, and 150 service sites throughout Utah, southern Idaho, and eastern Nevada. When we visited IHC, the system included 400 employed physicians and 1,500 who were directly affiliated. The majority of Utah physicians were impaneled by the IHC health plan. IHC had a 45–50 percent market share of its catchment area, of which 25 percent was paid directly to its system; the rest was contracted out to payers. IHC operated 50 percent of the hospital beds in Utah. The health plan covered 475,000 lives, with only a 6 percent rate of disenrollment after the first year.

IHC's purpose is to improve the health of the population it serves. It spends millions in direct charity care of over a hundred thousand patients. Intermountain Community Care Foundation supports clinics for homeless and low-income populations with a clinic serving over three thousand children in seven schools. IHC's policy is to keep premiums low to make quality care as affordable as possible.

IHC leadership can be viewed as a model for any organization of professionals trying to transform itself from a bureaucracy to a learning organization. IHC is moving from a traditional hospital-based bureaucratic system, with physicians essentially operating in a craft mode of production, to a knowledge mode that makes good use of information technology and quality tools to develop evidence-based health care. It's moving from specialty silos to clinical programs, from treating specific illnesses to solutions that sustain health. To do this, it's had an exceptional leadership partnership and a leadership system. At the top of the organization, Bill Nelson, the visionary CEO, has a background in finance, and Dr. Charles Sorenson, the emotionally intelligent and interactive chief medical officer, heads operations with the physicians.

At the program level, operational leaders—physicians working with nurses and administrators—work to persuade their colleagues to practice according to protocols (processes or pathways) that reduce variation, lower costs, and improve outcomes. These "doctor" (in the sense defined in chapter 6) leaders are helped in developing protocols and mapping processes by Drs. Brent James and David Burton, who provide the tools of quality management and informatics.

Our team interviewed seventeen leaders of the IHC system, culminating in a two-hour feedback session and discussion of the findings with Nelson and Sorenson. The people we interviewed all believe that IHC is moving in the right direction, up a learning curve. They appreciate Nelson's leadership and his focus on quality and Sorenson's interactive style of listening and responding to physician concerns.

A good example of an effective leadership partnership on the operational level of a clinical program comes from Dr. Don Lappé and Susan Goldberg, RN, who run the cardiovascular clinical program. Lappé has a weekly clinical conference at which data is presented on reasons to use a process or therapy. The doctors and nurses together set goals that are easy to measure. Lappé finds that physicians accept clinical pathways when they measurably improve patient care, so he provides timely, relevant, and easy-to-understand feedback. The data and methodology are placed on the IHC intranet.

Lappé is also taking on the task of cutting costs and limiting vendors to those who provide the best value. This means that some physicians will lose the free meals and vacations offered by vendors. However, the savings in the cost of stents, pacemakers, and intra aortic balloons are significant. Once the number of vendors is limited, it becomes possible to negotiate price reductions for quantity.

Lappé spends one-third of his time in clinical practice. He believes this is important if he is to maintain his credibility with physicians and, with the continual changes in practice, his knowledge of the field. Physician leaders say that once they stop practicing medicine, their colleagues no longer consider them real physicians. In a meeting on this report in Stockholm, Dr. Carola Lemne, CEO of Danderyd Hospital, remarked wryly that physicians will accept only other physicians as leaders, but once these doctors have become leaders, they're no longer considered to be physicians. Or as one chair said of a colleague who became a hospital head, "He's gone over to the dark side."

Brent James affirmed the outline I showed him of the movement from craft to manufacturing to knowledge modes of production in health care: "We can show that the craft style actually harms patients. Caring concern can lead to the wrong solution." For example, a surgeon defines quality in terms of a nurse following his orders. But if twenty surgeons give a nurse twenty different processes, she is likely to make a mistake. Working within standard processes reduces the possibility of confusion, and at the same time, leaves physicians free to exercise craftsmanship and to be caring.

Why hasn't the movement to evidence-based medical practice not gone more quickly? According to James, "We are dealing with relatively new knowledge. Physicians are still arguing about the scientific facts."[25] He went on to say that the tools to manage quality of care are new. So is the mind-set needed—systems thinking, since 50 to 75 percent of errors are not human error, but system problems. Physicians need to understand the elements of total quality management: root cause analysis, and statistical process control of variability. Furthermore, it's a mistake to try to impose pathways for all 610 common medical processes when 65 account for 95 percent of the variance. James also said that leaders are just starting to learn how to produce change, not by dealing one-on-one with doctors, but by gaining group consensus to protocols and persuading doctors of their value—changing mind-sets.

Another reason why hospitals are not driven to change, James noted, is that national surveys show that people choose providers on the basis of cost, convenience, and friendly service, not quality. The outcome study in New York State on coronary artery bypass surgery had no effect on patient volumes in hospitals with good or bad results. Patients typically stay with bad doctors who develop a good relationship with them—when you are worried about your heart, you're more likely to feel comforting transferential trust in the doctor you have who may not be the one you need.

Another important reason for slow change is disincentives for the providers. While protocols may lead to savings of 30 to 70 percent, the organization loses money because of reduced fees for service. James said: "You can only make a business case for quality if you can link quality to a payment strategy." This can be done in a capitated health plan (the patient pays a fixed amount each year to cover all services) with little turnover or a partnership with a company that's willing to invest in the long-term health of employees.

The Mayo-Intermountain Dialogue

On the surface, the Mayo Clinic and IHC organizations are very different. IHC is a large integrated delivery system with a health plan. To maintain its huge market share and not-for-profit status, it must demonstrate a commitment to "the best clinical practice" at "the lowest appropriate cost." Its hospital charges are 15 percent lower than the national average. Mayo-Scottsdale, by contrast, is part of a unique academic health center in which research and teaching are vital to the mission. Compared to IHC, Mayo-Scottsdale is a medical boutique for episodic treatment; its charges are among the highest in the Phoenix area.

Despite their differences, these organizations appeared to have complementary competencies, and it seemed that that they could provide valuable lessons for each other. IHC is a national leader in evidence-based medicine, and Mayo wanted to learn how IHC leadership went about this. In turn, some of the IHC physicians had asked us how they could create more of a Mayo-type group practice, with a patient-focused cross-disciplinary culture.[26] We thought that by bringing leaders of the two organizations together, they might learn from each other, and the CEOs of both organizations liked the idea.

What emerged from this encounter between two of the best health-care organizations in the world is that they are both approaching knowledge modes, but from different directions. The IHC leadership came from the world of bureaucratic hospitals—they are comfortable with large scale and with practices like rule-based management and performance incentives—but sought to reinvent themselves in a way that would create greater involvement of physicians and staff. The Mayo tradition comes originally from the craft world and has remained generally within a small-group, personalized framework. Mayo and IHC were interested in each other because both see that their approaches need to be further developed to deal with complex interdependence on a large scale. The Mayo physicians are interested in and wary of formalized process, while the IHC leaders are interested in, but also wary of, encouraging flexible local teamwork in place of some of their top-down rules.

These differences emerged most clearly around two issues.

- *Evidence-based medicine:* IHC leaders believe that EBM leads both to more consistent clinical excellence, reducing the rate of medical errors, and to maximum cost-effectiveness. In the dialogue, however, the Mayo doctors expressed resistance to EBM; they pointed out that they often deal with complex health problems that require cooperation across disciplines and do not fit standardized pathways. Although some Mayo chairs have begun to address systematic variability, the physicians as a whole are not yet convinced that the scientific literature is strong enough to provide consistent answers to many situations; they trust more in their peer interactions and mutual criticism focused on the patient to maximize quality. They will move to EBM only when their own research supports it. However, this will probably happen more quickly with IT systems that provide the medical staff with systematic information on both process and outcome performance.

- *The physician–administrator relationship:* At IHC, administrators and physicians often clash: the former focus on controlling costs and quality, while the latter continue to try to maximize their individual professional autonomy within the framework of a large organization. At Mayo, administrators explicitly serve physicians. The positive element in this approach is that the focus on patient welfare is unclouded; the negative element is that there is little opportunity to create a unified set of processes that would standardize the best learnings throughout the hospital and lead to continuous improvement of the whole.

One way of putting the problem is that the Mayo approach of physician interaction and consensus works very effectively to bring together varied resources around a specific problem; on a case-by-case basis, it is unmatched. At Mayo, groups have relied on peer review and discussion to work out consistency of procedures. The problem is to scale this capability to a larger system where doctors can't be expected to learn from each other informally.

IHC leaders seemed to be struggling to define an approach that reconciles the need for physician involvement and commitment with the need for procedural consistency and efficiency on a large scale. They were moving, with difficulty, toward a process in which medical protocols are developed through group consensus across the system. This may point the way to a resolution of the tension between collaboration based on case-focused discussion and more formalized processes.

Thus the two organizations show in different ways the difficulty of making the transition to a knowledge mode of production for the healthcare system as a whole. The Mayo example involves high levels of collaboration but on a small and personal scale, with much use of informal mechanisms; the IHC case involves large scale and an attempt to create greater involvement, but continues to struggle with the tensions between administrators and physicians. Both are trying to move beyond individual craft performance without getting stuck in an industrial mode.

As a result of the dialogue between these two systems, Sorenson continued in the role of "doctor," using the gap survey to lead the dialogue with physicians, responding to legitimate concerns, but emphasizing the logic of change. Mayo-Scottsdale planned to study IHC's approach and to design a version of EBM that fit its culture and values. In both places, the leaders recognized that they had to create collaborators, not followers, and this required them to persuade, using data and encouraging open discussion.

Visionary Leadership at Vanderbilt University Medical Center

What kind of leader can move traditional academic health centers with their craft baronies to a knowledge mode of production? Certainly, the ombudsman-type leader won't motivate change. I asked Roger Bulger for a good example, and he recommended a visit to Vanderbilt University Medical Center (VUMC), where Dr. Harry Jacobson was attempting this kind of transformation.

Jacobson is a visionary leader and a successful business entrepreneur. But he faced some tough opposition as he attempted to transform VUMC medicine to the knowledge mode of production. He has put together a first-rate leadership system with one of the leading medical IT innovators in the world, Dr. William Stead, Director of the Informatics Center. When we visited, Dr. Paul V. Miles, the Chief Quality Officer and Dr. Robert Dittus, Director of Internal Medicine, were teaching evidence-based medicine. But many faculty members were skeptical.

Some faculty argued that Jacobson was trying to force them into practicing "cookbook medicine," that his purpose was cutting costs, not doing what was best for patients. Others were wary that they'd be pushed into a group practice, like Mayo, where they'd become salaried and lose the right, as one orthopedic surgeon put it, to "eat what you kill"—meaning, get the payments from the patients you treat.

Jacobson recognized he needed a strategy for transformation. Education and dialogue were essential elements. But Jacobson knew he was better at strategizing and visioning than at managing. One big step he took was to hire an effective chief operating officer, Dr. Steve Gabbe, from the University of Washington, as dean. He also recruited a couple of physician ex-astronauts who helped teach faculty, nursing staff, and students/ residents to understand systems-based practice. Given their backgrounds, these physicians had instant credibility. They adapted airline crew resource training (CRT), and they were quite successful in getting their students to see the role systems and teamwork play in the quality of care. And Jacobson also made use of his leadership power to incentivize physicians to tackle variability and to place supporters in department chairs.

THE LESSONS OF LEADERSHIP
FOR KNOWLEDGE WORK

Leaders are essential to transform business bureaucracies and healthcare organizations to the knowledge mode of production. One type of leader alone can't do this. A system of leaders is needed: visionary strategists who are generally productive narcissists, obsessive systematic operational leaders, and interactive network leaders.

These leaders will face resistance, rooted in threats to self-interest and the bureaucratic social character. But they'll also find supporters among the Interactives. Resistances won't be overcome by warm, fuzzy leadership. But narcissistic visionaries also won't succeed by forcing knowledge workers to follow them. As one VUMC chair said, "If Harry forced people, they'd become disaffected and leave." Furthermore, as the power of paternal transference wanes, the key is to educate interactively, creating collaborators by persuasion and the generous use of supportive data as was done at Intermountain. Leaders must be "doctors" before they can become "democrats." They need to understand the people they lead so they can address resistance and recognize real support. But as doctors, leaders also need to use their powers of promotion and incentives to back up the message. Dr. Kenneth Kizer, who led the transformation of the VA system, said at a seminar I attended that some of the bureaucratic physicians and administrators never got the message: "I had candid discussions with them and facilitated their leaving."[27]

Leaders may sometimes need to engage unions as collaborators, as did Dr. David Lawrence, when he was CEO at Kaiser-Permanente, with the help of Pete DiCicco of the AFL-CIO. Lawrence also put a lot of effort into educating his board, and that can be crucial to support change.[28] Dr. Stan Pappelbaum, a visionary CEO at Scripps in San Diego, was shot down by his board when he began to threaten the sweet deals enjoyed by some physicians, especially by one doctor the board chairman believed had saved his life. Boards have to recognize that change in healthcare organizations can provoke some nasty resistance, and if they want change, they must support a courageous visionary leader.

Knowledge work organizations are not alike. They are social systems that differ according to their traditions and missions, and they select and socialize different values in their key actors. Even the best healthcare organizations like Mayo, IHC, and VUMC can't just copy each other. But they can learn from each other, if they adapt learnings to their own cultures. This also holds true for businesses.

Policy makers need to understand that solving the problems of healthcare delivery is not just a matter of different incentives, new technology, or government policy, but rather of transforming a craft mode of production to a knowledge mode in a way that incorporates the best craft values in collaborative learning organizations. This means that leaders should be selected not because they are distinguished experts, but because they understand the logic of business, quality, and interactive leadership and have the Personality Intelligence to select complementary partners and gain collaborators.

Gap survey: The leadership that's needed

How important are each of the following elements to the success of your organization?
*How **well** are you achieving them?*

	Importance		Level today	
	Low High		Low High	
Strategies				
• We provide excellent service to:				
Patients	1 2 3 4 5		1 2 3 4 5	
Health plan members	1 2 3 4 5		1 2 3 4 5	
Customers	1 2 3 4 5		1 2 3 4 5	
Physicians	1 2 3 4 5		1 2 3 4 5	
• We serve the diverse needs of:				
Young	1 2 3 4 5		1 2 3 4 5	
Old	1 2 3 4 5		1 2 3 4 5	
Rich	1 2 3 4 5		1 2 3 4 5	
Poor	1 2 3 4 5		1 2 3 4 5	
Urban	1 2 3 4 5		1 2 3 4 5	
Rural	1 2 3 4 5		1 2 3 4 5	
• Our services are cost-effective	1 2 3 4 5		1 2 3 4 5	
• We continuously improve the cost and quality of our services	1 2 3 4 5		1 2 3 4 5	
• We work to improve the health of the community	1 2 3 4 5		1 2 3 4 5	
• We provide our services with integrity	1 2 3 4 5		1 2 3 4 5	
• Our research and education strengthen the clinical enterprise	1 2 3 4 5		1 2 3 4 5	
• We learn from best practice	1 2 3 4 5		1 2 3 4 5	
• We attract exceptional individuals at all levels	1 2 3 4 5		1 2 3 4 5	
• We provide opportunities for personal and professional growth	1 2 3 4 5		1 2 3 4 5	
• We recognize and reward employees who achieve excellence	1 2 3 4 5		1 2 3 4 5	
• We give people appropriate responsibilities that make full use of their capabilities	1 2 3 4 5		1 2 3 4 5	
• We evaluate individual performance regularly	1 2 3 4 5		1 2 3 4 5	
• Our information systems support physician decision making	1 2 3 4 5		1 2 3 4 5	
• Physicians use clinical pathways and guidelines	1 2 3 4 5		1 2 3 4 5	
Leadership approaches				
• Communicating a vision	1 2 3 4 5		1 2 3 4 5	
• Practicing openness	1 2 3 4 5		1 2 3 4 5	
• Coaching	1 2 3 4 5		1 2 3 4 5	
• Empowering	1 2 3 4 5		1 2 3 4 5	
• Resolving conflicts	1 2 3 4 5		1 2 3 4 5	
• Holding people accountable	1 2 3 4 5		1 2 3 4 5	
• Developing relationships of trust	1 2 3 4 5		1 2 3 4 5	

CHAPTER 8

Leaders for Learning

OUR PROSPERITY AND WELL-BEING depend on our ability to learn. We humans have to learn how to make a living, how to take care of ourselves, how to relate to others. Yes, we are born with embryonic personality traits and talents, but we must learn to make use of these gifts, to adapt them to a particular culture. And now that our culture is in a turmoil of transformation, the learning needed to succeed is more demanding then ever before.

But while children from advantaged families are being shaped for success in the knowledge world, starting at home, children from disadvantaged families are not. Affluent children are developing the interactive social character that fits them for the knowledge workplace. From an early age, they know what's at stake. They are pushed by their parents, teachers, and peers to compete, and they're given the tools they need—books, computers, video games, cell phones, iPods. Disadvantaged children, especially African Americans and Latin American immigrants from the inner cities, are adapting to a different world, where success, such as it is, means dodging violence and gaining respect on the street. They may have dreams of making it big in sports or entertainment, but not in the knowledge workplace.

Educators argue endlessly about the best way for children to learn. The intellectual descendants of Jean-Jacques Rousseau believe children should be encouraged to follow their own instincts, to make their own decisions about what they want to learn. Variations of this view include learning by doing rather than rote learning or memorization. Others argue for more discipline and rigorous testing for basic skills. But none of the educational theorists has come up with a persuasive theory that serves the needs of all children in our turbulent society, especially those from disadvantaged backgrounds.[1]

However, in this chapter, we'll see that some schools do prepare at-risk children for success in the knowledge workplace, not only through their curriculum, but even more because their tough-minded leadership and organization are shaping their students' social character. This kind of leadership is not the same as that which works well with affluent kids. It could be considered transitional leadership, based on a clear understanding of the challenge of developing social character as well as intellect.

In the past, schooling was less essential for success. The children of traditional farmers could learn most of what they needed to know from their parents. The children of the industrial-bureaucratic age could get by with basic reading, writing, arithmetic, and learning to follow orders. People could get a good job in a factory with little education, and the schooling required for clerical and professional jobs seems simple compared with what is now needed in the age of knowledge work. The kids in this age won't succeed by copying their parents, and above all, they need to learn to keep learning.

The challenge to our schools is not limited to low-income minority children. On the national policy level, urgent voices warn us that we're falling behind China and India in producing the engineers and scientists needed for innovation and business success. As factory jobs migrate abroad and transactional service jobs—telephone operators, bank clerks, sales—are automated or replaced with Internet shopping, those higher-paying jobs that aren't automated or outsourced usually go to people with college diplomas.[2] Statistics show the wage gap between college and high school graduates is growing.[3] But increasingly, with the ease of Internet communication, global companies can even place higher-paying technical jobs in other countries.

However, there are good jobs that don't require a college degree. These are craft jobs in construction, service, and solutions: electricians, plumbers, mechanics, and carpenters. These vocations can pay very well, and they are not likely to leave the country. Yet, the politicians and policy makers who promote college for everyone seldom mention these jobs and don't encourage kids to aim for them. Why not?[4] Probably because people look down on them compared with white-collar jobs. While teaching executives at Ford, I heard the owner of a large Dearborn dealership complain that when he advertised for a mechanic at a starting salary of $80,000 a year, he didn't get enough applicants. But when he advertised for an office clerk at $40,000, there was a line of job seekers stretching around the block. Something is wrong with our values and educational alternatives when we don't give kids the option of learning a vocation that will provide them interesting work and a good income and that is unlikely to be either automated or shipped offshore.

There is no surefire education, even in science and technology, that prepares kids to succeed in a culture that calls for continual innovation in products, marketing, and organization. Consider that both Bill Gates and Steve Jobs dropped out of college because their thinking was ahead of what the professors were teaching. What Jobs got most out of his brief time at Reed College was the importance of product design. What Gates got from Harvard was an eventual partnership with his roommate Steve Ballmer, whose managerial skills complemented Gates's strategic brilliance. Consider that while Sony was loaded with engineers and programmers, the company fell behind because these experts didn't collaborate with each other. Howard Stringer, the first non-Japanese Sony CEO, who has an interactive marketing personality, sees himself as a bridge-builder, selecting and connecting the talent. It's not at all clear how he learned that leadership skill. It's not part of any school curriculum, but it does require both an interactive social character and high Personality Intelligence.[5]

WHAT CAN SCHOOLS DO?

The founding fathers recognized that an educated public is essential for a society that is both democratic and prosperous. And it follows that the members of the society need excellent education to prosper in this global economy. This means that without good schooling, they'll have little or no chance of making it; instead, they'll likely become a problem to society and a reproach to its promise of equal opportunity. But many kids are not being well educated, especially those from the inner cities. Because of this, a concerned policy industry has sprung up, producing theories and proposals about how to improve schools. Rather than trying to report on all the different views and arguments, as with health care, I'll describe programs I've seen up close where kids from disadvantaged backgrounds are learning. These success stories, like those in health care as described in chapter 7, result from great leadership. It seems obvious to me that policy makers should avoid trying to legislate change before they understand what the most effective educational innovators are doing. Policy should support proven excellence.

Before visiting these schools, let's stop and reflect on how many of us have learned what we've needed to know to succeed in our work. Some of us got a head start at home. My mother was a schoolteacher who taught me to read before I entered kindergarten, so that learning at school came naturally for me. This may also be the case at schools like the Sudbury Valley School, where kids are free to choose what they want to learn.[6] These kids feel liberated, and some who take pleasure in learning have gone on to college and the professions. But other alumni, including a professional skateboarder and a waiter, have not done so well.[7] Why not? Could they have done better in a more structured school?

Many inner city kids get taught as much or more by TV and on the street as they do in school. The discipline of reading and writing, memorizing facts and formulas, does not come easily for them as it did for many of us. And according to African American and Hispanic parents and students, schools often fail because the kids don't respect teachers, many of whom are unable to keep order in the classroom.[8] Possibly, we exaggerate the negatives. No more than 30 percent of African American children surveyed report serious levels of disruption and unrest in their schools. But this number is still much too large. And to succeed, these kids need more than passable, OK schooling. They need to be motivated to work hard, stretch themselves, and to enjoy learning and using what they learn.

A number of business leaders and their foundations have taken up the challenge of transforming inner city public schools, mostly with limited success. Bill and Melinda Gates have spent $1 billion funding twenty-two public schools, but according to an interview in *BusinessWeek*, they view their experience so far as research and development to learn what works and what doesn't, mostly what doesn't.[9]

THE EMOS AND KIPP

Hundreds of millions have also been invested, mostly by idealistic business leaders, in educational management organizations (EMOs). These are charter schools, started in the 1990s, which have been licensed by public school systems. Some, like Adventure and Edison Schools, promised to give venture capitalists a big return, but didn't. The most successful charter schools in terms of results have been the not-for-profits. As of January 2007, the top of the list are the forty-eight middle schools, two high schools, and two early childhood schools run by KIPP (Knowledge Is Power Program), a foundation that trains school leaders to open up schools and practice the KIPP approach to education.[10]

In 2005, I was asked by leaders of the KIPP Foundation to help them craft an effective national organization.[11] Besides working with Mike Feinberg and Dave Levin, KIPP's founders, and Scott Hamilton and Richard Greene, who were then running the Foundation, I visited KIPP schools in Houston; New York; Oakland, California; and Washington, D.C.

At each of these schools I was inspired by the students' and teachers' energy and spirit. I sat in classes where the kids were fully focused on their work, moving back and forth between independent and collaborative tasks. I read well-written essays and research reports pinned up on the walls. At KIPP Academy in the Bronx, I watched and heard a middle school orchestra practicing. At KIPP Bridge College Preparatory in Oakland, I saw the sets the kids had painted for the musical *The Wiz*, and I was given a CD of their spirited performance. At KIPP Academy Middle School in Houston, one of the first KIPP schools (opened in 1994), there are pictures on the wall of the original class. Over 80 percent have gone on to college.

On the walls of all these schools is the simple but powerful KIPP motto: "Work hard, be nice." Other mottos I saw were: "Team always beats individual," "Never give up!" and "I believe that success comes from doing the best I can do, not from winning."

How does KIPP succeed where other schools fail? Both leadership and organization make the difference. The founders who developed the KIPP approach joined the Teach for America Program founded by another exceptional innovator, Wendy Kopp, right after they graduated from college. Feinberg was then twenty-four years old and had graduated from Penn with a major in international relations; Levin was twenty-three and from Yale, where he had majored in the history of American education. Sent to teach middle school in Houston, Feinberg and Levin discovered they got results, loved teaching, and believed they could build schools where inner city kids would learn and succeed.

One night in 1993, while listening to U2's *Achtung Baby* on repeat play, they brainstormed until dawn and came up with a vision for a fifth grade. They started with the middle school because that's where they'd been teaching. It's also the place where so many at-risk kids entering puberty see themselves as failures and become turned off to learning.

Levin is more the educational philosopher, while Feinberg pushes ahead to create new schools. Feinberg says Levin is like a quarterback deciding on strategy and he's like a fullback, always charging ahead. Levin cites three factors essential to KIPP's success. The first is "talented" leadership, based on selection of promising leaders with classroom experience to become principals—called school leaders—who then go through an extensive year of apprenticeship and five weeks of training, starting with a two-week workshop at Stanford University (I'll come back to the qualities of leadership needed at KIPP schools later in the chapter). This is unlike most public schools, where principals are not academic leaders but rather administrators who have had little leadership training. A pillar of the KIPP edifice is the school leader's "power to lead"; power in both senses—authority and ability.

The second factor is more time used well, which allows for more time in classes and lets teachers finish their work before leaving; this also means there is more time for sports, games, music, salsa, and Shakespeare, subjects you don't need to motivate kids to learn and that spark creative fires. Keep in mind that charter schools like KIPP are public schools. Any child who applies will be admitted first-come, first-served. However, parents and students must sign a Commitment to Excellence form (see "Sample Commitment to Excellence Form" at the end of this chapter) that includes arriving at KIPP by 7:25 a.m. Monday to Friday, staying until 5:00 p.m. (4:00 p.m. on Fridays), coming to school some Saturdays from 9:15 a.m. to 1:05 p.m. for sports and the arts, and attending a month of summer school.

Parents all promise to check their children's homework and encourage them to call the teacher if there's a problem. A KIPP principle is: ask for help if you need it. Teachers agree to be available. Students also make a commitment to ask questions if they don't understand something. There's no excuse for not completing homework or not seeking help when it's needed. Furthermore, the kids commit to respecting others. In other words, "Work hard, be nice" is not just a motto; it's a behavioral norm that shapes a productive personality.

At KIPP, there are also consequences for not meeting commitments. Each week, the KIPPsters, as Feinberg and Levin call them, are given a few dollars' worth of KIPP money, or *scrip*, which they can use to buy KIPP materials, notebooks, shirts, etc. By saving up the scrip, they "pay" for excursions at the end of the year. If the kids fail to produce homework, they lose scrip. If they are disrespectful in class, they have to sit apart from the others and are not allowed to talk, but they still must do the work. There's also a dress code—not a uniform, but basic chinos and neat white or navy skirts, and blouses, some with KIPP logos, so there is no costly competition for clothes.

Levin's third factor is quality of instruction, but principals and teachers have the freedom to innovate on curriculum as long as they get results. Levin claims these three elements are what get KIPP the parental and community support.

I think there's more to it than three factors. Levin is a natural systems thinker. When asked which of his factors was most important, he correctly said they were interrelated. I see KIPP as a self-organizing learning organization bringing kids into the knowledge workplace and developing the interactive social character they need to succeed. The school leader, teachers, students, and parents accept rules like being on time and doing homework and internalize values like working hard and being nice. Furthermore, incentives like scrip and school excursions reinforce operating principles like availability of help and no shortcuts, no excuses.

Because of these shared values and KIPP practices, there are few other rules, and teachers can be trusted to innovate curriculum as long as they get results. However, each school has the same organizational culture—no innovation is allowed there—and as we'll see, these schools need an authoritative leadership to make certain that this culture of social character development is sustained.

The typical public school is more a bureaucracy and less a learning organization for Interactives in the knowledge age. Most public school principals are administrators, not leaders, and they run schools by enforcing rules—not modeling values or enforcing operating principles. Levin is right that it's a mistake to focus on any single element of the KIPP social system, because the definition of a system is that each of its parts can't be evaluated by itself, but only according to how well it furthers the system's purpose. And in KIPP's case, as in all public schools, the explicit purpose of the system is the measurable learning success of the students. It's my view that the implicit purpose is character development.

LEADING KIPP SCHOOLS

I first met Susan Schaeffler in 2005 when she was still the founding school leader of KIPP Academy, a middle school in southeast Washington, D.C. I was amazed at how well-written were the essays and book reports the kids had produced, and their test results showed significant year-by-year gains over the average in D.C. At that time, 70 percent of these inner city, mostly African American, children lived with a single parent, almost always the mother; 10 percent in foster families; 10 percent with their original parents; and 10 percent with one biological and one step-parent. Eighty percent of the families were under the poverty line.

Schaeffler has since become executive director of the three KIPP schools she helped develop in Washington, and she has gained chartering authority for three more elementary and two high schools. Clearly, the board of education has been impressed with KIPP results, and clearly Schaeffler, like the best KIPP leaders, is also an effective entrepreneur.

Schaeffler graduated from Colorado State University with a major in human development, specializing in adolescence. She started out in D.C. as a public school teacher after serving in the Teach for America program and teaching in Ethiopia for a year with International Foundation of Education and Self-Help (IFESH). Like Feinberg and Levin, she enjoyed working with kids. She had thought about becoming a lawyer ("getting a real job") but when she interned in the public defender's office, she didn't like the work. When Feinberg and Levin recruited her, she started a small program in an Anacostia church, which in 1991 became KIPP Academy, the highest-achieving public middle school in the country.

Schaeffler is an authoritative leader, and she's been good at selecting school leaders from the ranks of KIPP teachers. I asked her what kind of person she looks for and what she sees as the main developmental challenges of beginning KIPP principals. I've asked Levin the same question, and essentially, they agree that for teachers becoming school leaders, the major challenge is to accept their new authority, to "be the boss" without forgetting that they're also teachers. Good KIPP school leaders demand accountability from teachers and students. They don't let things lapse, and they don't shy away from conflict. Schaeffler notes that some excellent teachers "would be miserable with conflict" and would fail as school leaders. Furthermore, they'd avoid making necessary but unpopular decisions. I suggested these are the caring erotic personalities, and once I had explained this personality type, Schaeffler nodded and said, "They are not good school leaders." Nor are the obsessives who get caught up in details and micromanage the teachers. And the marketing types sometimes shy away from being authorities rather than interactive siblings. Schaeffler says she wants to find more interactive narcissists; her leader is the type of person who wants to change the world and who "embraces conflict, even enjoys it."

Levin and Schaeffler are describing a very different kind of leader from the bridge-builder facilitator admired by Rowena Davis (mentioned in chapter 6). Levin goes so far as to say that the best KIPP principals are "benevolent despots" who demand high performance from teachers as well as students. However, these despots are working within a set of agreed-on operating principles. The teachers they lead are collaborators, not followers, and the KIPP school leaders I've met move from being doctors who educate beginning teachers to democrats who involve them in key decisions. They can be compared to the best football coaches, described in chapter 2, who share responsibility and accountability with team members but also insist on peak performance and drive for results. At the same time, these school leaders have to be able to be authoritatively paternal with the kids and more siblinglike with the teachers. In effect, they're leading different social characters, and they need the Personality Intelligence to understand the people they lead.

I asked Schaeffler whether she thought there was a difference between male and female school leaders. After noting that all the school leaders she's chosen are women, she said, "Women need to work harder to gain respect. A female has to come out fighting from day one. You're not given anything." Possibly women have a harder time than men in leadership roles because they are more likely than men to run up against the mother transference—the expectation that they'll be nurturing and resentment when they're not. They may need to show they are going to be neither fairy godmothers nor wicked witches.

An excellent school leader with a well-developed Personality Intelligence is Julene Mohr, principal of the KIPP high school in Houston. She got her BA in sociology and anthropology, specializing in American culture, at the University of Michigan, then taught in the Teach for America program in Rio Grande Valley, Texas. Mohr joined KIPP in 1995 and started teaching fourth- and fifth-grade kids with learning disabilities. She says one thing that impressed her about Feinberg was that he was a principal who could think like a fifth-grader. Like Levin and Schaeffler, she says KIPP school leaders need to learn to accept authority, to be decisive with teachers. But she adds that principals also need to be able to defuse controversy; to be "charming with parents"; and to get teachers, parents, and students "to buy-in, make it seem win-win." The entrepreneurial

KIPP school leader has to gain collaboration from school superintendents, boards of education, foundations, and philanthropists.

For the children they lead, these school leaders are transitional leaders, more autocratic than the ideal leader in the knowledge workplace, but perhaps essential to transform the social character of the street into the motivated Interactives that graduate from KIPP schools.

CAN KIPP BE A MODEL FOR PUBLIC SCHOOLS?

The idea of charter schools came from a speech in 1988 by Albert Shanker (1928–1997), the visionary larger-than-life president of the American Federation of Teachers (AFT). I was hired by Shanker in the early 1990s to help AFT create a vision and structure for its future, based in large part on his thinking. Unlike union leaders who just focus on getting the most they can for their members, Shanker taught that society would not support a teachers' union that was only out for itself, not also for the success of the students. He understood before most people did that schools designed for an industrial-bureaucratic society were not preparing students for the knowledge age, and he conceived of charter schools as providing the R&D for the public school system of the future.

So do Feinberg and Levin. Feinberg told me he'd like KIPP to be the FedEx to the U.S. Postal Service, the mouse that pushes the bureaucratic public school system elephant to start dancing. But can public schools learn from KIPP? There are some critics who raise concerns about the degree of discipline and the scrip incentives at KIPP schools. Are students being bribed to learn by getting the scrip, and will they continue to learn when there are no "money" incentives? Levin responds that "some kids are interested and motivated from the word go, but the majority are not, so the rewards are like a crutch to get them working on their own." The scrip also gets the kids thinking about earning money and builds self-esteem when they succeed in saving enough for excursions. Money is a big factor in the knowledge workplace, and these kids need to connect it with good work.

Another concern about replication is the argument that KIPP parents are more motivated than parents of other public school kids. This is hard to prove one way or another, since it could be that they get more motivated once they join the KIPP family. Levin invites the doubters to compare the test scores of KIPP kids when they enter the program and after enrollment. The entering students have the same low scores and disciplinary problems as kids in other inner city schools; at KIPP, their scores rise well above the city average.

What about the teachers? Can they sustain the intensity, the long hours they put in? Levin says, "You can't build a system with martyrs." Teachers are paid for the extra time, and they are proud to be part of the KIPP family (Feinberg and Levin like to talk about team and family as KIPP values). Some teachers aspire to become school leaders. Others see KIPP not as a lifetime career but as a deeply meaningful learning experience. Schaeffler says that, of the seven teachers who started with her in 1991, two are running KIPP schools in D.C., two are still teaching, two are at home with their children, and one is in medical school. That's four of seven still with KIPP. However, 50 percent of new public school teachers leave teaching after five years. Another 12 percent transfer each year, and the percent who leave high-poverty schools is even higher.[12] Furthermore, 45 percent of all workers in America today say they want to change jobs at least every three to five years.[13]

Some union leaders voice concern that the funds given to charter schools are being diverted from improving the public school system. But I'd argue that KIPP is playing the R&D role that Al Shanker envisaged, at least for inner city schools. To be sure, KIPP schools raise private funds to get started, and some continue to raise up to $150,000 a year to support special activities. However, Susan Schaeffler says that in D.C., KIPP operates with the same amount allocated to any public school, once funds have been raised for buildings.

I doubt that all public schools can copy KIPP, and I question whether the KIPP schools are the right model for more affluent kids who might not need the strict discipline, whose social character has been shaped at home to prepare them for the knowledge workplace. But as we saw in chapter 7, organizations can learn from great models without copying them. In particular, there are two elements that all public schools can learn from KIPP. One is that to be effective for the knowledge age, schools must be learning organizations, self-organizing social systems powered by values and principles more than rules. The second is that these schools must have leaders with the authority and ability to lead, even though leadership methods may be different at schools for the more affluent kids. This calls for leadership education. Where will this education be found? It's a challenge for schools of education. Dave Levin wants to found an institute to train school leaders, and he deserves the chance to provide a model for schools of education.

BARRIERS TO CHANGE

What keeps schools from learning from KIPP? First of all, the public and even school boards are just beginning to hear about KIPP. When I met members of the prestigious National Academy of Education in the fall of 2005, two deans of major university schools of education I spoke with had never heard of KIPP. However, many supporters of charter schools blame the bureaucratic school system and especially the teachers' unions for resisting change. Steven F. Wilson's view is representative: "Organized interests have successfully resisted calls for radical change in the organization and delivery of public education, none more than the two national teachers' unions, the National Education Association (NEA) and the AFT. Today, the majority of K–12 public school teachers belong to a local union, nearly all of which are NEA and AFT affiliates. Together, the two unions count 3.5 million public school teachers, support staff, preschool teachers, and college faculty among their members."[14]

Wilson goes on to argue that collective bargaining and union rules promote bureaucracy and distrust and undermine the power to lead and a culture of collaboration based on shared purpose. No doubt this is the case in some school districts, but not all. Wilson notes in passing that Dave Levin gained agreement with UFT (United Federation of Teachers), the New York affiliate of AFT, to accept the KIPP rules and values. Underperforming teachers were induced to leave KIPP for less demanding schools, and Levin was able to use emergency and temporary certification provisions to hire qualified and motivated teachers who lacked formal credentials.

It all depends on leaders. Ed McElroy, president of AFT, states that union-management collaboration has resulted in better schools and improved results in Toledo, Cincinnati, Minneapolis, Rochester, and Pittsburgh. He maintains that the union contract allows teachers to feel safe about trying new approaches. All of those cities have had innovative and courageous AFT local presidents who took the initiative with school management.[15]

Diane Ravitch, Research Professor of Education at New York University, a senior fellow at the Hoover Institution at Stanford and at the Brookings Institution, and former assistant secretary of education in the George H. W. Bush administration, is a respected historian and a fair-minded observer of schools. In contrast to union bashers, she believes unions, by protecting teachers and giving them voice, play an essential role in school reform.[16] This role can even be creative, provided there are leaders people want to follow.

ABC UNIFIED SCHOOLS

An example of a positive union-management relationship is the ABC Unified School District in three California cities—Artesia, Cerritos, and Hawaiian Gardens—south of Los Angeles. The superintendent of schools, Dr. Gary Smuts, and the AFT local president, Laura Rico, collaborate in a partnership that has shifted the union-management relationship from what Smuts described as conflict over work rules to collaboration to improve education. The result: continual improvement of scores on the California state English language and math proficiency tests. The ABC scores are 10 percent higher than the state average (see table 8-1). In the Hawaiian Gardens Schools with over 80 percent Hispanic children, the annual percent improvement in results from 1999 to 2005 was 179.[17]

TABLE 8-1

ABC District scores compared with California average

	PERCENT PROFICIENT	
	State of California	**ABC District**
English language arts		
2002	33	43
2003	35	45
2004	35	46
2005	40	50
Math proficiency		
2002	35	50
2003	41	51
2004	42	52
2005	47	57

Source: These statistics were provided by the superintendent, Dr. Gary Smuts.

Smuts and Rico meet weekly, and union and management leaders meet periodically to review progress or participate together in leadership training. The guiding principles of the partnership emphasize common purpose.

Rico says that working on the partnership has been the hardest part of her job. I can understand that. When I served from 1980–2000 as consultant to the collaboration between AT&T and the Communication Workers of America (CWA), I learned that local union leaders can lose elections if members believe they are too close to management.[18] Some of Rico's members are suspicious of the partnership, but she reports everything discussed, all partnership activity and decisions. Rico sees her role very much in the way Al Shanker believed it should be: meeting the members' needs for fair wages, benefits, work rules, and professional development, and also furthering the success of the children they serve. "If you belong to the union," says Rico, "you never have to be afraid. There is someone there for you for help in coaching or improving skills. We won't let you fail." As a leader, Rico is a doctor with skeptical teachers and a democrat with those who share her purpose.

What about the school principals? Do they have the power to lead? Smuts, who was himself a teacher and principal, says that in the past, the principals' main role was administration. At meetings, they just talked business. Now the business is done on the Internet and meetings concentrate on leadership skills. Principals are involved in curriculum, but teachers run the committees, and Gary allows the different schools latitude in textbook selection. Union and management have together agreed on a new evaluation instrument for teachers which emphasizes their development, and Smuts believes principals have the power to get rid of nonperforming teachers, as long as they follow California's due process regulations. Do the ABC principals have optimal authority and ability? Rico thinks even with enough authority, many still don't know how to lead.

Few school districts can boast the collaboration of ABC, and this is a failure of leadership on all sides, including boards of education.[19]

NUESTROS PEQUEÑOS HERMANOS

Foundations and international relief organizations spend millions to save the lives of people in Africa, Latin America, and the Caribbean who suffer from disease—HIV/AIDS, tuberculosis, malaria—and malnutrition. But millions of children are orphaned or abandoned victims of war, crime, domestic violence, and the diseases that killed their parents. What about them? Even if they get food and medicines that save their lives, what will become of them? Will they become just like their parents? Will they join criminal gangs? Or will they develop the skills and social character to become successful and responsible members of their societies? Unless we focus on the development of these children, we can expect more crime and violence in the future. However, I have seen at first hand that these orphaned and abandoned children can be developed into productive citizens of their countries. But it takes leadership.

William B. Wasson (1923–2006), a Catholic priest, was the kind of leader needed to create the centers to educate these children. His work for more than fifty years in Latin America and the Caribbean (Mexico, Guatemala, El Salvador, Honduras, Nicaragua, Peru, Bolivia, Haiti, and the Dominican Republic[20]) produced thousands of successful graduates of the homes he founded. And most impressive, eight of nine directors of these organizations are themselves orphans raised by Father Wasson and his followers.

He didn't plan this career. Father Bill, as he was called, was born in Phoenix, Arizona, and received an MA in social science from San Luis Rey University in Santa Barbara, California. He entered a seminary with the intention of becoming a Catholic priest, but the presiding bishop refused to ordain him because of a thyroid condition. He then got a job teaching adolescent psychology at an English-language university in Mexico City. He met the innovative bishop of Cuernavaca, Don Sergio Méndez Arceo, who recognized his spiritual qualities, ordained him, and placed him in a church in the city's teeming marketplace.

Father Wasson's leadership journey started in 1954, when the poor box in his church was robbed by a ten-year-old child. The little thief was caught by the sacristan and sent to jail. Father Wasson went to the jail, and when he saw a small boy among hardened criminals, he told the warden that he wasn't pressing charges; the boy should be freed. The warden said the boy was an orphan who lived in the street and survived by stealing. If freed, he'd soon be back in jail. Father Wasson asked to take charge of the boy. The warden agreed and soon after brought him eight more orphaned boys. Nuestros Pequeños Hermanos (NPH) was born.

At first, Father Wasson didn't know where he'd get the money to feed his brood. He borrowed and begged and began to find donors among the American expatriates in Cuernavaca. As he collected more boys, he thought about building an orphanage. He visited Boys Town, which had been made famous by the popular film based on it. Father Wasson found Boys Town to be very well funded, with comfortable living conditions and good schools, but he was troubled by the strict policy of sending the boys away when they reached age eighteen. What if they weren't prepared to leave? In a good family, parents don't push their kids out just because they've reached a certain age. Father Wasson went back to Mexico with the idea that NPH should not be an orphanage; it should be a family where kids could expect unconditional love and stay as long as they wanted, but they would also be expected to do their share, to pitch in according to their abilities, and they'd be educated to the limit of their abilities. At first NPH was a home for boys, but after a few years, he added a girls' house and then a house for infants.

Like Dave Levin of KIPP, Laura Rico of AFT, and the most successful CEOs I've interviewed, Father Wasson was a natural systems thinker. He balanced principles of security, responsibility, hard work—in the fields, growing their own food; in the kitchen cooking; and in school, studying—and the cultural stimulation of sports, music, dance, and the arts. (Like KIPP schools, NPH homes develop exciting musical and dance groups.) He also infused these operating principles with teaching and modeling moral and spiritual development. From the start, Father Wasson preached a gospel of caring for your brothers and sisters and sharing what you have with them. He rightly saw the danger that these children, victims of violence and tragedy, could fall into a self-defeating fog of self-pity and depression. "Don't let yourself start thinking 'poor little me' [*pobre de mi*]," he preached, "that just makes you weak"; and the children don't let newcomers succumb to corrosive self-pity.

Erich Fromm introduced me to Father Wasson over forty years ago, when I was living in Cuernavaca, studying a peasant village, and learning to be a psychoanalyst. I was impressed by the spirit of cooperation and mutual responsibility, and the pride the children felt about being part of this extended family; the term *orphanage* gives the wrong impression—this vibrant community was nothing remotely like the institutions portrayed in *Oliver Twist* or *Little Orphan Annie*. Together with two students, Dr. Salvador Millan and Rolando Weissman, I studied the attitudes of the boys and girls. We found that the new arrivals were depressed, but after two years, they expressed hope and happiness, energy and enthusiasm. They felt lucky to be part of NPH. It was amazing to observe that there were hardly any discipline problems and the children were motivated to work and learn.

Pequeños, as they are called, arrive at different ages. The policy is to bring all brothers and sisters who are orphaned or abandoned.[21] At first, Father

Wasson allowed adoption, but because of the bad experiences with foster parents and because the children not chosen felt devalued, he stopped the practice and affirmed that NPH is a family.

For the small children (some arrive as infants), schooling begins at age two or three with a Montessori program and continues as long as the children are willing and able to learn. Some go on to university education and become doctors, dentists, lawyers, accountants, hotel managers, electronic and agricultural engineers. But they all must do a year of service after finishing secondary school and again after high school. During that year they supervise work groups and act as *tios* and *tias* (uncles and aunts) for the younger children.

In Mexico, NPH also has a program to educate children living in a garbage dump (*milpillas*) near the orphanage at Miacatlan, Morelos. One thirteen-year-old girl, sick with malnutrition, with orange-dyed hair and spots on her face, accepted the offer for schooling. After seven years, including a year of service, she had entered the University of Morelos.

Those pequeños who don't qualify for higher education are trained in craft skills as electricians, carpenters, dressmakers, leather workers, welders, and plumbers. In the older homes, Mexico (900 children) and Honduras (550 children), there are thriving apprenticeship programs so that NPH graduates go right into good jobs.

For those children who arrive at NPH with disabilities, physical or psychic, there are competent occupational and psychological therapists to help. Some of these are volunteers from the countries where friends and former volunteers raise the funds that support NPH through mailings and a godparents program: the United States, Germany, Austria, France, the Netherlands, Belgium, Switzerland, Italy, and Spain.

Father Wasson was the model for three volunteers who later took over the leadership of the NPH extended family. Reinhart Kohler came from Germany. He studied psychology, and combines a profoundly caring attitude with systematic obsessive traits. He made the Honduras home into a model for the others with his schools, a medical and dental clinic, social workers to find children in need, apprenticeship programs, and a farm that raises food for the family. There is also a home on the grounds for abandoned elderly people, some of whom act as grandparents to the small children. Kohler is now director of Family Services, responsible for the development of the newer homes according to Father Wasson's principles and the model educational system he established in Honduras.

Father Phil Cleary, a diocesan priest from Chicago, came to Mexico in June 1983 to volunteer for a summer. It's been a long summer. Father Wasson prevailed on him to stay, and Cardinal Joseph Bernadin gave permission after he had seen NPH. Father Cleary stayed because, as he says, "I love the kids." He also proved to be the careful, thorough administrator NPH needed.

When Father Wasson stepped up his travel to found new houses, he left Father Cleary in charge of Mexico. Then, when Joan Provencio, NPH's executive director, retired, Father Cleary took over running NPH. Now responsible for a growing budget, he tried to limit Father Wasson's drive to keep founding new homes. "Where will we get the money?" he'd ask. Father Wasson would answer, "I don't believe God will let us be more generous than he is." Like other productive narcissists, Father Wasson was eager to make the world a better place. Father Cleary, the obsessive and interactive operational leader, had to struggle to establish some order in an organization built willy-nilly by an inspirational, charismatic visionary. The challenge was how to do this while not transforming a creative family into a bureaucratic machine. He's had help from Reinhart Kohler and Father Richard L. Frechette, a visionary priest who belongs to the Passionist order, which has supported his work with NPH.

Father Frechette, better known as Father Rick, was considering becoming a volunteer when he came to see me in the early 1980s. Although he interviewed me about NPH and Father Wasson more than I questioned him, I immediately felt his dedication, combined with a brilliant smile and wicked sense of humor. Father Frechette joined Kohler in founding the Honduras home in 1986 and then in 1988 went to Haiti where he became director of Nos Petits Frères et Soeurs (NPFS), which now has over five hundred children in residence. Faced with the extreme poverty and disease in Haiti, Father Frechette decided spiritual healing was not enough, and he took time off in the 1990s to train as a physician at the New York College of Osteopathic Medicine of New York Institute of Technology in Westbury, Long Island. When he returned to Haiti, he put a former pequeño in charge of the home and focused on caring for the country's sick and the victims of violence. There were times he faced down gangs with guns pointed at him as he tended to the wounded and dying in Cité Soleil, a Port-au-Prince slum. In his trips back to the United States, he raised funds for a hospital with 150 beds in Port-au-Prince, which opened in 2006.[22] Father Frechette also developed a healthcare program for all the NPH homes, including immunizations, water and environmental health risk checks, and periodic examinations of all pequeños. Almost all the former pequeño leaders in Mexico, Guatemala, El Salvador, Nicaragua, Peru, and Bolivia have university degrees, as does NPH's chief financial officer, Miguel Venegas, who has an MBA, but they need leadership education to sustain the mission, and Reinhart Kohler orchestrates that ongoing process. He says that a common problem with NPH leaders is that they start out with an autocratic style, making decisions without explaining the reasons for them or even trying to orchestrate consensus, just saying, "That's the way we do things at NPH."

As do the leaders in the KIPP inner city schools, NPH country leaders have to be authoritative, to make sure everyone acts according to Father Wasson's principles. The social character that succeeds in Latin America is hardworking and, increasingly, interactive. But it's also more respectful, more concerned with dignity, and more identified with family and religion than in the United States and western Europe. The social character shaped at NPH combines elements of the bureaucratic and interactive, with strong sibling ties.

THE LEADERS WE NEED FOR EDUCATION

In this chapter, we have seen that it is demonstrably possible to educate disadvantaged children for success. But it's not easy, and it won't be achieved just by throwing more money into schools. Rather, it requires exceptional and dedicated leaders who love children.

These kids with an unformed social character need an authoritative, paternal type of leader with a high level of Personality Intelligence to give them a sense of security and hope. Unlike affluent kids who are ambivalent about authority and arrive at school already prepared for academic competition, disadvantaged children benefit from strong parentlike leadership that cements trust. Father Wasson went further than evoking transference from infancy. He became the real father to thousands of children and a model for the development of a productive social character. The challenge for his disciples, sons, and daughters is to sustain this development without the founding father.

One of these pequeños grew up to take a job running one of the NPH houses after having worked a few years in a global company, saying, "If God hadn't put Father Wasson in my path, I don't know what would have been my life. I would have been a delinquent maybe. I would have been in a jail, maybe I would have lived in misery, or simply maybe I would have been dead."

I've described organizations I've seen and leaders I've met and can vouch for. I am sure there are many others that demonstrate similar lessons of leadership. When I asked Dave Levin about other charter schools he'd put in KIPP's class, he named Achievement First, which has six schools in Connecticut and New York. These schools and NPH present a challenge to governments and foundations. It's great work to save lives, but what happens to the children who are saved?

To summarize this chapter:

- A major challenge of our time is educating children. This involves developing not only their intellects but also their personalities.

- Children from different backgrounds have different social characters and need different kinds of schools.

- The schools that succeed in developing disadvantaged kids need leaders with the Personality Intelligence to understand the people they lead and the personality qualities that combine love and authority.

- Schools can learn from the models presented here, even if they can't copy them. There is no excuse for schools of education, foundations, school boards, and teachers unions to ignore the evidence of what succeeds. We can see the kinds of leaders we need in education. Let's recognize, support and develop them.

Sample Commitment to Excellence Forms

Teachers' Commitment

We fully commit to KIPP in the following ways:

- We will arrive at KIPP every day by 7:15 a.m. (Monday–Friday).

- We will remain at KIPP until 5:00 p.m. (Monday–Thursday) and 4:00 p.m. on Friday.

- We will come to KIPP on appropriate Saturdays at 9:15 a.m. and remain until 1:05 p.m.

- We will teach at KIPP during the summer.

- We will always teach in the best way we know how and we will do whatever it takes for our students to learn.

- We will always make ourselves available to students and parents, and address any concerns they might have.

- We will always protect the safety, interests, and rights of all individuals in the classroom.

Failure to adhere to these commitments can lead to our removal from KIPP.

X _____

Please print name here.

Parents'/Guardians' Commitment

We fully commit to KIPP in the following ways:

- We will make sure our child arrives at KIPP every day by 7:25 a.m. (Monday–Friday) or boards a KIPP bus at the scheduled time.

- We will make arrangements so our child can remain at KIPP until 5:00 p.m. (Monday–Thursday) and 4:00 p.m. on Friday.

- We will make arrangements for our child to come to KIPP on appropriate Saturdays at 9:15 a.m. and remain until 1:05 p.m.

- We will ensure that our child attends KIPP summer school.

- We will always help our child in the best way we know how and we will do whatever it takes for him/her to learn. This also means that we will check our child's homework every night, let him/her call the teacher if there is a problem with the homework, and try to read with him/her every night.

- We will always make ourselves available to our children and the school, and address any concerns they might have. This also means that if our child is going to miss school, we will notify the teacher as soon as possible, and we will carefully read any and all papers that the school sends home to us.

- We will allow our child to go on KIPP field trips.

- We will make sure our child follows the KIPP dress code.

- We understand that our child must follow the KIPP rules so as to protect the safety, interests, and rights of all individuals in the classroom. We, not the school, are responsible for the behavior and actions of our child.

Failure to adhere to these commitments can cause my child to lose various KIPP privileges and can lead to my child returning to his/her home school.

X _____

Please print name here.

Student's Commitment

I fully commit to KIPP in the following ways:

- I will arrive at KIPP every day by 7:25 a.m. (Monday–Friday) or board a KIPP bus at the correct time.

- I will remain at KIPP until 5:00 p.m. (Monday–Thursday) and 4:00 p.m. on Friday.

- I will come to KIPP on appropriate Saturdays at 9:15 a.m. and remain until 1:05 p.m.

- I will attend KIPP during summer school.

- I will always work, think, and behave in the best way I know how, and I will do whatever it takes for me and my fellow students to learn. This also means that I will complete all my homework every night, I will call my teachers if I have a problem with the homework or a problem with coming to school, and I will raise my hand and ask questions in class if I do not understand something.

- I will always make myself available to parents and teachers, and address any concerns they might have. If I make a mistake, this means I will tell the truth to my teachers and accept responsibility for my actions.

- I will always behave so as to protect the safety, interests, and rights of all individuals in the classroom. This also means that I will always listen to all my KIPP teammates and give everyone my respect.

- I will follow the KIPP dress code.

- I am responsible for my own behavior, and I will follow the teachers' directions.

Failure to adhere to these commitments can cause me to lose various KIPP privileges and can lead to returning to my home school.

X _____

Please print name here.

CHAPTER 9

The President We Need

As DONALD KAGAN NOTES in his study of Pericles: "The paradox inherent in democracy is that it must create and depend on citizens who are free, autonomous, and self-reliant. Yet its success—its survival even—requires extraordinary Leadership."[1] Kagan's observation is an accurate expression of the issues at the heart of this chapter. At the top of government, we need extraordinary leaders who understand the historic changes that threaten us, who are fully aware of the dangers to human life on this planet, and who take the lead in addressing these dangers—nuclear and biological weapons of mass destruction in the hands of people who might use them and global warming caused by human activity. But understanding is not enough. We need a president who the American people will follow, even if that means being pulled out of their comfort zone.

The president we need can gain followers by bridge building, starting with issues on which there's potential agreement across party lines: developing alternative energy and freeing ourselves from dependency on Middle Eastern oil, protecting a sustainable environment, improving education, strengthening national security, and supporting the research in science and technology that will keep our economy innovative and competitive in global markets.[2] In so doing, the president we need will articulate a sense of purpose that sparks the hope that we'll use our wealth and ingenuity to enhance the quality of life in America and wherever we can to improve life in other parts of the world.

As *New York Times* columnist Thomas Friedman writes, we need political leaders who can explain the forces that are changing the world, are able to educate people about them, and galvanize a creative response. But, Friedman recognizes that the leaders we elect are not always the leaders we need. He writes, "We have way too many politicians in America who seem to do the opposite. They seem to go out of their way actually to make their constituents stupid . . ." He makes an essential observation that "politicians can make us more fearful and thereby be disablers, or they can inspire us and thereby be enablers."[3]

Yes, presidents can inspire and enable, as Franklin D. Roosevelt did during the bank panic right when he was elected president. And they can make us more fearful, as George W. Bush did in the 2004 presidential campaign by constantly ratcheting up the color-coded threat level. Psychologically, fear triggers anxious regression to infantile feelings of helplessness so that people express transferential attitudes of passive obedience to leaders who promise to protect them. Fear combined with loss of meaning can also drive people into embracing fundamentalist ideologies that explain the world to them, bind and direct their fear and anger, give them false hopes and real enemies.

Besides global warming, I believe the greatest danger in this time of complex change and confusion comes from people with extremist ideologies that, closed to evidence and reason, justify destructive actions. Some of these ideologies are religious, promising rewards in a future life to destroyers killed in acts of terrorism. But secular ideologies can also be dangerous, such as unquestioning belief that communism, democracy, or market forces will magically solve economic and social problems. The goal of America's remarkable founding brothers was the development of free, educated, and productive citizens. Democracy and freedom from intrusive government were the means not the end of their purpose.

WHO SHOULD BE PRESIDENT?

What kind of national leader will be able to recognize our threats and opportunities, infuse people with hope by engaging them to rise to the challenge? I'd like to be able to name people who would clearly be the president we need, but history shows it's not possible to predict with any accuracy how someone will act in the office of president. No one predicted that Franklin Delano Roosevelt would become the inspirational leader who gave Americans hope during the dark days of the Depression and rallied the country after the attack on Pearl Harbor. Before FDR was elected president, Walter Lippmann called him "an amiable boy scout" and H. L. Mencken wrote that he was "somewhat shallow and futile."[4] No one expected Lyndon B. Johnson, who rose to leadership in the U.S. Senate on the shoulders of Southern racists, to bully that body to pass the Voting Rights Act of 1957 and later lead Congress to pass the Civil Rights Acts of the 1960s. No one expected Richard Nixon, who gained office by attacking Communism, to meet Mao in China. No one expected Ronald Reagan to hasten the end of the evil empire not by force but by dealing face-to-face with Mikhail Gorbachev. Yet, these politicians turned out to be the leaders we needed to rally the nation, right the wrongs of discrimination, improve chances for peace, and expand the realm of freedom.

In contrast, other American presidents did not rise to the occasion and give America the leadership needed. Woodrow Wilson, for all his brilliance and idealism, proved too rigid to lead the country to support the League of Nations after World War I. Although George W. Bush brought America together after 9/11, he ended up dividing the country over the ill-conceived war in Iraq.

If past achievement doesn't tell us enough, is there any other way to decide who we should support for president? Or course, we all see things through the lenses ground by our unique experiences. My view of what's important will be seen through the prism of this book's argument.

What I look for in a political leader who wants to be president is someone who understands the challenges facing us in social and human as well as economic and security terms, and has the combination of emotional and intellectual qualities—personality and brains—to shape solutions and galvanize the country to implement them. I write this with the belief that the Interactives, more than the bureaucrats, will recognize the importance of evaluating candidates in terms of their personal qualities, including their ability to both listen to and educate the public, rather than their résumés. Interactive leaders look at what people can contribute to a team, and in that spirit, we all need to ask what a presidential candidate will do for the country. And that depends even more on a candidate's personal strengths and understanding than the espoused policies that may change once the president takes office and has to share power with Congress.

What kind of personality should we look for? Both psychology and history provide clues.

Obviously we want a president who is gifted temperamentally with qualities of openness, agreeableness, emotional stability, and conscientiousness—qualities that make us feel good about a leader. FDR had them all. It was sometimes said that he had a second-rate intellect but a first-rate temperament. However, Lincoln was sometimes depressed, Nixon was suspicious and disagreeable, and Reagan wasn't very curious, even though they all had the other positive elements of temperament. So clearly, while desirable, good temperament is not enough for a president to deal with the challenges we face.

Almost all the leaders who have moved America in new directions have been gifted productive narcissists, like Lincoln, FDR, LBJ, Nixon, and Reagan. That's because this personality type, not wedded to the past, wants to change the world and has a deep need plus the skill to recruit others to make it happen.[5] Narcissists can combine a hopeful vision for the common good with political cunning, guiltlessly using people and tossing them aside when they're no longer useful, pragmatically shifting positions while appearing to stand for basic principles. (How many people know that Reagan, the revered icon of the Right, as California governor signed the first bill in the United States that legalized abortion?)

Narcissists are extremely competitive, and the most effective ones enjoy the combat of a campaign. They get sharper when stressed. Watch for this in the primaries. The productive narcissists will not be defensive, but will turn aside attacks with clever counterattacks or, like FDR and Reagan, sometimes with disarming and dismissive humor. I saw this close up in 1967, when I was a professor at the University of California at Santa Cruz. Reagan, who was then governor, visited the campus, and one of my students, a radical rebel, tried to bait him.

Student: Is it true you said trees cause pollution?

RR: You have a beautiful campus here.

Student, pulling me over to meet RR: Can you believe it? This man is the governor of the whole state of California.

RR, smiling: Well, at least you learned a little civics.

The best of our narcissistic presidents have formed strong convictions about key issues facing the country. These aren't based on opinion polls or what consultants advise them, but on their own study and experience; or like FDR, they invite the best minds on different sides to debate an issue, which can be as good as doing the research themselves. These presidents persuade and inspire others because they persuade and inspire themselves to take action. They bring the public into their internal dialogue. A powerful example is Abraham Lincoln's speech at Cooper Union, which was essential in gaining him the Republican nomination for president. Lincoln spent months studying the views of the framers of the constitution on slavery before crafting a speech that argued that while ending slavery would be like cutting out a cancerous growth and risking death by bleeding, letting it grow was certain to destroy the patient, by which he meant the spirit of the Republic.[6] In conclusion, Lincoln made it clear that he was ready to lead a righteous struggle, saying, "Let us have faith that right makes might, and in that faith, let us, to the end, dare to do our duty as we understand it."

Intellectuals had little respect for Ronald Reagan's intellect. But they were wrong. George Schultz, his secretary of state, reports that when Mikhail Gorbachev took over the U.S.S.R., Reagan studied everything he could get on Gorbachev and the Soviet Union for over a year. And when Reagan and Gorbachev had their first meeting, the senior staff was horrified that the president was meeting the chairman with only a translator present. But Schultz points out that Reagan knew what he wanted, he'd been a labor negotiator in Hollywood, and after studying Gorbachev for a year, he knew him better than any member of his staff.[7]

Reagan had transformed himself from a self-styled bleeding-heart liberal to the spokesman for free enterprise and against Big Government when he was the TV face of GE from 1954 to 1962. Thomas W. Evans, a lawyer who served in the Reagan administration, tells the story of Reagan's conversion through discussions with GE executives and workers that caused him to rethink his views.[8] The famous speech for Barry Goldwater at the 1964 Republican convention that made Reagan the leader of the Right expressed the result of his own internal dialogue.

Of course, the danger with narcissists is lack of control over their appetite for power (in Bill Clinton's case, it was sex). They ignore laws and constitutional limits that hamper their purposes, for example, Lincoln with *habeas corpus*; FDR trying to pack the Supreme Court and interning Japanese-Americans during World War II; Nixon trying to harass political opponents with the IRS; Reagan and the Iran-Contra deal.

At an *Economist* Leadership Forum I attended in Rome on "Narcissistic Leaders," Fausto Bertinotti, president of the Chamber of Deputies, stated a bit facetiously that only narcissists can be visionary leaders, but they'd be wise to learn to act humble.[9] We rightly fear grandiose visionaries, and we appreciate visionaries who can keep their egos in check.

But other personality types, even those obsessives with high moral standards like Herbert Hoover and Jimmy Carter, haven't moved the country to address the challenges of their time. Our one great obsessive president, George Washington, was needed to manage two great narcissists with clashing visions, Thomas Jefferson and Alexander Hamilton. Obsessives like Hoover and Carter act like know-it-all experts, which does not stir followers. A similar attitude turned some voters away from Al Gore and is still a source of satire about him, even though he has performed a huge service in raising our awareness of global warming. While effective narcissists bring the public into their own internal debate, with a conclusion that demands action, obsessives sermonize in ways that leave people feeling inadequate or guilty, like Carter's famous speech about the national "malaise," which just made people feel bad and mad at him. Both Hoover and Carter were great humanitarians, leading admirable projects before and after their terms in office, but neither was the leader the country needed, and of course, neither was reelected.

What about George W. Bush's personality? Starting with temperament, he is low on curiosity; he reads little and gets his information digested for him by his staff.[10] He's been emotionally stable since he stopped drinking—but alcohol can make anyone unstable. He's conscientious and sticks with things to a fault, and he's extraverted, sociable, and agreeable, although he lacks the dazzling brightness of FDR and Reagan. All in all, it's a positive temperament for a national leader, except for the lack of interest in learning, a gap we'll consider further. However, we can't tell whether Bush's stubbornness is a personality trait or whether he is just sticking to a script written for him. Possibly, it's a combination. People who knew him at school and college remember he had to win, even if that meant taking big risks. He wouldn't quit.

In my book on narcissistic leaders, I described Bush as a marketing personality with a bit of a loving (erotic) quality, which explains both his warmth and the machismo typical of the erotic who doesn't want to seem soft. My view was based on his history of shaping his persona to fit his audience. He was a uniter as governor and ran for office in 2000 as a healer, a bridge-builder. But in 2004, his persona, as outlined by his political guru Karl Rove in a campaign brief, was a "Strong Leader" who favors "Bold Action" and "Big Ideas."[11] Of course, part of this had to do with his post-9/11 role of a war leader. However, after my book was published, a reporter who had talked with Bush in the White House said to me that he felt Bush had also become a visionary with his idea of spreading democracy. Didn't I think my characterization was wrong, that he really had a narcissistic personality?

No, Bush seems to me a counterfeit narcissist who outsources his visions. Lincoln, FDR, and Reagan studied and worked hard to develop their visionary ideas; they convinced others because it was evident they had convinced themselves. Bush tried to sell concepts he hadn't worked through. His speechwriter David Frum told a TV interviewer that he had hoped that by writing visionary language for Bush, the president would then internalize the vision and act on it. Frum was disappointed.[12]

A good example of lack of thought is the idea of spreading "democracy." Bush uses the term as though its meaning were self-evident, when in fact there are many variations of democracy and it's not at all clear what would be evidence for him that a country was truly democratic. Nor has he seemed aware that the authors of our Constitution debated the strengths and weaknesses of democratic systems and some argued that democracy can be dangerous. In the Federalist Papers, published before the Constitutional Convention of 1787, James Madison argued that direct democracy can result in factionalism and tyranny of the majority, that the United States should be a republic, with checks and balances to protect individual liberty. Furthermore, Madison and many of the other framers of the Constitution believed that without an educated electorate, democracy would be vulnerable to dangerous demagogues. American democracy has evolved over two hundred years as the central ideal of individual freedom has been gradually expanded. The American experience is that democracy needs to be continually tended and developed. The purpose of our republic isn't democracy but liberty as the basis for the fullest development of all Americans, the opportunity to realize our creative potential in the pursuit of happiness. Democracy is important, but not the only means to this end.

Tocqueville observed in 1830 that American democracy was rooted in local town meetings and the emotional attitudes of Americans, their "habits of the heart," or in the language of this book, their social character.[13] A Russian delegation found this out when they visited America after the fall of Soviet communism to study democracy. When I met the group at the end of their study trip and asked what had most impressed them, they described meetings they'd witnessed in Protestant churches where each person was able to express an uninterrupted view on an issue. In Russia, they said, this never happened. People interrupted each other and the loudest or strongest person dominated. (Think of the television's *McLaughlin Report*.) They returned home with the sober view that Russian democracy would be fragile until cultural attitudes changed. During the G8 summit in St. Petersburg in July 2006, after suffering a lecture by Vladimir Putin, George W. Bush allowed that democracy had a different meaning and tradition for Russians than for Americans.

Bush assumed wrongly that building democracy is the first priority in every country. Of course, people everywhere want to be free of oppressors. But they also want freedom from want and fear. If they had the choice, would people in developing countries choose political democracy before security and material well-being? In Singapore and Chile, autocratic governments established free markets that stimulated economic growth before allowing political freedom. China has taken a similar path. Leaders in these countries believe that a stable democracy depends on sustainable economic success.

And keep in mind Erich Fromm's analysis in *Escape from Freedom* of why the German people voted for Hitler.[14] A people who have felt humiliated are vulnerable to leaders like Hitler who preach revenge, combined with hope of future greatness. Isn't this what motivates supporters of Hamas, Hezbollah, and Shiite militants in Iraq?

Put Bush's thin vision of exporting democracy together with his ill-considered idea of turning social security into a risky investment scheme and the persona of a visionary leader becomes just that, a *persona*, which comes from the Latin word for mask, or, in Jungian terms, taking on the archetypal role of visionary without the underlying substance. Unlike true visionary presidents, Bush has taken big gambles without fully understanding the odds or the consequences of failure.

Arguably, George W. Bush seems to be our first interactive president, with both the strengths and weaknesses of this social character. As a campaigner, his agreeable temperament and marketing traits are winning. In good interactive style, he's both collaborative and decisive. But his decisiveness seems more like a video-game "decider," a term he gave himself, than someone who takes deep dives into the material. In a conversation among journalists and writers who have covered the Bush White House, he comes across as someone with only a superficial grasp of the decisions he makes. For example, Bob Woodward of the *Washington Post* says, "You can't help but look back at Clinton's famous late nights at the dorm when he would pick through details and ask questions and keep people well past midnight . . . And if you look at Bush, he's kind of, you know, meeting starts at 9, the meeting is over at 10. That's it." Thomas Ricks, author of the best seller *Fiasco*, adds, "He [Bush] should be a central figure in decision making. And again and again, there's never any one key meeting." Says Woodward, "And in this whole story, he's been the cheerleader."[15] Or better said, the salesman for decisions made with or by Vice President Dick Cheney and Secretary of Defense Donald Rumsfeld.

Under Bush, the interactive marketer, the White House staff enjoyed remarkable collegial collaboration among the inner team, unlike the competitive conflict among advisers typical with narcissists like Roosevelt, Nixon, and Clinton. But interactive collaboration doesn't guarantee good policies, and conflict can be creative. Bush picked close advisers who were hard-liners like Cheney and Rumsfeld. His guru Rove had him campaign on fear of terrorists, gay marriage, the specter of social security bankruptcy. He was directed in 2004 to market to his base, to play on their fears and prejudices. But in his message, there was little of the hope generated by FDR's "We have nothing to fear but fear itself" or Reagan's "It's morning in America." Once in the White House, Bush backed policies that rewarded his base of the rich and socially conservative. Policies on national security, meant to protect the country from its enemies, threatened democratic values, and even our allies came to view Bush's democratic rhetoric as hypocritical. America's reputation fell to new lows, depressed by Bush's insulting macho style. But Bush finally lost the support of most Americans when his reasons for invading Iraq and promise of a quick victory both proved false and his response to the devastation of hurricane Katrina was inept, demonstrating that a winning personality can take a politician only so far.[16] And by the start of 2007, the persona of a strong leader had faded; the majority of the public considered Bush neither strong nor effective.[17]

STRATEGIC INTELLIGENCE

Personality is just one part of the equation for an effective president. We should also evaluate the intellectual capabilities required to lead the country. Of course, no one gets to be president without a certain level of analytic intelligence or IQ, but in our complex world this is not enough. A president also has to have foxlike street smarts and should have enough emotional intelligence in terms of self-control to block impulses that get leaders like Clinton into trouble. But more important for the well-being of the country is the president's judgment and, beyond that, wisdom—the ability to foresee the future implications of present decisions. Although judgment has to do with qualities of both head and heart, which I'll discuss in chapter 10, presidential wisdom depends in large measure on a kind of braininess I've termed *Strategic Intelligence,* a set of five interrelated qualities—foresight, systems thinking, visioning, motivating, and partnering. These are qualities found in the most effective corporate CEOs.[18] Here's what we should look for in a presidential candidate.

Does the candidate describe the forces shaping the future? Does he or she seek the views of people at the forefront of business, the natural sciences, and social sciences? Is what's learned integrated into a view or scenario of what is likely to happen? Politicians often predict the future by just extrapolating from the past. But we live in an age of discontinuity. Extrapolations can be way off the mark. Just look at past predictions by Ford and GM executives. In the mid-1990s Ford was discussing how to keep growing 15 percent a year, and now its trying to stop red ink from flowing.

Having foresight doesn't mean predicting the future. It does mean trying to shape the future to take advantage of dynamic forces like changes in technology, global trade and the nature of work with implications for education, and jobs, demographic changes and their effect on healthcare and pensions.

It's not enough for politicians with foresight to just describe forces. They should be skilled communicators, teachers who explain future threats and opportunities and how they plan to deal with them, simplifying complexity to mobilize support. They should show people why changes will benefit them, telling illustrative stories rather than giving lists of policy initiatives. They should emphasize principles rather than detailing legislation that, in any case, has to be crafted together with Congress.

To explain the interplay of forces shaping our future, a president also needs the other interrelated elements of Strategic Intelligence: systems thinking, visioning an ideal future, motivating the public to play its role. Bill Clinton told an interviewer that "intellect is a good thing [for a president] unless it paralyzes your ability to make decisions because you see too much complexity. Presidents need to have what I would call a synthesizer intelligence," which is similar to what I mean by systems thinking.[19] The president can't do this alone. He or she needs to partner with strong people who complement his/her abilities, as FDR did by putting together his "brain trust" and Nixon did by recruiting Henry Kissinger for foreign policy and Daniel Patrick Moynihan for domestic policy. Ideally, a president would have the Personality Intelligence demonstrated by Lincoln in choosing and managing his cabinet of strong and contentious rivals.[20]

As I write this in 2007, candidates are declaring their intention to run for president. What should determine our choice of a candidate? These are the questions I'll ask as I listen to the candidates.

- Do they respond to the challenges and stress of the campaign with grace and a sense of humor?

- Do they understand the threats and opportunities we face, and do they have a vision of America that will mobilize people? Do they spark hope and not fear? Do they bring us into their internal dialogue in a way that inspires confidence?

- Do they emphasize issues that bring people together, as has Arnold Schwarzenegger (a productive narcissist), who rebounded from blaming his opponents for California's problems to championing the environment, education, and universal health insurance?

- Do they show courage to stand up for the common good against special interests?

- Will they rebuild America's moral authority in the world and our relations with our European allies? Do they understand the importance of cultural differences? Do they recognize the influence of social character (although they might not call it that)? And are they able to see issues from different points of view?

- Will they bring into their administration the best of advisers? Interviewers should ask them to tell us the names of people they look to for counsel and ideas and the reasons why they would choose these people. Do they demonstrate Personality Intelligence in their evaluation of friends and foes?

But even a brilliant visionary with the best of brain trusts can't provide all the leadership needed to shape policies and energize the American people to rise to the challenges we face. And if the president is an interactive marketing type, it's even more essential that public pressure for new policies becomes a powerful political force. In particular, we need policy leaders, either elected or in nongovernmental organizations (NGOs), and journalists who publicize new ideas from researchers and intellectual entrepreneurs and mobilize the public to put pressure on the president and Congress. It's up to all of us to get the president we need.

CHAPTER 10

Becoming a Leader We Need

THE THESIS OF THIS BOOK is that in these tumultuous times, we urgently need leaders who will mobilize people for the common good. The turmoil of transformation in technology, global markets, shifts in offerings from products to solutions, demands for better education and health care, and threats to our security all call for leadership that creates collaboration. But in this new context, the age of knowledge work, would-be leaders can't get people to follow them in ways that worked in the past. That's because historic changes in culture are forming a social character in the advanced globalized economy that is more interactive and less bureaucratic. Where once father transferences linked followers to leaders, now sibling transferences undermine hierarchical authority. Interactives may reluctantly follow a leader because they feel they have to, but they'll only want to follow a leader who makes them respected collaborators.

Although Interactives fit the needs of flatter, networked businesses, these organizations now need a combination of leadership types—transformational visionaries, operational obsessives, trust-creating bridge-builders—requiring the different styles and psychological profiles I've described in this book.

Yet the traditional questions about leadership remain. Why do people become leaders? Are leaders born or made? What are the qualities of mind and heart that will enable our needed leaders to gain collaborators? And how can these qualities be developed?

WHY PEOPLE BECOME LEADERS

Clearly, genetic qualities like curiosity, conscientiousness, agreeableness, and emotional stability make a difference in why people become leaders. Upbringing can strengthen these qualities, and school, sports, and other activities can provide opportunities to practice leadership. Natural leaders seem from an early age to get people to follow them, but in different ways. Some future operational types are like Mark Twain's character, Tom Sawyer, who cleverly got Ben, Bill, and Johnny to pay him for the chance to whitewash Aunt Polly's fence by pretending the work was fun. Another operational type has command presence, like George Washington, whose height, strength, and courage attracted followers early on. As a farmer, general, and president, Washington was a great operational leader. While we don't know what he would have been like grown up, Tom Sawyer also had the makings of an effective operational leader, a supermotivator.

Strategic visionaries may not show their abilities right away, as I noted about FDR in chapter 9. Some only show their leadership qualities by responding courageously to a difficult challenge, like Martin Luther King Jr., who stood up against the injustice of racial discrimination in America and created a visionary movement. Or Mohandas Gandhi, who started out as a barrister and responded to British discrimination in South Africa and India by leading a revolution. Business leaders with visions of new products that change the way we work and live, and the strategic skills to turn the vision into a successful business, may emerge when young, like Bill Gates, or when older, like Henry Ford.

Networking leaders are typically less commanding than the other two types. But they are natural facilitators and mediators—we recognize them as people who are good at helping to resolve conflicts.

Of course, among our cousins, the chimpanzees, natural leaders are the rule. What differentiates us from other primates is that we humans have reasons for becoming leaders. To this day, some individuals have tried to satisfy their thirst for power and glory by becoming leaders, and people have followed them, either seduced by promises or out of fear. Almost everyone who has worked in a bureaucratic organization has at one time or another suffered a dictatorial boss. And we'll continue to suffer them.

But power and glory are not the driving motives of the leaders we need. We need leaders who want to improve the common good or the well-being of people—like Moses who became a leader by reacting to the injustice of Egyptian slave masters; like Lincoln, who became a leader by challenging the injustice of slavery in America; like Gandhi, King, and Nelson Mandela, who became leaders by opposing the injustices of racial segregation and oppression; like Father William Wasson and Mother Teresa, who became leaders by responding with love to helpless outcasts.

The exemplary leaders in health care and education I've described in this book became leaders by responding effectively to social needs. They wanted the power to lead in order to get results, to further the common good, not to lord it over others. Some, like Mike Feinberg and Dave Levin, attracted collaborators who found meaning for themselves in what Feinberg and Levin were doing. Other leaders, like Harry Jacobson of Vanderbilt University Medical Center, have had to persuade skeptical physicians to become willing collaborators.

To be sure, even the best of business leaders want wealth and recognition. And many good leaders find meaning in making organizations work well and bringing out the best in people. But what most inspires them and their collaborators is the vision of furthering the common good, empowering people (Bill Gates of Microsoft; Steve Jobs of Apple; Larry Page and Sergey Brin of Google), building a modern nation (Mukesh Ambani of Reliance Industries) or a cleaner environment (Jeff Immelt of GE).

Lao Tzu's statement, written twenty-five hundred years ago, is, for me, the best description of an ideal leader, because it describes a leader who strengthens people so they become independent and doesn't need to be made into an idol. The description can be improved only by making it neutral in terms of the leader's sex, which I've done by changing "leader" and "he/him" into "leaders" and "they/them":

> *The best of all leaders are the ones who help people so that eventually*
> *   they don't need them.*
> *Then come the ones they love and admire.*
> *Then come the ones they fear.*
> *The worst let people push them around (and therefore aren't leaders*
> *   at all).*
> *People won't trust leaders who don't trust them.*
> *The best leaders say little but people listen to what they say,*
> *And when they're finished with their work, the people say we did it*
> *   ourselves.*[1]

Lao Tzu and Confucius gave their advice about ideal leadership in a different context. They were trying to make despots benevolent, and these rulers, with unquestioned authority, didn't need to promote themselves. They didn't need courses in self-presentation. But even in this context, Lao Tzu saw the leadership wisdom of knowing and trusting followers, and of understanding their needs and helping them to meet those needs, and of empowering them.

UNDERSTANDING PEOPLE—A HEART THAT LISTENS

We often hear that global competitiveness calls for more and better training in science and technology, but arguably, it depends as much or more on leaders who understand people, including their social character. Management researchers estimate that virtual teamwork in global technology companies is 90 percent about people and 10 percent about technology.[2]

As understanding people has become more important, it has also become more difficult than in the past. In traditional villages, everyone shares the same social character, and variations from the norm stand out like sore thumbs.[3] Peasants observe each other closely, catching expressions of jealousy, envy, greed, or anger. Their gossip mill grinds relentlessly, spreading news about neighbors. Yet peasants have a sour view of human nature and are suspicious of each other. A Mexican villager who worked with a neighbor for over twenty-five years said he didn't trust his *compadre*. Why not? In a dream, this man knifed him. Was the dream acutely sensing a potential attack? Or was it more likely expressing distrust of anyone not part of his immediate family? (Another interpretation is that the dreamer was thinking about cheating his neighbor and feared revenge.)

For historic reasons, peasants have reason to distrust people who don't belong to their village. They aren't good at understanding outsiders, and they've been taken in by slick snake-oil salesmen, as in the cautionary fairy tale of *Jack and the Beanstalk*. But suspiciousness doesn't hamper farm work and is an effective protection against getting fleeced. The gossip network informs everyone about each other so that fear of public disapproval and shaming keeps villagers on the straight and narrow.

In the industrial age, managers of bureaucracies avoided having to understand individuals by using formulas to control behavior. Individual jobs were formatted, results were measured, and incentives—the carrots and sticks—were used to motivate people who were typed according to their results and how well they served the boss. These incentives reinforced strong father transferences that made subordinates want to follow the boss.

But at IBM, AT&T, and the other large companies I studied in the 1970s, few managers could describe the personalities of their bosses or peers. Furthermore, top managers often put subordinates in their place with humiliating teasing, put-downs, and ridicule—behavior that would be considered abusive in the diverse workforce of the knowledge era, maybe even grounds for a lawsuit. But people swallowed these insults with forced smiles. It was all part of solidifying the hierarchy.

In the knowledge age, there are still many bureaucratic organizations, but as firms become more like collaborative communities, there is a cacophony of transferential feelings. To gain a following, leaders must be "doctors" and role models rather than parents. Furthermore, the interactive social character doesn't take kindly to abusive bosses, and that accounts for the popularity of emotional intelligence (EI). This concept, popularized by Daniel Goleman in the 1990s, includes qualities such as empathy and self-control.[4] Managers with EI communicate more effectively and have smoother relationships with subordinates. EI is especially important for operational and bridge-building network leaders. It matters less for strategic leaders; some of the most successful strategic visionaries—Bill Gates, Steve Jobs, and Larry Ellison, to name the most well-known—have been reported by subordinates as blowing up in meetings and ridiculing people for ideas they call stupid. Even those productive narcissists who are gifted with empathy aren't particularly self-aware or caring with their underlings. Empathy can be used tactically to seduce people into thinking a leader understands them and sympathizes with their plight, but feeling your pain doesn't mean a leader cares about you or even understands you.[5]

Although EI is a significant element in understanding people, it's only a part of Personality Intelligence. To understand people means to understand how they think and what motivates them, their personality. It's intellectual as well as emotional. Some people are gifted with this kind of understanding. Great novelists and playwrights create believable personalities, some of whom become prototypes for how we view people, for we don't recognize anything we can't name or categorize. For example, Suomis in the north of Scandinavia see and name different colors of reindeer skin that others just see as a kind of yellow-brown, and the trained botanist sees variations in plants and flowers that don't register for the rest of us. So it is with personality. By describing characters, their personality and passions, Shakespeare, perhaps the greatest writer in terms of Personality Intelligence, teaches us to see some of the personalities we meet in our own lives, the Hamlets and Horatios, Othellos and Iagos, Romeos and Juliets, Macbeths and Lady Macbeths. In this sense, Freud's personality types can be considered a systematic approach to describing a universal cast of characters.

The most astute princes, presidents, and generals, from antiquity to the present, have tried to understand personality, to predict the behavior of key lieutenants or adversaries. For them, knowing the people they must fight and those they depend on was a matter of life and death. Some used astrology, which offers an elaborate set of personality descriptions based on date and time of birth. Now, organizational leaders use personality questionnaires, which, while less rich in description than astrology, boast a bit more test validity.[6] But people can game these paper-and-pencil tests. They can consciously or unconsciously give answers they think put them in the best light. Having a good theory of personality types and understanding social character, cultural values, and identities are essential for understanding people, but Personality Intelligence also requires the ability to directly experience another person's emotional attitudes.

Can anyone fully understand another person? Heraclitus, the pre-Socratic philosopher, wrote, "You could not in your going find the ends of the soul, though you traveled the whole way: so deep is its law."[7] Even though we may never fully know another person, to begin to know others in their uniqueness, to understand their psyches, to have some sense of how they see the world, requires a combination of a good theory and experiential capability, qualities of both head and heart.

In traditional thinking about wisdom, the heart is a metaphor for the kind of experiential knowledge that should combine with conceptual knowledge to develop Personality Intelligence. In the bible, King Solomon dreams that God asks him, "What shall I give thee?" and he answers, "Give thy servant, therefore, a heart with skill to listen, so that I may govern thy people justly and distinguish good from evil."[8]

People think that qualities of the heart are opposite to those of the head, that heart means softness, sentiment, and generosity, while head means tough-minded, realistic thought.[9] But in pre-Cartesian thought, the heart was the true seat of intelligence and the brain the instrument of logic and calculation. The head alone can decipher codes, solve technical problems, and keep accounts, but it can't resolve emotional doubt about what is true, good, or beautiful. The head alone can't give emotional weight to knowledge, and therefore, can't fire up courage based on knowledge of what is right to do. *Webster's New International Dictionary's* first definition of courage, with its root in the Latin *cor* and French *coeur.* "The heart as the seat of intelligence or of feeling . . ." The head can be smart, score well on an IQ test, but cannot be wise, certainly not about people. That takes a heart that listens.[10]

Intellectually, it's possible to observe patterns of behavior that fit the personality types, for example, the obsessive's neatness and controlling moves, the erotic's pleasure at inclusion and affirmation, the narcissist's self-involvement, and the marketing person's sensitivity to interpersonal cues.[11] Even body language can express type of personality, like the tight-lipped obsessive with elbows close to the body or wagging his finger as he lectures us. But knowing personality types can't help us to know that a person is sad or happy, loving, angry, resentful, envious, doubtful, or insincere. Yes, to a certain extent we can recognize emotions like anger and fear from facial expressions and body language. Indeed, Paul Ekman, a professor of psychology at the University of California Medical School, San Francisco, teaches people to recognize at least seven facial expressions: sadness, anger, fear, surprise, disgust, contempt, and happiness.[12] But we are only sure about what we see when we can experience these feelings directly in others, just as in ourselves. That takes a developed heart.

Intellect alone organizes data from and about other people, but it doesn't experience them. Knowledge from the head alone is laundered of emotion. The more we experience what we observe, the more information we have to understand others. We use our heads fully to reason and affirm only when our hearts are engaged. Of course, the term "heart" doesn't mean just that one organ that pumps blood. Rather it's a synecdoche (like all hands on deck) to represent all of our body parts focused on experiencing and understanding not only others but also ourselves. Goleman describes recent research on mirror neurons, which allow us to experience another's emotions. He cites Giacomo Rizolatti, the Italian neuroscientist who discovered mirror neurons, who says these systems "allow us to grasp the minds of others not through conceptual reasoning but through direct simulation; by feeling, not by thinking."[13]

But by knowledge of the heart, I also refer to self-understanding. With a detached heart, we remain unaware of our own feelings. I've had patients who, when I ask what they feel, say, "I'm feeling fine," even though I (through my mirror neurons) experience directly their sadness or anger. This repression of feeling leaves them anesthetized, half asleep.

When both head and heart develop together, the result is heightened experiential perception and expanded understanding of others, enhanced awareness of truth versus sham, increased energy and courage to act on our convictions.

Developing both head and heart doesn't guarantee always being right about people. We can be fooled by another's charm or our own wishful thinking. However, the opposite of doubt isn't certainty, but rather faith in our ability to get to the truth and willingness to risk being wrong or gullible, because we know we can learn from our errors. Nor does Personality Intelligence guarantee always doing what's right. There will always be ethical dilemmas to consider, even for someone with the clearest vision and best moral values.

When executives are asked to list the competencies of an effective leader, they mention skills like good decision making, strategic thinking, coaching, team building, communicating complex messages, and selecting and developing talent. Although all of these skills can be learned to some degree, how well they are done depends on a person's intellectual and emotional qualities, their personality and brains.

I have discussed the kind of personalities that fit the three types of leadership roles needed in the knowledge workplace. And I've mentioned the new kinds of intelligence—Strategic and Personality—that equip leaders for the challenges of our time. Let's now consider how to develop these intellectual abilities, beginning with Personality Intelligence.

DEVELOPING PERSONALITY INTELLIGENCE

Personality and Strategic Intelligence are the new leadership qualities for the age of knowledge work. But both are extremely difficult to develop, and someone who is strong in Strategic Intelligence will not necessarily be as accomplished in Personality Intelligence and vice versa. Although both require analytic and practical intelligence, Personality Intelligence builds more on Emotional Intelligence, Strategic Intelligence more on systems thinking and practical intelligence.[14] Rather than expecting all leaders, even the best ones, to score at the top range of both types of intelligence, we can also think of developing these qualities in a leadership team where different members are respected for their distinctive strengths. Of course, to make this work, the whole team needs to understand what these qualities are and why they are both essential to strategy and visioning on the one hand, and on the other, improving relationships, dissolving distorting transferences, selecting talent, and motivating and partnering effectively. Even though some members of a team will excel more than others, everyone can improve both Personality and Strategic Intelligence. Here's how, starting with Personality Intelligence.

First of all, *develop the heart.* Recognize that figuratively as well as literally the heart is a muscle. Without exercise, it won't get strong. Overly protected, it's easily hurt. There's a term for a person with a weak heart and a strong sense of guilt: a bleeding heart, typically an erotic personality with liberal beliefs who doesn't understand others but wants to help the underdog. When the object of these good intentions isn't grateful, the bleeding heart feels taken in.

All social characters and personality types can develop their hearts, but there are typical differences in attitudes to fully experiencing self and others. The bureaucratic social character, brought up in a more or less close-knit nuclear family, typically has strong emotional ties that cause strong transferences. To avoid feeling vulnerable or being misled by their emotions, bureaucrats sometimes build a shell around their hearts. For example, one such CEO said to me, "If I opened myself up to people, they would eat me alive." Another said, "I've a shell around my heart, and even my children feel and resent it." But the lack of Personality Intelligence caused by an overprotected heart cramped their effectiveness. It made these two executives vulnerable to countertransferences whereby they overvalued inadequate but admiring subordinates. This self-protectiveness leaves the unexercised heart flabby and causes managers to obsess over decisions when they need to be decisive.

In contrast, Interactives tend to be more detached. At an early age, they don't expect parents to always be there for them, and they become emotionally more independent. It's easier for them to break off unsatisfying relationships, but it's also harder to commit themselves to others. Although they may have radarlike interpersonal intelligence, they use their gut rather than their hearts in deciding about people. This leads to valuing people too much on appearance, on whether or not they look good, present themselves well, seem confident. Underneath these quick judgments often lurks unresolved doubt. Interactives, especially marketing types, know who's on their side only as long as they're playing the game together. However, the most productive Interactives are self-developers, and just as they recognize they need to keep mind and body up to speed, so they may grasp the benefits of developing their hearts.

Of course, some people don't just protect a tender heart, but harden their hearts in the pursuit of power, revenge, or an ideology that justifies terrorism. These are the most dangerous leaders, who are not moved by others' feelings. An example is Fidel Castro, who was "remorseless and unforgiving of his perceived enemies" and wrote from prison, "I have a heart of steel."[15]

Developing the heart means exercising it, being willing to experience strong and painful feelings; it means leaders should not ignore the guilt they may feel when making an unpopular decision, firing people, or otherwise causing grief in order to further the common good, and not ignore the anger of those who are hurt. No muscle gets strengthened without painful exercise.

Just as there are disciplines to develop the intellect, such as mathematics, logic, and scientific methods, so there are disciplines to develop the heart.[16] They are: *clearing the mind* to see things as they are, *deep listening* to get in touch with ourselves, and *listening and responding to others*.

Clearing the Mind

Clearing the mind to see things as they are means frustrating the cravings that cloud the mind, avoiding fantasy and all forms of escapism. Heraclitus wrote that when we dream, we are all in different worlds, but awake, we are in the same reality. Only when we are fully awake do we see things as they are, and many people go through life half-asleep because they repress uncomfortable perceptions and feelings.

Furthermore, we can't see people as they are when our minds are clouded by emotions like lust, anger, or jealousy. For example, a lustful man doesn't see a beautiful woman's spiritual qualities, just as a glutton isn't the best judge of gourmet cooking.

To see things as they are, first of all, we have to practice frustrating the fantasies and passions that keep us from being clear-eyed and fully awake. But we can't frustrate irrational passions if we repress them. At an early age, we naturally repress thoughts and impulses that make us feel crazy or could get us into trouble. But the habit of repression can spread, blocking self-awareness.

Deep Listening

Deep listening to get in touch with ourselves means experiencing what we would feel and think if we weren't defending ourselves from these unpleasant feelings and thoughts. Freud's motto, taken from the poet Horace, was "Nothing human is alien to me." We have within us all the human potentialities and passions, creative and destructive. If we were fully in touch with ourselves, we'd experience murderous madness and dark despair, but also transcendent love and cosmic consciousness. The great mystics like Meister Eckhardt, St. John of the Cross, and the Buddhist masters journey to the depths of the soul to free the self from enslaving needs and affirm the human capacity to find transcendent relatedness to the universe, to overcome the illusion, as Einstein put it, that we are isolated beings. In the Judeo-Christian tradition, the goal is oneness with God. In the Buddhist, nontheist tradition, it's enlightenment—being fully awake and present. An essential function of religious and philosophical thinking is to contain and give meaning to what we can experience when we become aware of powerful and troubling repressed feelings. Freud tried to substitute a psychoanalytic framework, but I think his insights need to be understood within a more spiritual context. This is what Erich Fromm tried to do in his approach to humanistic psychoanalysis.

But although there's a limit to how much we can, at the same time, function in the rough and tumble world and also explore the depths of our psyches, we can practice getting in touch with what we really experience with other people and not repress uncomfortable thoughts and feelings. In his book *Blink*, Malcolm Gladwell cites studies of how first reactions are often more accurate than studied evaluations.[17] We sometimes repress our first negative perceptions of people. As we saw in chapter 3, unconscious transference projections can cover the real personalities of bosses or subordinates. Of course, sometimes it's inconvenient to admit to ourselves what we really feel about people we need to get along with. But we can't do anything about improving bad relationships if we don't see people as they are.

Getting in touch with oneself, self-awareness, is a goal of psychoanalysis, especially uncovering transferences that distort how we see others. But analysis is a costly process, and unless a person is suffering from psychological causes, it's not practical for most people. Furthermore, when I taught and supervised analysts, very few showed the talent for or interest in exploring the unconscious any more than was necessary to alleviate a patient's anxiety or depression. And even with the deep analysis I underwent with Erich Fromm for eight years, I still found it helpful to practice the Zen Buddhist form of daily meditation to get in touch with myself. Besides Zen, there are other forms of meditation and prayer that help to connect us to our feelings and silence the noise that muffles the small voice of truth that's in all of us, but is often ignored.

Listening and Responding to Others

Listening and responding to others when we have cleared the mind and are awake frees us from the obsession with self, so we can see others more clearly. This kind of listening is active, reaching out with head and heart to understand what we are hearing. Paradoxically, egocentrism is reinforced by obsessing about what others think of us. That just keeps us in ourselves. We only overcome egocentrism when we get out of ourselves to see things from another's point of view. That doesn't mean assuming that others feel what we'd feel in their place. Rather, we need to make an effort to understand how others view things through their own lenses, even experience directly what they experience, an effort of both head and heart. Beyond understanding is courageous service, reaching out to others, responding with intelligence and passion to social needs, as we have seen with the leaders profiled in this book.

Not only do we strengthen our ability to understand and act by practicing these disciplines, but also, as Albert Schweitzer wrote, only those who have sought and found how to serve well will be truly happy.[18] By realizing a vocation of service, we strengthen our hearts and also attract others who find meaning in the same missions.

DEVELOPING STRATEGIC INTELLIGENCE

In my earlier study of narcissistic leaders, I found that the most successful strategic visionaries demonstrate Strategic Intelligence, an interactive mix of analytic, practical, and creative elements.[19] Now, when we need visionaries to take on the challenges of health care, education, alternative energy, environmental protection, and national security, these leaders should be able to anticipate future trends, think systemically, understand how to architect effective social systems, communicate meaning and purpose to motivate and educate collaborators, and partner with other types of leaders who complement their strengths.

The largest gap in the intellectual ability needed for effective leadership in the knowledge age is systems thinking. Without it, leaders can't understand the relation of global forces to local pressures, macro policy to micro implementation, and social character to individual personality. Without it, their organizational vision will lack coherence. When linear thinkers connect the dots, they draw straight lines rather than the dynamic interactive force field that represents a knowledge-age organization.

After I first wrote about Strategic Intelligence, a group of interested consultants joined me to interview over thirty top executives about it.[20] These leaders agreed that the elements of Strategic Intelligence were essential for a CEO's effectiveness. They told us that a major part of the CEO's role is to think about the future, and all of them worked on their foresight, using tools like scenario planning. In one way or another all these executives scanned the relevant business environment. Large companies and government agencies teach "what-if" thinking. U.S. naval officers are even graded on their foresight.

But with few exceptions, these executives told us that among the elements of SI, they were weakest on systems thinking. Their knee-jerk approach to a problem was to attack and analyze, to break it into clearly manageable pieces—stacked rather than integrated—and to manage the parts of their organization rather than the interactions. Why is systems thinking so hard for many executives? And can it be taught?

Some people are natural systems thinkers, while others think in terms of clearly definable details and simple cause-and-effect relationships.[21] Productive narcissists tend to be systems thinkers because they like global visions, while obsessives are more inclined to make lists. Contrast Freud, the narcissist, who conceived of behavior as resulting from the interaction of passions (id), conscience (superego) and self-interest (ego) with obsessive psychologists who list behavior traits they can measure but that have no obvious relationship to each other. Some of the great business entrepreneurs have been systems thinkers, like Henry Ford, who designed the model system for the industrial age, and Toyota's Taiichi Ohno, who transformed Ford's system—pushing out a standardized product—to a pull system of lean production and just-in-time delivery of varied products demanded by customers. And some business leaders have had a meteoric ride to failure because they lacked systems thinking.[22]

In this book, we've met natural systems thinkers like Dave Levin of KIPP, Father William Wasson of NPH, and Dr. William Mayo of the Mayo Clinic. Each of these leaders designed social systems with a distinct purpose—the well-being of the people they served. Each of their organizations became collaborative cultures based on shared values and principles, with processes and measures that reinforced the purpose. Sure, they still needed some bureaucratic-type rules, but these were kept to a minimum. A role of leaders in the organizations they've built is to educate and persuade people to internalize the principles so the rules won't be needed.

As corporate executives try to transform bureaucracies, to twist silos into networks, they can learn from the Mayo Clinic that organizational culture can be more effective than formal rules in strengthening the role of network leaders. When patients arrive at Mayo, internists are assigned as the leaders of their treatment. In complex cases, these doctors bring together the specialists who decide on and integrate their treatment. They form an effective team not because the internist-leader has any power over them, but because they believe that working together is the best way to achieve the Mayo Clinic's purpose, patient care.

One way to learn systems thinking is to study business cases like the Mayo Clinic. At the high point of the industrial age, the Toyota system became the gold standard for car companies, the model most others tried to copy.[23] Toyota is an exceptional example of an advanced industrial company that employs and teaches systems thinking. Recently, I visited a supplier to a number of automobile companies. I asked whether there was any difference in how Toyota related to them as compared to other car companies. There was. When the supplier had a quality problem, other customers just told the supplier to fix it. "Toyota," the plant manager said, "is deeply involved. They won't relent until they understand how the system is causing the problem. The other companies just want the problem to go away. We sometimes work around the problem and that adds cost. Toyota partners with us. Their system solutions improve quality and cut costs."

In the knowledge age, there is no best way to organize work. We saw in chapter 8 that knowledge organizations can learn from, but not copy, each other. However, to learn from the best cases of effective organizational systems, case writers at business schools should be systems thinkers who are sensitive to the interaction of roles, processes, competencies, operating principles, and values and be able to evaluate all these elements in terms of how well they work together to further the system's purpose. Few of the business school cases I've seen, where I've worked within the company or government agency described, meet this test.

Toyota tries to teach systems thinking to its suppliers in their *kaizen* workshops. The engineering manager of the supply company I visited said, "Getting people to learn systems thinking is hard. In the workshop, they may suddenly get it. But then they go back to their factory and try it out. Sometimes they can't do it, or it doesn't work right and the other managers discount it. You can't develop and use it without top management support."

A way to develop systems thinking in a company is for top management to organize workshops in which teams made up of managers from different divisions apply systems thinking in creating a new offering or business. Together with Russ Ackoff, who begins the workshop by teaching principles of systems thinking, I've led workshops like these where we've also focused on the kinds of leadership capable of creating the collaboration needed to design and implement innovative visions.

The most direct way to educate managers about social systems is to get them to take part in transforming their own organizations. I've facilitated this process in a few companies, including the MITRE Corporation, which does technical consulting and R&D for the military and Federal Aviation Administration. Faced with increased competition and complaints from MITRE's clients, then-CEO Barry Horowitz recognized the need for change and asked me to help. In the past, MITRE had developed new technology and then sold it to its clients who sometimes had trouble using it. Now, clients wanted business solutions integrating the technology, and that called for better understanding and collaboration, both with clients and within MITRE. The essential story is that Horowitz and the MITRE vice presidents redesigned the organization to achieve the new purpose. This called for new client relationships, adapting organizational structure, evaluating MITRE professionals on marketing and managerial as well as technical skills, and instituting supportive training programs. MITRE had the advantage of a tradition of working with technical systems, so there was a relatively easy acceptance of the need to understand social systems. Furthermore, some MITRE executives—like Jack Fearnsides, who was trying to transform the air-traffic control system, and Lydia Thomas, who became president and CEO of the company's Mitretek Systems spin-off—also learned to apply knowledge of personality and social character in placing managers and coaching them to collaborate.

An essential quality for leaders in the knowledge age is the ability to keep learning, and specifically to keep developing and employing their Personality and Strategic Intelligence. Change—whether new technologies, competition, or political and environmental dangers—never ends, and new people constantly come on stage. The time is long past when executives could preside over a smooth-running stable bureaucracy, or national leaders could ignore the larger world. However, the good news is that there are many people with leadership qualities ready and willing to respond to the challenges of our time, to become the leaders we need. Those of us who study and teach leadership have the challenge of helping them to succeed.

As much as they might want it, they won't be helped by getting new techniques and lists of things to do. Some need help to change mind-sets formed in the bureaucratic-industrial era. Others, the technical professionals who chose careers in technology to escape the messy world of people, need help to move out of their comfort zones to connect with the human side.

A final reminder to would-be organizational leaders: keep in mind that the people you need to help you succeed aren't all just like you. Increasingly, they won't follow the good parent model of leadership. To make them willing collaborators, especially the Interactives, first of all you'll have to engage and convince them of the purpose of your work together. Then, by understanding them and fitting them into roles where they can demonstrate and develop their strengths, you'll gain their respect, maybe even their trust. Only then will the people you lead become collaborators who help you succeed.

Social Character and the Life Cycle

For those readers seeking a more comprehensive understanding of the social character shift, I'll zoom in on the differences between the bureaucratic and interactive social characters and how each develops through the life cycle.

I've used Erik H. Erikson's theory of personality formation through eight stages of life to contrast how the bureaucratic and interactive social characters are formed.[1] Erikson, like Fromm, is among the rare breed of psychoanalysts who have tried to revise Freud's theory of personality by factoring in cultural influences. Erikson based his stages on the idea that people had to respond to the challenges of both their maturing bodies and their culture's expectations of them at different ages. How they met these challenges formed their competencies, values, emotional attitudes, and identity. Table A-1 illustrates positive life-cycle development of bureaucratic and interactive social characters, where those challenges are successfully met. Table A-2 lays out the negative implications of these life stages.

But what Erikson first wrote in 1950 and revised in 1963 was in a context that has changed almost beyond recognition, a culture that formed the bureaucratic social character. If you were born in the 1970s or '80s, it's hard to imagine a culture where two-thirds of families were headed by

TABLE A-1

Positive life-cycle development: Bureaucratic and interactive social characters

	Bureaucratic	Interactive
Basic trust	Focused on parents	Focused on parenting network
Autonomy	Self-directed conformity	Negotiating with parents
Initiative	Knowing your place, learning the role	Interpersonal competence, team-work
Industry	Passing the tests	Learning to learn
Identity	Choosing a career and belief system	Seeking a vocation, finding a center
Intimacy	Mutual care and focus on male success	Mutual development, building a network together, and focus on male and female success
Generativity	Parenting, protecting	Coaching, facilitating
Ego integrity	Playing the bureaucratic role with dignity and effectiveness, resisting illegitimate commands and corrupting pressures, detachment	Pragmatic development of ideals, living with contradictions and uncertainty without losing hope, staying engaged

a single wage earner, the father; where few women in this pre-pill era of *The Feminine Mystique* aspired to leadership roles in business and government, and most of those who did identified with their fathers.[2] At that time, even the most educated women were repeatedly told their role was to create the warm culture of the home, a haven from the rough and tumble of the corporate battlefield. That's what Adlai Stevenson, the Democratic presidential candidate, advised the graduating class of Smith, the elite women's college, in 1955. Of course, all that has changed. The twenty-first-century emphasis at Smith is strengthening the department of engineering so women can gain management jobs in technology companies.

At the present time, when most couples are both in the workforce and there are as many families headed by single women as there are traditional families of the 1950s, it's much harder to describe a typical experience for a child growing up. Clearly, these different types of families also differ in

TABLE A-2

Typical developmental problems: Bureaucratic and interactive social characters

	Bureaucratic	Interactive
Basic trust versus basic mistrust	Dependency on mother; hothouse environment	Feeling abandoned; detachment
Autonomy versus shame and doubt	Obsessive conformity	Lack of boundaries; impulsiveness
Initiative versus guilt and anxiety	Oedipal struggle and over-identification with parents	Anxiety about group acceptance causing over-conformity
Industry versus inferiority	Loss of self-confidence—poor grades, performance	Overestimation of self as defense against loss of self esteem
Identity versus role confusion	Compulsive conformity to parental role model or peer group	Self-marketing and lack of a center
Intimacy versus isolation	Tribalistic relatedness	Superficial coupling
Generativity versus stagnation	Becomes a narrow role	Nothing to teach
Ego integrity versus despair	Tolstoy's *Death of Ivan Illich*—the lost self	Burnout; anomie

wealth and opportunities for children to succeed, and, as I'll note, richer parents get involved early on in their children's careers. Yet, with universal access to current events through TV, radio, movies, and the Internet, few children are unaware of what they have to do to succeed in a world of fierce competition and global business where capability for knowledge work is the key to success.

As we contrast the eight stages of life of bureaucratic and interactive social characters, what it takes to prosper in this new world will become clearer.

Do national cultures make a difference? What I've concluded after interviewing managers in Europe and Asia is that while national differences exist, the common culture of global business is pulling the most educated young people toward a common interactive social character.

Erikson's stages were a speculative framework, and in building on it, I've made use of studies from developmental psychology and sociology that were made after Erikson's time, combined with my own observations and those of colleagues.[3]

The eight stages with approximate ages are:

- *Trust versus mistrust:* From birth to age 1

- *Autonomy versus shame and doubt:* From 1 to 3 years

- *Initiative versus guilt:* From 3 to 6 years

- *Industry versus inferiority:* From 6 to 12 years

- *Identity versus role confusion:* From 12 to 20 years

- *Intimacy versus isolation:* From 20 to 40 years

- *Generativity versus stagnation:* From 40 to 65 years

- *Ego integrity versus despair:* From 65 on

These stages should not be thought of mechanically, as though we moved through life on a track, stopping at fixed stations to wrestle with psychosocial challenges. Although our success in mastering the challenge of each stage increases greatly the chances of our success at the next level, failure at a particular stage doesn't mean we are forever blocked in developing ourselves. Despite early setbacks, some people, often with help, can recover and find their way back on the path.

BASIC TRUST VERSUS MISTRUST

We're all born with a rudimentary sense of identity, me versus not-me, but up to two to three months of age, "me" includes mother. Then we begin to recognize ourselves in the mirror and even recognize other babies. In the bureaucratic family, the infant is focused almost exclusively on the mother. The attitude of basic trust and love of life grows from connection with a loving mother and expectation that she'll satisfy basic needs. Ideally, the bond between mother and child includes a deep sense of knowing each other, sensing and responding to each other.

The typical developmental problems at this stage have to do with overdependency—failure to break the umbilical cord—sometimes because a mother is so intensely attached to her children. Of course, problems with basic trust also stem from a cold, frightened, inadequate mother or a rejecting or ambivalent mother who resents the mothering role that keeps her trapped at home.

In the interactive family, mother usually starts out as the main infant caretaker, continuing the physical symbiosis of childbearing. But early on, when she returns to her paid work, others share this role. (Over 60 percent of women with children under age six work outside the home.[4]) Increasingly, the father also participates in caring for the baby, and babies may also be put in day-care centers or in the care of hired nannies.

On the positive side, as infants receive care from others, trust is expanded beyond the mother. On the negative side, children may lack the security of deep maternal attachment. Feeling insecure and abandoned, they become more distrustful, anxious, and self-protectively avoidant. Later in life, this makes it harder for them to develop intimate relationships and accept the deep feelings of need for others that they've repressed.[5] While the quality of day care also makes a difference for the infant's trust and sense of well-being, studies show that "a mother's sensitivity to her infant had a lot more to do with attachment security than whether or not an infant was in alternative care. Moreover, under some circumstances, high-quality day care appeared to counteract the negative effects of parenting."[6]

There is still debate about day care, and some conservatives blame absent and working parents and day care for belligerent and aggressive children, juvenile obesity, psychoactive drug use, and teenage sex, among other problems of the young in our time.[7] However, the psychologist Diane F. Halpern, in her presidential address to the American Psychological Association in 2005 wrote that "there is an emerging consensus that effects are more likely to be negative when the work schedules of the caretaking parents (usually the mother) [are] erratic and unpredictable; the hours are long and she faces other significant stressors, such as poor health, poverty, and little control over work-related events. In other words, children, families, and work suffer when the parent has few sources of support and stress is high."[8] Professor Halpern believes that it's time to end the "mommy wars" and "games of mother blame" and focus on basing policy on the best evidence of what benefits children and families.

I fully agree.

AUTONOMY VERSUS SHAME AND DOUBT

About the age of two, children want to act on their own, and they show a rebelliousness to adult authority, the start to achieving a sense of autonomy. Kids want to do things for themselves, express themselves without losing loving support from parents. By this self-expression, children try to avoid the shame of being seen as babies who can't control their bodily functions, dress themselves, or handle a fork and spoon. They want to be able to feel good about themselves. Parents should treat this rebelliousness by setting limits and giving reasons why.

But not all parents respond this way. In the bureaucratic family, some parents impose overly strict demands, such as too-early toilet training. The danger is that the child will avoid humiliating shame by obsessive compliance, the uptight, superclean, and humorless anal character described by Freud. Alternatively, the child is plagued by doubt and needs constant reassurance that he or she is doing the right thing. But all shaming isn't bad. Although extreme shaming of a child at this age can cause deep hurt and anger, which may be repressed, without some homeopathic shaming, children don't learn to conform to social expectations and are vulnerable to more serious humiliations later in life.

The child in the interactive family may have to deal with various parenting figures, less consistency, and less certainty. Sensing their parents' insecurity about standards and their guilt about not being around when needed, two-year-old children begin to negotiate with parents for more freedom, playthings, or a later bedtime.

Many interactive children seem to have responded to parental indecision with a loss of respect for adults. According to an Associated Press-Ipsos poll in the fall of 2005, "nearly 70 percent of Americans said they believed that people are ruder now than they were 20 or 30 years ago and that children are among the worst offenders." In 2002, according to surveys by Public Agenda, only 9 percent of adults saw children as "respectful toward adults."[9]

In a *New York Times* interview by Judith Warner, Dan Kindlon, a Harvard University child psychologist, said that while most parents today would like their children to be polite, considerate, and well-behaved, they're too tired, worn down by work, and personally needy to demand proper behavior. " 'We use kids like Prozac,' he said. 'People don't necessarily feel great about their spouse or their job but the kids are the bright spot in their day . . . They don't want to feel bad. They want to get satisfaction from their kids. They're so precious to us. What gets thrown out the window is limits. It's a lot easier to pick their towel up off the floor than to get them away from the PlayStation to do it.' "[10]

So, as on the TV show *Nanny 911*, unbridled nagging children run family dictatorships where mom and dad are there to serve them at all times. Parents have become so disempowered that they need help from experts like Brian Orr, a pediatrician and author, who runs workshops north of Boston on how to say "no" to children. Think of the future transference to bosses when these kids get to the workplace. They won't idealize bosses and they may shy away from becoming a parental-type boss. Who wants to deal with a bunch of demanding kids?

However, while parents of Interactives let their kids disempower them about everything else, they do teach children to compete for success, whatever it takes. When it's about achievement, parents get serious and take charge. According to Kindlon, " 'We're insane about achievement . . . Schoolwork is up 50 percent since 1981, and we're so obsessed with our kids getting into the right school, getting the right grades, we let a lot of things slide.' "[11]

And that brings us to the next two stages.

INITIATIVE VERSUS GUILT AND ANXIETY

This is the age where kids take the initiative and start to play together. Traditionally, preschool boys and girls play separately, boys being more aggressive and girls focused more on creating group harmony.[12] This is the age at which kids also start comparing themselves, forming an identity based on being smarter, cuter, a better athlete, and so on.

In the traditional family, children up to ages five or six are still essentially egocentric and see things only from their own point of view. Although they may rebel against adult commands, the grown-ups rule and other kids are rivals for the authority's love and approval.[13]

When this pattern is reproduced in bureaucracies, it causes childlike emotions in employees who compete for the boss's favor. In the traditional family, rebellion against authority is resolved by boys identifying with father and his outlook on life (what Freud called the resolution of the Oedipus complex) while girls identify with mother and take on her values. Going against these internalized parents (the superego) causes guilty feelings. In bureaucracies, when subordinates identify with the CEO, even copying his dress and mannerisms, they no longer feel childlike with the boss; rather, they feel just like the boss, especially when dealing with their own subordinates.

Children of interactive families, less emotionally dependent on adults, are quicker to forge ties with other kids. While the psychological pitfall for the bureaucratic character was fear of parents' disapproval, which becomes internalized as crippling guilt, for the interactive character it's anxiety about not being in with the group.[14]

This anxiety can drive kids into overconformity in their urgency to be accepted. Alternatively, children may totally reject the group and form alliances with other "outcasts" whose resentment curdles into fantasies of revenge. These feelings may return with a vengeance in adolescence as was the case in Littleton, Colorado, in the spring of 1999, when kids like these went on a murderous and suicidal rampage. Part of the guilt belongs to teachers, administrators, and parents who didn't step in when these kids were being ostracized and bullied.

Of course, most kids do learn to fit in. But while normal bureaucratic conformity results from identification with older role models, the interactive child becomes increasingly alert and responsive to changing fads and fashions among peers. In his 1950 book, *The Lonely Crowd*, David Riesman was the first sociologist to see that the traditional obsessive and inner-directed American whose internal gyroscope determined right and wrong was being challenged by a new type who was other-directed and whose interpersonal radar signaled the appropriate way to act.[15] By the 1990s, other-direction combined with peer transferences was becoming the dominant form of social control for the interactive social character.

By the end of this stage, bureaucratic children were cooperating at play to work out conflicts with authority in central person games like hide-and-seek and Red Rover, where the group bands together to escape "It," the oppressive authority. In contrast, the interactive child is much further along in forming relationships at play and on the Internet, more concerned with getting grown-ups to serve him or her than to escape from authority.

INDUSTRY VERSUS INFERIORITY

When children reach the age of six or seven, they are ready to become workers. But their first work depends on the mode of production in their culture. In peasant villages, boys follow their fathers to the fields and girls help their mothers with cows, pigs, and chickens; caring for younger siblings; cooking; washing; and cleaning.

In the bureaucratic world, the main work is schoolwork, and the tools kids must master are tools for reading and understanding, writing clearly, and solving abstract problems. The peasant child sharpens physical skills, and develops a keen observation of nature and people, common sense; the bureaucratic child learns internal discipline, to sit still for long periods and concentrate, and to memorize concepts and formulas, construct arguments, and take tests.

In the bureaucratic world, boys begin to play team sports where they develop a capacity for reciprocity—the ability not only to understand and follow fair rules, but also design them.[16] In games like baseball, kids learn not only to play by the rules but also to put themselves in another person's role, not only to play but also to execute plays that require cooperation (like the double play). Reciprocity expressed as fairness tempers both egocentric competition and authoritarian hierarchy.

But bureaucratic managers don't make use of reciprocity. They divide to conquer and provoke egocentric rivalry. Even in the most cooperative organizations, there will still be conflict about being a team player versus individual achievement. In professional sports, this tension is resolved by evaluating individuals on both individual statistics and contribution to the team.

To succeed in the interactive world, a child's industry is essential, but so are her talents. As factory jobs and, increasingly, knowledge work moves offshore, and transactional jobs—operators, bank clerks, salespeople—are automated, the jobs that remain are either low-paying service jobs—cleaning, fast-food counters—or high-salaried knowledge work. Unlike jobs that require formulaic intelligence, manual dexterity, or muscle power, the jobs that have increased during the past ten years call for analytic reasoning, imagination and creativity, people skills, and emotional intelligence.[17] Of course, construction workers, truck drivers, garbage collectors, and baggage handlers will remain on these shores, as well as well-paying work for skilled electricians, carpenters, and plumbers, but the difference in wages and wealth between knowledge work and other types of jobs has been increasing.[18]

A troubling finding from social psychologists is that while upper-middle-class parents have become career directors for children this age and younger, working-class parents are much less involved in their children's lives—and their success. These richer parents know what's coming for their children, and their anxiety about their kids' future ability to maintain their status drives the kids on—from supervised learning experiences to little league games. Sociologist Annette Lareau, who has been observing parents and children for over twenty years, finds that the upper-middle-class kids are prepared to succeed in the world of knowledge work by parents who are more facilitators and coaches than authorities, who allow kids to talk back, express their negative feelings (as long as they do the homework), shine on the stage, and show they can make a good impression at an interview to get accepted into a program.[19]

While working-class parents are more likely to give orders and demand respect, they also let their kids play freely. There is less anxiety, less manipulation, more autonomy. But Lareau shows the anxious, driven kids become successful professionals, while the working-class kids don't.[20]

The knowledge mode of production demands continual learning and collaboration, and traditional forms of schooling that may have served for the bureaucratic era have now been found wanting. There's been a lot of debate about the best way to prepare children to succeed in the knowledge economy, much too much for me to try and summarize here. However, I believe the debate between proponents of rigorous teaching to tests versus "learning to learn" falsely opposes the need for kids to memorize and practice basic arithmetic, languages, scientific facts, historical events, and so on, to the need to develop critical thinking, communication skills, and the motivation to learn. Some of the progressive educators seem like piano teachers who ask pupils to express emotion in their playing before they've mastered the keys and learned the scales, while the conservative educators seem like piano teachers who never inspire their pupils to put their heart into their art.

Kids today benefit from teachers who combine discipline with challenge, rigor with fun, respect for precision with love of life, and this is especially true for disadvantaged children in the inner cities whose future opportunities depend on good schooling. I describe in chapter 8 how the KIPP (Knowledge Is Power Program) is providing this kind of education to mostly African American and Hispanic kids in about fifty charter schools in the inner cities.

For the affluent, some schools are taking the lead in preparing children for what they believe will gain them success in the interactive economy. One such school is St John's School and Community College in Marlborough, Wiltshire, England. Patrick Hazlewood, the headmaster, says, "The national curriculum kills learning stone dead by compartmentalizing subjects as if they have no relation to each other."[21] The school bases teaching around five competences for business proposed by the Royal Society for

Encouragement of Arts and Manufactures—learning, citizenship (ethics and society), relating to other people, managing situations, and managing information (critical thinking and finding things out).

Industrious future bureaucrats risked becoming narrowly focused and unimaginative. Industrious interactive children risk becoming glib and shallow, and under the illusion of knowing more than they do because knowledge seems the click of a mouse away. In the bureaucratic classroom, the unsuccessful child would lose self-confidence and self-esteem, triggering a vicious cycle of poor performance. While this might also happen to the interactive child, denial of failure is supported by the antibureaucratic popular culture and pop psychology, which inflates the self and puts down authorities. Defending against the loss of self-esteem, these children overestimate their capabilities and become impervious to coaching. Caring teachers who help these children understand that the discipline required for learning and self-expression makes a huge difference in their future ability to learn and play a productive role in the interactive society.

Of course, a profound influence in shaping the interactive social character is the Internet, facilitating interaction (combined with cell phones) as well as finding things out. The first thing the typical eleven- or twelve-year-old does after school is connect with correspondents all over the world and play video games. For these kids, global networking comes naturally. We're also learning how video game playing shapes attitudes to leaders.

There has been concern about the effects of game playing on kids. Some games are extremely violent. Are they making kids aggressive? Do games detach kids from reality? Can they train kids to kill? So far, according to a report in the *Economist*, the evidence is inconclusive.[22] Kids who tend toward violence may be pushed over the edge by violent games like *Grand Theft Auto*.[23] However, these games do require players to learn a great deal. They must construct hypotheses about the intra-game world and test them. They learn the game rules through trial and error, solve problems and puzzles, develop strategies, and get help from other players via the Internet when they're stuck. They also learn to share leadership roles.

Of course, the bureaucratic child played at different roles and identities, being a grown-up or a policeman, fireman, model, nurse, or doctor.

But the interactive gamester moves in alternative realities and takes on alternative personalities. That can be a strength, but only as long as game players know the difference between the game and a reality that doesn't end when the game is over, where it's not so easy to change identities. And that takes us to the next developmental stage.

IDENTITY VERSUS ROLE DIFFUSION

Youth begins. Individuals should have gained basic skills for work and relationships. But in puberty and adolescence, rapid body growth and genital maturity cause confusion about identity. Youths struggle with the physiological revolution inside them and the grown-up tasks ahead of them. Who are they becoming? How do others view them? How to connect the roles and skills they have practiced with the occupational prototypes that appeal to them? How to discover a vocation?

Youth is a time of exuberance and experimentation, sometimes grandiose fantasies and ambitions, daredevil risk taking—what I've called a "narcissistic moment."[24] This is a time of freedom, when children feel the whole world is open to them and they can do anything they put their minds to. They are invulnerable. For the bureaucratic personality, it may mean rejecting their father's or mother's plans for them—their parents' ideas of what they should do for a living—or rebelling against the tyranny of the peer group. When bureaucratic teenagers imagine adult life, they often think in narcissistic terms, turning jobs that require years of rote study and training, such as doctor or lawyer, into heroic, high-wire acts: They'll become a world-famous surgeon, or a lawyer who overwhelms the Supreme Court with brilliant arguments.

For interactive youth, fantasies often include getting rich, but they are also more likely to envision being part of a great team: a new Google or The Dust Brothers or Dreamworks.[25] Ultimately, however, the inner discipline and real-world skills formed in earlier stages make the difference between fantasy and reality, success and failure. Few people ride the narcissistic moment into a lifetime adventure, creating a world-class career or a great company that does change the world.

A challenge of youth is to integrate all the pieces of identity that make up a self. We all have attachments—to family, nation, religious groups, even teams—with which we identify. But for adolescents, the roles and identities of the child at home and the youth outside can clash. Erikson wrote that the main psychological danger of this stage was role confusion, not only between home and the peer group, but also possibly confusion about sexual identity. It could also be confusion about settling on an occupational identity. He saw falling in love at this stage as an attempt to gain a sense of identity by being defined and affirmed in a passionate relationship.

He wrote that "young people can also be remarkably clannish, and cruel in their exclusion of all those who are 'different,' in skin color or cultural background, in tastes and gifts, and often in such petty aspects of dress and gesture as have been temporarily selected as *the* sign of an in-grouper or out-grouper."[26] He saw this intolerance as the dark side of defense against identity confusion and as a way of testing loyalty and trust.

Erikson also described youth as a time of idealism, of committing oneself to an ideology or religion. Soon after he wrote this, in the 1960s, the enlarged cohort of baby-boomer youth began to undermine the bureaucratic social character. They attacked "dehumanizing" bureaucratic rules, roles, and technology with an ideology of libertarianism. The youth that survived this self-indulgent orgy were somehow able to combine pleasure seeking with pragmatism. The losers were the ideological extremists, revolutionaries who became disillusioned cynics, tribalistic cultists, and drug addicts.

In contrast to Europeans, whose identities are more tightly tied to social class and place of birth, Americans have had more freedom in shaping identities. I think of two American icons: Robert Frost, born in San Francisco and educated at Dartmouth and Harvard, failed as a farmer in New Hampshire and went to England, where he made himself into the craggy prototype of the rural New Hampshire farmer-poet. And Robert Allen Zimmerman, the middle-class Jewish boy from Duluth and Hibbing, Minnesota, became Bob Dylan, the folk-rock balladeer and figurehead of the 1960s.[27]

The Interactives go even further than a single change of identity in their protean ability to take on and shed identities that serve their needs, just like the characters in video games. Madonna is a prototype, constantly reinventing herself to fit the fashions of the times. Furthermore, their idealism often gets mixed with self-interest as they join identity groups based on occupation, politics, business, race, religion, disabilities, or sexual orientation.

While the challenge for bureaucratic social character was constructing an individual identity and not just putting on the identity laid out by parents and other authorities, the challenge for Interactives is to find meaning. In large part, this has to do with finding a vocation, work that engages talents and values. However, many Interactives feel a need for more than a vocation to provide a sense of meaning. The UCLA Higher Education Research Institute reports that three-quarters of the 112,000 students surveyed, from a sample of 236 colleges in 2004, indicate that they are "searching for meaning and purpose in life."[28] That's why they seek help from therapists, Eastern spiritual disciplines like Yoga, or religions. That's why Rick Warren's *The Purpose-Driven Life: What on Earth Am I Here For?* has sold millions of copies.[29]

Finding a meaningful purpose, a center to anchor changing identities and protean role taking can become a platform for the next stage.

INTIMACY VERSUS ISOLATION

The challenge for younger adults, from ages twenty to forty years, is to achieve an intimate, trusting relationship; to do this they have to be able to trust themselves as much as they trust the other person. This is not just a matter of faithfulness. Without a firm identity, intimacy is threatening: people can be taken over by an other, losing their identity as well as their freedom. However, to become a mature person, an essential task is to establish a loving relationship, overcome loneliness, and create a family.

Ideally, a family supports the positive development of all its members, and by development I mean the increased capability to both determine and satisfy those needs that strengthen us—needs to know and understand, to create, and to love. In contrast, compulsive or addictive needs enslave us, making us dependent not only on drugs or sex but also on constant reassurance, protection, applause—whatever limits free choice. Achieving maturity means becoming more aware of our needs, able to reinforce those that are developmental and frustrate those that are addictive.[30]

In the bureaucratic era, the goal of this stage was forming a unit for mutual care and success, with clearly differentiated male and female roles. The danger was that this intimate family might isolate itself, become a tribalistic haven, held together by narcissistic self-inflation ("We're better than everyone else").

The interactive family at its best avoids this pitfall and builds a network that reaches beyond blood ties to connect with others who share its developmental values. But there are two kinds of pitfalls for Interactives. One is the inability to fully commit, to fully trust. Perhaps this is caused by lack of identity integration; however, a deeper cause may go back to early attachment issues. Detached, avoidant adults repress strong needs for mothering, but are driven into relationships and then repelled by infantile yearnings and behavior, either their own or the other person's. This attraction and repulsion can cause superficial coupling and frequent break-ups.

The second pitfall has to do with the pressure two careers put on a relationship. A major cause of divorce for Interactives is that women who are economically independent won't stay in a bad relationship. In the past, their need for a breadwinner might have kept them from leaving. Not now. So if both partners are economically independent, mature understanding and compromise are urgently needed to sustain their relationship, especially when they both feel career pressures.

Freud once described psychological health as *lieben und arbeiten*, to love and to work. This is a formula that fits any social character, but it seems to me essential for Interactive well-being. Interactives want to love their work and many of them need to work at love. As Erich Fromm wrote in *The Art of Loving*, there is little education or understanding about the kind of love that strengthens self and other and deepens trust.[31] Relationships built on narcissistic love, the projection of one's ideal onto the other, collapse when the mutual illusion fades, and then the prince and princess become frogs in each other's eyes. It's the difference between infatuation and *agapé*: deep knowledge and caring about what's best for the other person.

Trust is strengthened not only by affirmation but also by the kind of love that refuses to collude or ignore the danger when the other person strays from the path that both believe is best for his or her well-being.

During this period, young people are also establishing themselves at work. In the bureaucratic era, the ideal was to move up corporate or government hierarchies, make partner in law or accounting firms, or establish a professional practice. Interactives still want status and power, but they are now more likely to view corporations and government as postgraduate training for more freewheeling careers. Like professional athletes, they see themselves as assets that can be bought but not owned by companies, and their commitment is to meaningful projects, not powerful organizations.

GENERATIVITY VERSUS STAGNATION

The next period is when, with the achievement of a productive role at work and sustainable intimate relationships, individuals face the challenge of bringing along the next generation, as parents, teachers, coaches, or institution builders who articulate and defend good values—possibly as the kind of leader we need.

Erikson first thought this period lasted from about ages forty to sixty-five, but that was when he was in his forties. In his eighties and still active, he realized that people can now stay generative for a longer time. However, the generative role was clearer in the bureaucratic era, especially for men who could move up the hierarchy and mentor promising younger men who in turn were attracted to them as father figures. The productive bureaucrat who identified with father figures took pride in being an expert who could teach the younger generation. Mentor and mentee enjoyed the transferential relationship and helped each other succeed. When women first took management roles, the ones able to create father-daughter relationships were best able to find mentors.

The traditional bureaucracies allowed, even encouraged, middle managers to be mentors, both at work and in voluntary organizations. There was less pressure, more time for bonding. In contrast, in companies today, there is little time and even less energy for these forms of sociability. But even when there is time, the new social character is uneasy in the role of mentor or protective authority. Other than success, Interactives' highest value is tolerance in terms of race, religion, and ideology. Their moral code: "Judge not that you be not judged." And they've told me they don't think they should have to defend organizational values they didn't have a say in framing, saying, "Those are not my values and I'm not the police." But on a team or task force, they aren't tolerant about poor performance. One value everyone shares is results.

The most generative of the Interactives may take leadership roles as facilitators or bridge-builders, preferably for a project. They want it to be clear they are adding value for others, not trying to dominate them. They don't want to seem power hungry.

Ultimately, both Bureaucratics and Interactives who fail the test of generativity stagnate. The bureaucrat becomes his narrow role, like a character in one of Franz Kafka's novels or Max Weber's "specialists without spirit."[32] Interactives never deepen their knowledge or commit themselves to others. They have nothing to teach and no one wants anything from them. Keep in mind that we all need to feel needed, and a person who feels needed by no one will feel like a total failure.

And this is more than a personal failure. The more Interactives fail the test of generativity, the more our society suffers. We need generative leaders who defend the values that support a free, productive, and environmentally sustainable society. The well-being of the next generation depends on whether Interactives understand and accept the challenge of generativity.

EGO INTEGRITY VERSUS DESPAIR

Erikson first wrote about the final stage of life in his forties and revised it first in his eighties, and again finally before he died in his early nineties, when he wrote, "Lacking a culturally viable ideal of old age, our civilization does not really harbor a concept of the whole life."[33] He thought that elders in our society (now called seniors) are no longer seen as bearers of wisdom, but as embodiments of shame.

But, writing this at age 73, I can testify that that's not always the case. Erikson himself contradicted the statement by his continued generativity. Another example was W. Edwards Deming, the statistician who brought total quality management first to Japan and then to the United States; he was still teaching at age 90. At that time, he invited me to discuss leadership with him. We met periodically over a three-year period, and each time, he took notes (as did I); he was still learning. And John Gielgud, the great English director and actor, was still acting in films at age 95. Peter Drucker was active when he died at age 96. At age 93, his wife Doris is still running the company she started at age 80. Sidney Harman was running Harman International at age 88. Surely, these people had the luck of good genes, but I believe staying engaged kept them from the collapse common to old age that begins in the 80s.

It's too early to see how the Interactives will deal with old age. However, populations in the advanced economies are aging, and people who used to retire at age 65 or earlier may remain in the workforce up until and beyond age 70. In 2005 28 percent of retirement age adults, ages 65 to 69 were either still working or looking for work.[34] Furthermore, companies are offering part-time projects to valuable employees this old and even older.[35] And, of course, a number of people in their 60s, 70s, and 80s do volunteer work for charities and nonprofits, demonstrating that generativity doesn't necessarily stop with retirement from paid work. Programs like Civic Ventures' Experience Corps, which has placed eighteen hundred tutors and mentors to children, connect seniors with "good work" where they're needed.

This is all to the good. Research indicates that working during retirement together with exercise and diet can help us live longer and healthier.[36] And there's evidence that retirement without active engagement can cause the despair Erikson wrote about. A study of retired people by psychologist Ken Dychtwald emphasizes the benefits for old people of "reinventing" their lives after retirement. He writes, "Having a vision for the future and planning for that vision are as important as money in achieving a fulfilling retirement."[37]

Erikson focused on how people might view themselves at the end of life. A sense of integrity means one has not betrayed one's ideal self, or if so, has repented and found the path again. Despair means losing one's way and, what is more devastating, any hope of regaining it. Those who have betrayed themselves live with self-disgust, and the rationalizations they devise don't overcome their depression when they have lost their love of life.

In contrast, a sense of integrity is gained by mature realism, understanding what has been possible to do, given one's opportunities and abilities, always taking luck into account. This includes remaining engaged and generative as long as physically possible, concerned and hopeful about the future, related to what is alive and needs protection—especially children and the environment that sustains us—as opposed to resigning from the present and retreating into the past.

The integrity of the bureaucrat meant playing his role with dignity and effectiveness, resisting illegitimate commands and corrupting pressures. After retirement, it meant continued learning, reading, traveling, and voluntary activities. For women, it meant providing care and emotional support while staying sharp in voluntary organizations and cultural activities.

The despairing bureaucrat was like Tolstoy's Ivan Illich, who realizes only on his deathbed that he has never stood up for what he thought was right, never really been himself, only what others expected him to be. Tolstoy wrote:

> *His mental sufferings were due to the fact that that night, as he looked at Gerásim's sleepy, good natured face with its prominent cheek-bones, the question suddenly occurred to him: "What if my whole life has really been wrong?"*
>
> *It occurred to him that what appeared perfectly impossible before, namely that he had not spent his life as he should have done, might after all be true. It occurred to him that his scarcely perceptible attempts to struggle against what was considered good by the most highly placed people, those scarcely noticeable impulses which he had immediately suppressed, might have been the real thing, and all the rest false. And his professional duties and the whole arrangement of his life and of his family, and all his social and official interests, might all have been false. He tried to defend all those things to himself and suddenly felt the weakness of what he was defending. There was nothing to defend.*

"But if that is so," he said to himself, "and I am leaving this life with the consciousness that I have lost all that was given me and it is impossible to rectify it—what then?"

Perhaps the despairing interactive character will be more like Ibsen's Peer Gynt, who confuses self-indulgence with self-actualization and self-marketing with intimacy, and ends up alone and burned out. Acting out all his greedy impulses, Peer Gynt mistakenly believes he's being true to himself. In the end, "the button-maker" who comes for his soul tells Peer Gynt that he has no self. By never committing himself to anyone or anything and never responding with his heart, Peer Gynt has become a blank. His expressions of love and sorrow were never felt; his heart has never developed.

Maintaining integrity in the market-dominated world calls for principled pragmatism—continually testing one's views and values in terms of results. For those who have been engaged in the complex market world, it means living with contradictions and uncertainty without losing hope. This requires a faith that gives meaning to creative engagement with one's community, which in the interactive age may include people throughout the world who share a common purpose: to protect the environment, keep destructive extremists in check, and work to improve the quality of life for all.

Notes

Acknowledgments

1. Michael Maccoby, "Toward a Science of Social Character," *International Forum of Psychoanalysis* 11 (2002): 33–44.

2. Charles Heckscher and Paul S. Adler, eds., *The Firm as Collaborative Community: The Reconstruction of Trust in the Knowledge Economy* (New York: Oxford University Press, 2006).

3. Michael Maccoby, "Why People Follow the Leader: The Power of Transference," *Harvard Business Review*, September 2004, 76–88.

Preface

1. John W. Gardner, *On Leadership* (New York: The Free Press, 1990).

2. For example, John P. Kotter, "What Leaders Really Do," *Harvard Business Review,* May–June 1990, 103–112.

3. James McGregor Burns, *Leadership* (New York: Harper & Row, 1978).

4. *Knowledge worker* is a term coined by Peter Drucker in 1959 as a person who works primarily with information or someone who uses or develops knowledge in the workplace.

Chapter 1

1. Jack Weatherford, *Genghis Khan and the Making of the Modern World* (New York: Crown, 2004).

2. For example, a survey by the National Opinion Research Center, University of Chicago conducted between August 2004 and January 2005 found only 22 percent of the public expressed a "great deal of confidence" in the executive branch of the federal government, 29 percent in banks and financial institutions and 25 percent in leaders of organized religion. Reported in the *New York Times Magazine,* December 11, 2005, 25. In the United Kingdom, less than 20 percent of the public expressed either "a fair amount" or "a great deal"

of trust in the heads of large companies and even less in labor government ministers and senior civil servants ("Trust Me, I'm a Judge," *The Economist,* U.S. edition, May 5, 2007, 71).

3. The socio-psychoanalytic concept of social character was conceived by Erich Fromm (1900–1980). Fromm saw personality as the human equivalent of animal instinct. Another way of putting it is that personality shapes our instincts. To some extent, this is true of other mammals. But it is even more so for us humans, with our larger brains, longer period of dependency, and greater need for learning. If humans had to decide each action, we'd be overwhelmed by the choices. Personality structures our attitudes to work and how we relate to others, what we find most satisfying and dissatisfying and what we expect from others in our culture. While part of our personality is genetically determined, particularly temperament, character can be considered the part that is learned. The social character is that learned part of our personality we share with others in our culture or subculture.

4. Bureau of Labor Statistics report: *Employment Status of Parents by Age of Youngest Child and Family Type, 2003–2004 Annual Averages,* Table 4, "Families with own children, father employed, not mother (married-couple families): 7,867, Families maintained by women: 8,161 (numbers in thousands).

5. Erich Fromm and Michael Maccoby, *Social Character in a Mexican Village* (Englewood Cliffs, NJ: Prentice-Hall, 1970; reprinted with new introduction by Michael Maccoby [New Brunswick, NJ: Transaction Publishers, 1996]).

6. Of the fifty most generous philanthropists in 2005, fifteen, including these innovators, support new schools. *BusinessWeek,* November 28, 2005, 61.

7. Sigmund Freud, *The Dynamics of Transference,* vol. XII, *The Standard Edition of the Complete Psychological Works of Sigmund Freud* (London: The Hogarth Press, 1958), 97–109 (orig. pub. 1912); Michael Maccoby, "Why People Follow the Leader: The Power of Transference," *Harvard Business Review,* September 2004, 76–85.

8. In *The Moral Basis of a Backward Society* (Glencoe, IL: The Free Press, 1958), Edward Banfield describes similar dynamics in Southern Italian peasant families.

9. Michael Maccoby, *The Leader: A New Face for American Management* (New York: Simon & Schuster, 1981).

10. Michael Maccoby, *The Gamesman: The New Corporate Leaders* (New York: Simon and Schuster, 1976).

11. Michael Maccoby, *The Productive Narcissist: The Promise and Peril of Visionary Leadership* (New York: Broadway Books, 2003), released in paperback edition with a new preface by author as *Narcissistic Leaders: Who Succeeds and Who Fails,* (Boston: Harvard Business School Press, 2007).

12. Michael Maccoby, *Why Work: Leading the New Generation* (New York: Simon and Schuster, 1988; 2nd ed. *Why Work? Motivating the New Workforce* [Alexandria, VA: Miles River Press, 1995]); Charles C. Heckscher et al., *Agents of Change: Crossing the Post-Industrial Divide* (Oxford: Oxford University Press, 2003).

13. Charles Heckscher and Paul S. Adler, eds., *The Firm as a Collaborative Community: The Reconstruction of Trust in the Knowledge Economy* (Oxford: Oxford University Press, 2005).

14. Rakesh Khurana, *Searching for a Corporate Savior: The Irrational Quest for Charismatic CEOs* (Princeton, NJ: Princeton University Press, 2002).

15. Erich Fromm, *Escape from Freedom* (New York: Rinehart: 1941).

16. Erich Fromm, *The Working Class in Weimar Germany: A Psychological and Sociological Study*; trans. Barbara Weinberger, ed. Wolfgang Bonss (Cambridge, MA: Harvard University

Press, 1984); see also Richard J. Evans, *The Third Reich in Power, 1922–1939* (London: Penguin, 2005).

17. In "Employees Want to Hear It 'Straight' from the Boss's Mouth," *Financial Times*, December 1, 2006, Alison Maitland reports: "What employees really want, according to a new survey, are straight-talkers who keep them up to date with bad, as well as good news instead of putting on a performance or preaching through PowerPoint."

Chapter 2

1. These qualities were cited by CEOs and other leaders in speeches given at The World Business Forum in New York, September 13–14, 2005.

2. Thomas H. Davenport, *Thinking for a Living: How to Get Better Performance and Results from Knowledge Workers* (Boston: Harvard Business School Press, 2005).

3. Betsy Morris, "Genentech: The Best Place to Work Now," *Fortune*, January 11, 2006, 79–86.

4. See, for example, Donald Roy, "Quota Restrictions and Goldbricking in a Machine Shop," *American Journal of Sociology* (March 1952): 427–442.

5. Elton Mayo, *The Problems of an Industrialized Civilization* (Boston: Division of Research, Harvard Business School, 1933); F. J. Roethlisberger and William J. Dickson, *Management and the Worker: An Account of a Research Program Conducted by the Western Electric Company, Hawthorne Works* (Cambridge, MA: Harvard University Press, 1939).

6. See the description of my work at AT&T in Charles C. Heckscher et al., *Agents of Change: Crossing the Post-Industrial Divide* (New York: Oxford University Press, 2003), chapter 2.

7. Richard Gillespie, *Manufacturing Knowledge: A History of the Hawthorne Experiments* (Cambridge, UK: Cambridge University Press, 1991), 79. In his fascinating history of the Hawthorne studies, Gillespie goes back to the original field notes and memos and finds that the researchers differed among themselves about the findings and the workers argued about the conclusions.

8. Douglas McGregor, *The Human Side of Enterprise* (New York: McGraw-Hill, 1960); Abraham Maslow, *Motivation and Personality* (New York: Harper, 1954).

9. Abraham Maslow, *Eupsychian Management* (Homewood, IL: R.D. Irwin, 1965), 36. Maslow's examples of evolved versus unevolved people compare Americans to people from the third world. For example, referring to Peter Drucker's elaboration of Theory Y, management by objectives, he writes, "Where we have fairly evolved human beings able to grow, eager to grow, then Drucker's management principles seem to be fine. They will work, but only at the top of the hierarchy of human development. They assume ideally a person who has been satisfied in his basic needs in the past, while he was growing up, and who is now being satisfied in his life situation. He was and now is safety-need gratified (not anxious, not fearful). He was and is belongingness-need satisfied (he does not feel alienated, ostracized, orphaned, outside the group; he fits into the family, the team, the society; he is not an unwelcome intruder). He was and is love-need gratified (he has enough friends and enough good ones, a reasonable family life; he feels worthy of being loved and wanted and able to give love—this means much more than romantic love, especially in the industrial situation). He was and is respect-need gratified (he feels respect-worthy, needed, important, etc.; he feels he gets enough praise and expects to get whatever praise and reward he deserves). He

was and is self-esteem-need satisfied. (As a matter of fact this doesn't happen often enough in our society; most people on unconscious levels do not have enough feelings of self-love, self-respect. But in any case, the American citizen is far better off here, let's say, than the Mexican citizen is" (p. 15).

10. Michael Maccoby, *The Leader: A New Face for American Management* (New York: Simon & Schuster, 1981), 75.

11. Ibid., 166; see also Heckscher et al., *Agents of Change,* chapter 2.

12. Anabel Quan-Haase and Barry Wellman, "Hyperconnected Network," in *The Firm as Collaborative Community,* ed. Charles Heckscher and Paul S. Adler (New York: Oxford University Press, 2006), 314.

13. Edward E. Lawler III, *Motivation in Work Organizations* (San Francisco: Jossey-Bass, 1993), 43.

14. See Michael Maccoby, *Why Work? Motivating the New Workforce,* 2nd ed. (Alexandria, VA: Miles River Press, 1995).

15. Jean Piaget, *The Moral Judgment of the Child* (New York: The Free Press, 1965; orig. pub. 1932); Jean Piaget, *Play, Dreams and Imitation in Childhood* (New York: Norton, 1951).

16. For a fuller description of Kohlberg's stages of moral reasoning and other views on the subject see Daniel K. Lapsley, *Moral Psychology* (Boulder, CO: Westview Press, 1996).

17. It is dedicated to Lorenzo de'Medici, Duke of Urbino (1492–1519). This was not Lorenzo the Magnificent of Florence, the great patron of the arts who died in 1492, but a grandson who ruled as a dictator and whose claim to fame is his tomb in Florence, sculpted by Michelangelo. By dedicating his book to Lorenzo, Machiavelli hoped, vainly as it turned out, that the duke would revive his political career and end his exile from France.

18. Niccoló Machiavelli, *The Prince,* trans. Harvey C. Mansfield Jr. (Chicago: University of Chicago Press, 1985), 69.

19. Niccoló Machiavelli, *The Discourses,* Book 3 (London: Penguin Classics, 1984), chapter 20. However, Machiavelli writes that for a republic, it's better to have a harsh commander like Manlius because he reinforces republican values of discipline and justice without regard for rank or riches. Valerius's method is harmful, he writes, because it prepares the way for tyranny. How so? What Machiavelli doesn't mention but history tells us is that Valerius Corvinus while originally a republican went over to join Octavian (who became emperor Augustus) to destroy the republic. This message may be that a considerate general can become a popular politician, think of Dwight D. "Ike" Eisenhower, and might become a dictator while a tough general, think of George Patton, sticks to the military and is no such threat.

20. Machiavelli, *The Discourses,* 468.

21. Machiavelli, *The Prince,* chapter XXV.

22. Michael Maccoby, "Trust Trumps Love and Fear," *MIT Sloan Management Review* 45, no. 2 (Winter 2004): 14–16.

23. Alan Deutschman, "Psychopathic Bosses," *Fast Company,* July 2005, 44–51.

24. Jim Collins, *Good to Great* (New York: Harper Collins Business, 2001), 127.

25. Ibid., 27.

26. Michael Maccoby, *Narcissistic Leaders: Who Succeeds and Who Fails* (Boston: Harvard Business School Press, 2007). Neither Collins nor Jack Welch mentioned the other personality types I've observed: the caring and marketing types. I'll discuss these types in chapter 5.

27. Jack Welch with Suzy Welch, *Winning* (New York: Harper Business, 2005), 181–184.

28. This research on professional football players was done on the San Diego Chargers by Dr. Arnold T. Mandell, then chairman of the Department of Psychiatry, University of California, San Diego ("A Psychiatric Study of Professional Football," *Saturday Review*, October 5, 1974, 12–16).

29. Michael Maccoby, *The Gamesman: The New Corporate Leaders* (New York: Simon and Schuster, 1976), chapter 6.

30. Andrew Pollack, "Hewlett's 'Consummate Strategist,'" *New York Times*, March 10, 1992.

31. Personal communication from Martin C. Faga, CEO of MITRE in McLean, Virginia, June 22, 2006.

32. Leonard Shapiro, "NFL Coaches Take a Gentler Approach," *Washington Post*, November 6, 2005.

33. Carol Hymowitz, "Two Football Coaches Have a Lot to Teach Screaming Managers," *Wall Street Journal*, January 29, 2007.

34. John Brauch, "NBC Gives Barber the Ball and He Runs with It," *New York Times*, February 14, 2007.

35. Reported by Jena McGregor, "Game Plan: First Find the Leaders," *BusinessWeek*, August 21–28, 2006.

Chapter 3

1. This chapter builds on my article "Why People Follow the Leader: The Power of Transference," *Harvard Business Review*, September 2004, 76–85.

2. Sigmund Freud, *Character and Anal Eroticism*, vol. IX, *The Standard Edition of the Complete Psychological Works of Sigmund Freud* (London: Hogarth Press, 1958), 167–177 (orig. pub. 1908).

3. Sigmund Freud, *Observations on Transference Love*, vol. XII, *The Standard Edition of the Complete Psychological Works of Sigmund Freud* (London: Hogarth Press, 1958), 168 (orig. pub. 1915).

4. http://www.cps-ltd.co.uk.

5. Michael Maccoby, "Achieving Good Governance for Psychoanalytic Societies," *American Psychoanalyst* (Winter/Spring 2004): 9, 13.

6. Lydia Thomas, interview with author, August 5, 2004.

7. I've disguised all names and possible identifying aspects of my clients.

8. Freud, *Observations on Transference Love*, 196.

9. This thesis of the increases of sibling transferences linked to the changing family structure is based on my experience and that of colleagues, including academic researchers and psychotherapists who report that their patients from these family backgrounds express these transferences in therapy.

10. Along with the emphasis on protecting Americans from terrorists were ads projecting a paternal image of George W. Bush. One widely broadcast TV ad was "Ashley's story," in which Bush comforts a teenage girl who lost her mother in the 9/11 attacks. The transferential appeal reaches its peak when Ashley says about Bush, "He's the most powerful man in the world, and all he wants to do is make sure I'm safe, that I'm OK." Cited by Kevin Lanning,

"The Social Psychology of the 2004 U.S. Presidential Election," *Analyses of Social Issues and Public Policy* 5, no. 1 (2005): 150.

11. Michael Maccoby, *Narcissistic Leaders: Who Succeeds and Who Fails* (Boston: Harvard Business School Press, 2007).

Chapter 4

1. Michael Maccoby, *Narcissistic Leaders: Who Succeeds and Who Fails* (Boston: Harvard Business School Press, 2007). In the village, the entrepreneurs bought the land these people had been given after the revolution in order to build weekend houses for rich people from Mexico City. Left landless, these villagers soon used up the money and were forced to become day laborers.

2. Alexis de Tocqueville, *Democracy in America* (New York: Vintage Books, 1958), 330.

3. Peter F. Drucker, "Management and the World's Work," *Harvard Business Review*, September–October 1988, 75.

4. Charles Dickens, *Little Dorrit* (1857; New York: The Modern Library, 2002), 114.

5. "Public officers in the United States are not separate from the mass of citizens; they have neither palaces nor ceremonial costumes. This simple exterior of persons in authority is connected not only with the peculiarities of the American character, but with the fundamental principles of society . . . A public officer in the United States is uniformly simple in his manners, accessible to all the world, attentive to all requests, and obliging in his replies. I was pleased by these characteristics of a democratic government; I admired the manly independence that respects the office more than the officer and thinks less of the emblems of authority than of the man who bears them." Tocqueville, ibid., 214–215.

6. Max Weber, *The Protestant Ethic and the Spirit of Capitalism* (New York: Scribner, 1958), 182 (orig. pub. 1904–1905).

7. Cited by Robert K. Merton, "Bureaucratic Structure and Personality," in *Personality in Nature, Society, and Culture*, ed. K. Kluckhohn and H. A. Murray (New York: Alfred A. Knopf, 1961), 378.

8. Erich Fromm, *The Anatomy of Human Destructiveness* (New York: Harper and Row, 1970), 294.

9. Merton, "Bureaucratic Structure and Personality," 363–376.

10. Ibid.

11. Drucker, "Management and the World's Work."

12. Michael Maccoby, *Why Work? Motivating the New Workforce* (Alexandria, VA: Miles River Press, 1995).

13. In Melvin L. Kohn and Carmi Schooler's *Work and Personality* (Norwood, NJ: Ablex Publishing, 1983), a massive study of 3,100 men at all levels of corporations and government, the authors found that the ideal job for these bureaucrats is one that allows autonomy. Notably, labor unions in the United States bargained to give workers the rights to ownership of their jobs, in effect giving them a certain autonomy and protection from arbitrary authority. In contrast, European unions tended to bargain for influence at the executive level while allowing management more flexibility in running the shop floor. As a result, American industry suffered from elaborate contracts that detailed a worker's job and made

clear that the worker could not be asked to do anything else. This led to the ridiculous and costly situation in American industries like steel where one electrician only would do work on a wall up to a certain height while above that a different electrician owned the job.

14. Kenneth Blanchard and Spencer Johnson, *The One Minute Manager: Increase Productivity, Profits, and Your Own Prosperity* (New York: William Morrow and Company, 1982).

15. According to 2003 U.S. Census statistics, 67 percent of Americans work in private service producing industries, 17 percent in government, and 11 percent in manufacturing. That's a lot of organizations.

16. Michael Maccoby, *The Gamesman: The New Corporate Leaders* (New York: Simon & Schuster, 1976).

17. William H. Whyte Jr., *The Organization Man* (New York: Simon & Schuster, 1956).

18. Maccoby, *The Gamesman,* 120.

19. Jack Welch with Suzy Welch, *Winning* (New York: Harper Business, 2005).

20. Among AT&T's well-known bad decisions were: giving up cellular telephony after inventing it, trying to compete in computers, buying NCR, and deciding the Internet was a fad.

21. Maccoby, *Why Work?*

22. John C. Beck and Mitchell Wade, *Got Game? How the Gamer Generation Is Reshaping Business* (Boston: Harvard Business School Press, 2004). Beck, in a private talk, said that 100 percent of Harvard undergraduates were video gamers.

23. But these gamesters can lose touch with reality. A research laboratory director told me that one of them she directed kept playing with the data until he got the "right" result. When she questioned its accuracy, he said, "But that's the result you asked for."

24. Beck and Wade, *Got Game?* 154. Surveys of video gamers show a drop-off in play as the gamers age and have to focus more on work and family. It remains to be studied whether or not these attitudes toward work and leadership are sustained; see Nick Wingfield, "Game Companies Worry as Players Grow Up, Grow Bored," *Wall Street Journal,* February 14, 2007.

25. Beck and Wade, *Got Game?* 121–122.

26. I've found that they do appreciate, even enjoy, the kind of co-coaching designed by Marshall Goldsmith, where neither person is superior to the other. See for example, Marshall Goldsmith, "Try Feedforward Instead of Feedback," http://www.marshallgoldsmithlibrary.com.

Chapter 5

1. Although few managers have advanced very far in understanding people, almost all have taken and discussed the Myers-Briggs Type Indicator test, which is based on the theories of C. G. Jung, the Swiss psychoanalyst. However, test-retest studies of the Myers-Briggs don't show high reliability. Even so, since introversion-extraversion is genetically determined, Myers-Briggs taps into a valid trait. See, for example, Leslie A. Thomas and Robert J. Harvey, "Improving Measurement Precision of the Myers-Briggs Type Indicator" (paper presented at the Annual Conference of the Society for Industrial and Organizational Psychology, Orlando, FL, May 1995).

2. This is the questionnaire in chapter 1 of *Narcissistic Leaders: Who Succeeds and Who Fails* (Boston: Harvard Business School Press, 2007).

3. "Expanding the Innovation Horizon, the Global CEO Study 2006," IBM Business Consulting Services.

4. For examples of types of collaboration in the knowledge workplace, see Charles Heckscher and Paul S. Adler, eds., *The Firm as Collaborative Community: The Reconstruction of Trust in the Knowledge Economy* (Oxford: Oxford University Press, 2006). Also by Heckscher, *The Collaborative Enterprise: Managing Speed and Complexity in Knowledge-Based Businesses* (New Haven, CT: Yale University Press, 2007).

5. Lynda M. Applegate et al., "IBM: Uniting Vision and Values," Case 9-805-116 (Boston: Harvard Business School, 2006).

6. This research finding by Mitzi Montoya-Weiss of NC State University and Anne P. Massey of Indiana University was reported in CIMS Technology Management Report, Center for Innovation Management Studies (NC State University, Winter 2006–2007).

7. Kwame Anthony Appiah, *The Ethics of Identity* (Princeton, NJ: Princeton University Press, 2005), 117. Appiah goes on to write: "The social identities that clamor for recognition are extremely multifarious. Some groups have the names of the earlier ethnicities: Italian, Jewish, Polish. Some correspond to the old races (black, Asian, Indian); or to religions (Baptist, Catholic, Jewish). Some are basically regional (Southern, Western, Puerto Rican). Yet others are new groups that meld together people of particular geographic origins (Hispanic, Asian American) or are social categories (woman, gay, bisexual, disabled, Deaf) that are none of these. And, nowadays, we are not the slightest bit surprised when someone remarks upon the 'culture' of such groups. Gay culture, Deaf culture, Chicano culture, Jewish culture: see how these phrases trip off the tongue. But if you ask what distinctively marks off gay people or Deaf people or Jews from others, it is not obviously the fact that to each identity there corresponds a distinct culture. 'Hispanic' sounds like the name of a cultural group defined by sharing the cultural trait of speaking Spanish; but, as I've already pointed out, half the second-generation Hispanics in California don't speak Spanish fluently, and in the next generation the proportion will fall. 'Hispanic' is, of course, a category that's as made-in-the-U.S.A. as black and white, a product of immigration, an artifact of the U.S. census. Whatever 'culture' Guatemalan peasants and Cuban professionals have in common, the loss of Spanish confirms that Hispanic, as a category, is thinning out culturally in the way that white ethnicity has already done."

8. Allison Maitland, "Le Patron, der Chef and the Boss," *Financial Times,* January 9, 2006.

9. These were Thailand, Taiwan, South Korea, China, Hong Kong (then independent), Malaysia, Singapore, Indonesia, and the Philippines. When Lindahl first asked me to go to these countries, I wasn't sure that Asians would be open with me. I said I'd test my ability by trying Thailand and Taiwan. Before leaving, I read as much as I could about the culture and history of these countries. I went first to Bangkok and was pleasantly surprised how open the Thai managers were, giving frank opinions about the expats. I remarked on this to one Thai manager who said, "Most foreigners come and just tell us what they want us to do. You understood how important to us is Buddhism, and you listened."

10. The Chinese government has recently become more favorable to Confucius as a means of indoctrinating respect for their authority. Richard McGregor, "The Pursuit of Harmony—Why Fast-Changing China Is Turning Back to Confucius," *Financial Times,* April 12, 2007, 11.

11. Geert Hofstede, "Cultural Constraints in Management Theory," in *Leadership: Understanding the Dynamics of Power and Influence in Organizations,* ed. Robert P. Vecchio (Notre Dame, IN: University of Notre Dame Press, 1997), 479.

12. Marcus Buckingham and Donald O. Clifton, *Now Discover Your Strengths* (New York: The Free Press, 2001).

13. Adapted from P. T. Costa Jr. and R. McCrae, "Trait Psychology Comes of Age," in *Psychology and Aging,* vol. 39, *Nebraska Symposium on Motivation, 1991,* ed. Theo B. Sonderegger (Lincoln, NE: University of Nebraska Press, 1992), 169–204.

14. Richard Olivier uses this theory in his mythodramas (www.oliviermythodrama.com), as does Carol Pearson in her books and seminars (www.herewithin.com).

15. Michael Maccoby, *Narcissistic Leaders: Who Succeeds and Who Fails* (Boston: Harvard Business School Press, 2007).

16. Descriptions of the mixed types can be found in the appendix of *Narcissistic Leaders.*

17. Sigmund Freud, *Libidinal Types,* vol. XXI, *The Standard Edition of the Complete Psychological Works of Sigmund Freud* (1931; London: Hogarth Press, 1961), 215–220.

18. Ibid.

19. The questionnaire is published in chapter 1 of *Narcissistic Leaders.* Richard Margolies used the questionnaire in leadership workshops with the U.S. Army Corps of Engineers. Most of the business media managers at VNU have marketing personalities. Matt Downs and Michael Anderson, while students at Stanford Business School under the direction of Charles O'Reilly, gave the questionnaire to executives of Bay Area businesses. Nine of ten high-tech entrepreneurs were narcissists and six of seven manufacturers were obsessives.

20. Tony Barclay, interview with author, March 9, 2007.

Chapter 6

1. Stefan Stern writes "When 50 executive MBA students at a leading international business school were asked recently what word they would use to describe themselves, they opted for labels such as 'catalyst', 'change-agent', 'consultant' and 'leader.' None of them wanted to be thought of as a 'manager.'" *Financial Times,* December 19, 2006.

2. Dee Hock, *One from Many: VISA and the Rise of the Chaordic Organization* (San Francisco: Berrett-Koehler, 2005).

3. Bryan Huang, interview with author, August 1, 2005.

4. Ibid.

5. Judith Block McLaughlin and David Riesman, *Choosing a College President, Opportunities and Constraints* (Princeton, NJ: The Carnegie Foundation for the Advancement of Teaching, 1990).

6. Paul S. Adler, "Beyond Hacker Idiocy: The Changing Nature of Software Community and Identity," in *The Firm as Collaborative Community: The Reconstruction of Trust in the Knowledge Economy,* ed. Charles Heckscher and Paul S. Adler (Oxford: Oxford University Press, 2006), 179–198.

7. Michael Maccoby, "Learning to Partner and Partnering to Learn," *Research Technology Management* 40, no. 3 (May–June 1997): 55–57.

8. Jay R. Galbraith, "Mastering the Law of Requisite Variety with Differentiated Networks," in Heckscher and Adler, *The Firm as Collaborative Community,* 179–198.

Chapter 7

1. See, for example, Anna Bernasek, "Health Care Problem: Check the American Psyche," *New York Times,* December 31, 2006.

2. Richard Normann and Niklas Arvidsson, eds., *People as Care Catalysts: From Being Patient to Becoming Healthy* (Chichester, UK: John Wiley & Sons, Ltd., 2006).

3. This failure is described in Haynes Johnson and David Broder, *The System: The American Way of Politics at the Breaking Point* (Boston: Little Brown, 1997).

4. Simmons benefited from a talented and dedicated staff. Margaret Rhoades, PhD, and later Patricia Q. Schoeni were executive directors of the coalition, and Mark A. Goldberg was the policy expert.

5. *Building a Better Health Care System: Specifications for Reform* can be found at www .nchc.org.

6. The commission Simmons first organized also discussed the self-inflicted causes of illness such as smoking, obesity, and lack of exercise. Clearly, if Americans improved their habits—eating, drinking, exercise—the cost of health care would be reduced. One political leader, Mike Huckabee, former Republican governor of Arkansas, instituted programs to reward employees for healthy behavior. At a Coalition meeting on July 10, 2006, he pointed out that companies now reward employees for being sick, giving them time off and health care. Huckabee believes that if comprehensive reform can be shown to work in a state, its chances increase of being adopted by Congress.

7. Stanford University economist Allan C. Enthoven has written extensively on what it would take to create the conditions that would allow for a competitive market that could control costs while increasing quality. These include: (1) universal coverage; (2) a standard insurance package, so consumers could compare price and quality; (3) at least three independent insurance or provider systems competing in every part of the country; (4) transparent information about price and outcomes measures; and (5) government oversight and regulations. (A. C. Enthoven, "Market Forces and Efficient Health Care Systems," *Health Affairs,* March–April, 2004, 25–27.) Michael Porter, the distinguished Harvard business strategist, is a strong advocate of market competition among providers on the basis of measured results. We are a long way from getting the necessary measurements, but even if they were available, this would not necessarily control costs, since the most effective doctors could raise their rates. (M. E. Porter and Elizabeth Olmsted Teisberg, *Redefining Health Care: Creating Positive-Sum Competition to Delivery Value* [Boston: Harvard Business School Press, 2006].)

8. The Hospital Experimental Payment (HEP) program was cutting costs in Rochester hospitals that agreed not to compete in areas requiring costly technology, but rather allow each hospital to specialize. This program was initiated by community leaders. See J. A. Block, D. I. Regenstreif, and P. F. Griner, "A Community Hospital Payment Experiment Outperforms National Experience: The Hospital Experimental Payment Program in Rochester, New York," *Journal of the American Medical Association* 257, no. 2 (1987): 193–197. Griner told me that the cooperation/collaborative started to unravel when George Pataki was elected governor. He was a strong proponent of competition in the healthcare field. At about the same time, HCFA (Health Care Finance Administration) decided that the experiment had gone on long enough, and the experiment was a success (HCFA had granted a waiver for Medicare and Medicaid to participate in the experiment). So, fracture lines were already present when Kodak then took a public position favoring a more competitive environment.

The program ended with the result that costs rose as all hospitals bought the same expensive technology.

9. Paul Griner et. al., *Managing Change* (Washington, DC: Association of American Medical Colleges, 2000).

10. These included: Polly Bednash, PhD, RN, FAAN, Executive Director, American Association of Colleges of Nursing; Roger Bulger, MD, President, Association of Academic Health Centers; Paul Griner, MD, former President, American College of Physicians and Vice President and Director, Center for the Assessment and Management of Change in Academic Medicine, Association of American Medical Colleges; Federico Ortiz Quesada, MD, Director, International Relations, Mexican Ministry of Health; Stan Pappelbaum, MD, former CEO, Scripps Health; Richard Riegelman, MD, MPH, PhD, Dean, School of Public Health and Health Services, George Washington University; Henry Simmons, MD, President, National Leadership Coalition on Health Care.

11. The full report *Leadership for Health Care in the Age of Learning* was published by the Association of Academic Health Centers in 2001. It can be found at http://www.maccoby .com. Parts of this chapter have been published in Michael Maccoby, "Health Care Organization as Collaborative Learning Communities," in *The Firm as Collaborative Community: The Reconstruction of Trust in the Knowledge Economy*, ed. Charles Heckscher and Paul S. Adler (Oxford: Oxford University Press, 2006), 259–280.

12. Although I have a PhD rather than an MD, I went through psychoanalytic training together with psychiatrists and apprenticed under Erich Fromm and practiced in my own cottage industry. I can appreciate the traditional physicians' point of view.

13. Roger Bulger, *The Quest for Mercy, the Forgotten Ingredient in Health Care Reform* (Charlottesville, VA: Garden Jennings Publishing, 1998).

14. Paul Starr, *The Social Transformation of American Medicine* (New York: Basic Books. 1982); George Rosen, *The Structure of the American Medical Profession, 1875–1941* (Philadelphia: University of Pennsylvania Press, 1983).

15. Louis M. Savory and Clare Crawford-Mason, *The Nun and the Bureaucrat: How They Found a Simple Elegant Solution to a Deadly National Problem* (Washington, DC: CC-M Productions, Inc., 2006).

16. "How the VA Healed Itself," *Fortune*, May 15, 2006.

17. After the Institute of Medicine reported almost 100,000 Americans die each year in hospitals due to mistakes and poor practice, Donald Berwick, MD, a professor at Harvard Medical School led an eighteen-month campaign that engaged 3,100 hospitals ("Hospital Initiative to Cut Errors Finds About 122,300 Lives Saved," *Wall Street Journal*, June 15 2006); see also Donald M. Berwick, MD and Lucian L. Leape, MD, "Perfect Is Possible," *Business Week*, October 16, 2006, 70–72.

18. Ian Urbina, "Rising Diabetes Threat Meets a Falling Budget," *New York Times*, May 16, 2006.

19. Clyde H. Evans and Elaine R. Rubin, eds., *Creating the Future* (Washington, DC: Association of Academic Health Centers, 1999).

20. Normann and Arvidsson, *People as Care Catalysts*.

21. *In Pursuit of Greater Value: Stronger Leadership in and by Academic Health Centers* (Charlottesville, VA: University of Virginia Health Center, 2000).

22. From the Mayo clinic Web site: www.mayoclinic.org/about/history.html.

23. Ibid.

24. Mayo's tax-exempt status is based on its research mission; IHC's is based on its willingness to serve patients without regard to their ability to pay.

25. Brent James, interview with author, November 16, 1999.

26. Other Mayo-type integrated healthcare organizations that we did not study are the Scott-White Clinic in Albuquerque, New Mexico, and Dartmouth-Hitchcock Clinic in Hanover, New Hampshire, which has been a leader in sharing information on quality.

27. Quotation from Brookings Institution Leadership Laboratory, September 16, 2005.

28. I haven't described Kaiser-Permanente in this chapter, mainly because it has taken a similar path to that of Intermountain. However, many observers view Kaiser as a model for the future of health care. See Steve Lohr, "Is Kaiser the Future of American Health Care?" *New York Times,* October 31, 2004.

Chapter 8

1. For example, fourteen urban school districts have on-time high school graduation rates lower than 50 percent; they include Baltimore, Detroit, New York, Milwaukee, Cleveland, Los Angeles, Miami, Dallas, Denver, and Houston; see Gregg Toppo, "Big-City Schools Struggle with Graduation Rates," *USA Today,* June 20, 2006.

2. See *Tough Choices or Tough Times: The Report of the New Commission on the Skills of the American Workforce* (Washington, DC: National Center on Education and the Economy, 2007).

3. Lawrence Mishel, Jared Bernstein, and Sylvia Allegretto, *Economic Policy Institute: The State of Working America 2006/2007,* http://www.epi.org/content.cfm/datazone_dz national.

4. The report of the New Commission on the Skills of the American Workforce doesn't even mention these jobs. Yet, there is a shortage of competent skilled workers. This is the case also for factory work as reported in Barbara Hagenbaugh, "Wanted: Factory Workers," *USA Today,* December 5, 2006..

5. My description is based on the profile by Mark Singer in *The New Yorker,* June 5, 2006; and the article by Yukari Iwatani Kane and Phred Dvorak, "Howard Stringer, Japanese CEO," *Wall Street Journal,* March 3, 2007.

6. Daniel Greenbert, *Free at Last: The Sudbury Valley School* (Framingham, MA: Sudbury Valley School Press, 1995).

7. Nick Anderson, "Learning on Their Own Terms, Maryland School With No Curriculum Challenges Conventions," *Washington Post,* April 24, 2006.

8. "Reality Check 2006, How Black and Hispanic Families Rate Their Schools," *Public Agenda,* http://www.publicagenda.org.

9. Jay Greene and William C. Symonds, "Gates Gets Schooled," *BusinessWeek,* June 26, 2006.

10. http://www.KIPP.org. Steven F. Wilson of Harvard's Kennedy School of Government evaluates the charter schools in *Learning on the Job* (Cambridge, MA: Harvard University Press, 2005). As of 2005, there were 240,000 students in 535 charter schools, far fewer than the over one million who are home schooled. However, some KIPP schools are public

schools, contracted with school districts. Examples are Tulsa, Oklahoma; Oakland, California; and Memphis, Tennessee.

11. The main funding for the KIPP Foundation has come from Donald and Doris Fisher, cofounders of Gap, Inc. They have worked closely with the KIPP founders to create a national organization.

12. "Seeking Success with Students," *American Educator* (Summer 2006): 7.

13. Spherion's 2003 Workplace Study, http://www.spherion.com.

14. Wilson, *Learning on the Job*, 12.

15. Personal communication, July 13, 2006.

16. Ravitch writes, "We need independent teachers unions to protect teachers' rights, to sound the alarm against unwise policies, and to advocate on behalf of sound education policies." Diane Ravitch, "Why Teacher Unions Are Good for Teachers," *American Educator* (Winter 2006–2007), 8.

17. These statistics were provided by the superintendent, Dr. Gary Smuts.

18. For a description of my work with AT&T and CWA, see Charles Heckcher et al., *Agents of Change Crossing the Post-Industrial Divide* (Oxford: Oxford University Press, 2003).

19. A different kind of union response to the challenge of charter schools is a UFT Charter School in Brooklyn. In contrast to KIPP's emphasis on strong leadership, the UFT school emphasizes teacher participation in decision making on curriculum, discipline, and staffing. Rita Davis, who would be called a principal in other schools, holds the title of instructional leader. This elementary school, which serves 150 students in a middle-to-low-income Brooklyn neighborhood, makes parental involvement and student discipline operating principles. The seventeen teachers are enthusiastic, but they've only been in business for a year, and it's too early to evaluate the results of this model, which deemphasizes the role of the leader,

20. http://www.nphi.org.

21. At the beginning Father Wasson had the policy of only accepting children whose mothers were no longer alive. He reasoned that if she were alive, the children would never feel fully part of the new family. Also, she might come to claim them. The tie to the father, especially in Latin America, is weaker. In fact, we have found that when the mother is alive, the children usually do want to be reunited with her.

22. Dr. Paul Farmer is another noted medical leader in Haiti. While still a student at Harvard Medical School, he founded Zanmi Lastane, a clinic in the central plateau, where he showed that health could be improved with clean water and by training villagers to treat their neighbors. In Haiti, however, the limits to success aren't a matter of health and education but are imposed by poverty, violence, and the lack of jobs. That's why Father Rick Frechette is now trying to establish businesses for the NPFS graduates. Their future depends not only on their formal education but also developing entrepreneurial skills and finding the resources to get started.

Chapter 9

1. Donald Kagan, *Pericles of Athens and the Birth of Democracy* (New York: The Free Press, 1991), 9.

2. Norman R. Augustine, chair of the National Academies committee that produced the report *Rising Above the Gathering Storm: Energizing and Employing American for a Brighter*

Economic Future writes that "between 50 and 85 percent of the growth in America's per capita over the last half century is attributable to science and technology, much of it having roots in basic research performed either by the government's funding or by the government itself"; "Competitiveness: Late but Not Too Late," *Research Technology Management* (January–February 2007): 9.

3. Thomas L. Friedman, *The World Is Flat* (New York: Farrar, Straus and Giroux, 2005), 281, 283.

4. Quoted in Jonathan Alter, *The Defining Moment: FDR's Hundred Days and the Triumph of Hope* (New York: Simon & Schuster, 2006), 80, 82.

5. They all share a family constellation common to male narcissists: a weak, failed, disliked, or absent father and a powerful and supportive mother. This explains the absence of the strong superego, produced by internalized identification with the father, which is found in the obsessive type.

6. Harold Holzer, *Lincoln at Cooper Union: The Speech That Made Abraham Lincoln President* (New York: Simon & Schuster, 2004).

7. Cited by Newt Gingrich in "Transformational Leadership," The James E. Webb Lecture, November 21, 2003, Washington, DC.

8. Thomas W. Evans, *The Education of Ronald Reagan* (New York: Columbia University Press, 2007).

9. This took place at Villa Miani on May 20, 2006.

10. This is described by David Frum in *The Right Man: The Surprise Presidency of George W. Bush* (New York: Random House, 2003).

11. Michiko Kakutani, "Critic's Notebook: All the President's Books," *New York Times*, May 11, 2006.

12. *CNN Late Edition*, November 19, 2006.

13. Alexis de Tocqueville, *Democracy in America,* trans. George Lawrence (New York: Anchor Books, 1969).

14. Erich Fromm, *Escape from Freedom* (New York: Rinehart, 1941).

15. "The Real War," *Time*, December 25, 2006–January 1, 2007, 162.

16. Unlike psychiatrist Justin A. Frank (*Bush on the Couch: Inside the Mind of the President* [New York: HarperCollins, 2004]), I don't try to get into Bush's head. Rather, my personality diagnosis interprets patterns that anyone can see. However, based on Bush's history, I have speculated that he has strong erotic or loving tendencies and that he defends himself from feeling soft and vulnerable by assuming an aggressive, macho attitude. This pattern is common among alcoholics. Bush recovered from his addiction admirably, helped by a combination of religion and a strong, loving wife. Like many marketing types, he suffered from a lack of a spiritual center until he found it in religion.

17. Washington Post/ABC News Poll, "On Shaky Ground," *Washington Post*, January 23, 2007.

18. Michael Maccoby, *Narcissistic Leaders: Who Succeeds and Who Fails* (Boston: Harvard Business School Press, 2007).

19. David Rennick, "The Wanderer," *The New Yorker*, September 18, 2006, 65.

20. See Doris Kearns Goodwin, *Team of Rivals: The Political Genius of Abraham Lincoln* (New York, Simon & Schuster, 2006).

Chapter 10

1. My adaptation; from Lao Tzu, *Tao Te Ching*, XVII, trans. D. C. Lau (New York: Penguin Books, 1963).

2. Gale Cutler, "Mike Leads His First Virtual Team," *Research Technology Management* (January–February 2007): 67.

3. However, in the Mexican village Fromm and I studied there were three types of social character: descendants of free farmers,descendants of hacienda peons, and the small group of entrepreneurs.

4. Daniel Goleman, *Emotional Intelligence* (New York: Bantam Books, 1995).

5. Missing from descriptions of EI is a quality I do find in some narcissists who are neither particularly empathic nor self-aware. That's a sense of humor, the emotional equivalent of a cognitive sense of reality. Life is often absurd and, as noted in chapter 9, some of the most effective leaders bring people down to earth, defuse tense situations, even puncture their own self-importance with humor. We should be wary of humorless would-be leaders. They tend to be the rigid ideologues or holier-than-thou moralists.

6. Some questionnaires probe for behavioral strengths. The questionnaire I designed is based on psychoanalytic types, dynamic styles of relatedness which underlie both strengths and weaknesses. See Marcus Buckingham and Donald O. Clifton, *Now Discover Your Strengths* (New York: The Free Press, 2001); and Michael Maccoby, *Narcissistic Leaders: Who Succeeds and Who Fails* (Boston: Harvard Business School Press, 2007), chapter 2.

7. Kathleen Freeman, *Ancilla to the Pre-Socratic Philosophers* (Oxford: Basil Blackwell, 1947), 27.

8. 1 Kings 3:5-15 (New English Bible).

9. I first presented this discussion of head and heart in *The Gamesman* (New York: Simon & Schuster, 1976), chapter 7.

10. As a result of King Solomon's asking God for a heart that listens, "all the world courted him, to hear the wisdom which God had put in his heart" (1 Kings 10:24 [New English Bible]).

11. Recent research suggests females, more than males, are more observant of facial expressions and that this difference is hardwired in the brain. See Louann Brizandine, "The Female Brain," *New York Times*, September 10, 2006.

12. Paul Ekman, *Emotions Revealed: Recognizing Faces and Feelings to Improve Communication and Emotional Life* (New York: Times Books, 2003).

13. Daniel Goleman, *Social Intelligence: The New Science of Human Relationships* (New York: Bantam Dell, 2006), 43.

14. For a description of the difference between analytic, practical, and creative intelligence, see Robert J. Sternberg, *The Triarchic Mind: A New Theory of Human Intelligence* (New York: Viking, 1988); and *Successful Intelligence: How Practical and Creative Intelligence Determine Success in Life* (New York: Plume, 1997).

15. Ann Louise Bardach, "Letters from Prison: Castro Revealed," *Washington Post,* February 25, 2007, *Outlook*, 5.

16. I first learned of this reading the *Muqaddimah* of Ibn Khaldûn, the 14th-century Moroccan philosopher and social historian (trans. Franz Rosenthal, Bollinger Series XLIII

[Princeton, NJ: Princeton University Press, 1958]). I have taken off from his theory to develop my own interpretation of the discipline of the heart.

17. Malcolm Gladwell, *Blink: The Power of Thinking Without Thinking* (New York: Little, Brown and Company, 2005).

18. Albert Schweitzer, *Reverence for Life* (New York: Philosophical Library, 1965), 34 and throughout the book.

19. Maccoby, *Narcissistic Leaders.*

20. They included: Richard Greene, Richard Margolies, Edith Onderick-Harvey, Mark Paulson, Mark Paulson Jr., and Gary Wolford.

21. I first discovered this when I gave Rorschach tests to corporate managers for the study that became *The Gamesman: The New Corporate Leaders* (New York: Simon and Schuster, 1976). The systems thinkers saw ink blots as a whole, rather than as clearly distinct but unrelated parts. The most creative systems thinkers described action, a story about how the parts were interacting.

22. See examples in Maccoby, *Narcissistic Leaders.*

23. Honda is an exception with a culture that emphasizes cross-functional teamwork. Many of the attempts to copy the Toyota system have been partially successful at best, because the copiers have only focused on the economic and technical elements of the system and ignored the social and human element. See Michael Maccoby, "Is There a Best Way to Build a Car?" *Harvard Business Review*, November–December 1997, 161–171.

Appendix

1. Erik H. Erikson, *Childhood and Society* (New York: Norton, 1950).

2. See Betty Friedan, *The Feminine Mystique* (New York: Dell, 1964); Margaret Henning and Anne Jardim found that those women who succeeded in management in the 1970s were almost invariably close to their fathers (Margaret Henning and Anne Jardim, *The Managerial Woman* [New York: Anchor/Doubleday, 1978]). The father-daughter transference often went both ways, as father-fixated women became the protégés of paternalistic bosses.

3. Carol K. Sigelman and Elizabeth A. Rider, *Life-Span Human Development*, 4th ed. (Belmont, CA: Thomas-Wadsworth, 2003).

4. "Employment Characteristics of Families in 2006," BLS report, http://www.bls.gov/news.release/famee.toc.htm

5. Mauricio Cortina and Mario Marrone, eds., *Attachment Theory and the Psychoanalytic Process* (London: Whurr Publishers Ltd., 2003).

6. Sigelman and Rider, *Life-Span Human Development*, 382. According to Department of Labor Statistics about 30 percent of infants of working mothers are cared for by their parents, 30 percent by a relative, 20 percent in family day-care homes (typically run by a woman in her own home), 10 percent in large day-care centers, and a small percentage with hired nannies.

7. Mary Eberstadt, *Home-Alone America: The Hidden Toll of Day Care, Behavioral Drugs and Other Parent Substitutes* (New York: Sentinal, 2004).

8. "Psychology at the Intersection of Work and Family," *American Psychologist* 60, no. 5 (July–August 2003): 400.

9. Judith Warner, "Kids Gone Wild," *New York Times*, November 27, 2005.

10. Ibid.

11. Ibid.

12. E. E. Maccoby, *The Two Sexes: Growing Up Apart, Coming Together* (Cambridge, MA: Harvard University Press, 1999).

13. Jean Piaget, *The Moral Judgment of the Child* (New York: The Free Press, 1965 (orig. *Le Jugement Moral Chez l'Enfant* [Neuchâtel, Switzerland: Editions Delachaux & Niestlé, 1932]).

14. Sigelman and Rider, *Life-Span Human Development*, 382.

15. David Riesman, *The Lonely Crowd* (New Haven, CT: Yale University Press, 1950).

16. Piaget, *The Moral Judgment of the Child*.

17. W. Michael Cox, Richard Alan, and Nigel Homes, "Where the Jobs Are," *New York Times*, May 12, 2004. These knowledge worker jobs include financial service sales, recreation workers, nurses, lawyers, teachers and counselors, actors and directors, architects, designers, photographers, hair stylists and cosmetologists, legal assistants, medical scientists, and electronic engineers.

18. Bradford C. Johnson, James M. Manyika, and Lareina A. Yee, "The Next Revolution in Interactions," *McKinsey Quarterly* no. 4 (2005).

19. Annette Lareau, *Unequal Childhoods: Class, Race, and Family Life* (Berkeley: University of California Press, 2003).

20. Ibid.

21. "The New School in Alternative Learning," *Financial Times.* November 7, 2005, http://search.ft.com/nonFtArticle?id=051107000791.

22. "Breeding Evil?" *The Economist*, August 4, 2005.

23. An example was Devon Moore of Fayette, Alabama, a teenage minor who killed three policemen in a way that seemed to mimic what he did in the game. After his capture, Moore reportedly told the police, "Life is like a video game. Everybody's got to die sometime." However, Moore, who was brought up by various foster parents and was a poor student, had the risk factors that predict criminal behavior. *60 Minutes,* March 6, 2005.

24. Michael Maccoby, *Narcissistic Leaders: Who Succeeds and Who Fails* (Boston: Harvard Business School Press, 2007).

25. According to a survey of Washington, D.C., area teens, 60 percent of whites and 81 percent of African Americans say it's likely that they'll someday be rich. Richard Morin, "What Teens Really Think," *Washington Post Magazine,* October 23, 2005.

26. Erik H. Erikson, *Childhood and Society* (New York: Norton, 1950).

27. "One thing for sure," writes Dylan, "if I wanted to compose folksongs I would need some kind of new template, some philosophical identity that wouldn't burn out." Bob Dylan, *Chronicles*, vol. 1 (New York: Simon & Schuster, 2004), 73.

28. "Spirituality in Higher Education: A National Study of College Students' Search for Meaning and Purpose (2004–2005)," www.spirituality.ucla.edu/reports.

29. Rick Warren, *The Purpose-Driven Life: What on Earth Am I Here For?* (Grand Rapids, MI: Zondervan, 2002).

30. I have described these needs in *Why Work? Motivating the New Workforce*, 2nd ed. (Alexandria, VA: Miles River Press, 1995).

31. Eric Fromm, *The Art of Loving* (New York: Bantam Books, 1963; orig. pub. 1956).

32. Max Weber, *The Protestant Ethic and the Spirit of Capitalism* (1904–1905; New York: Scribner, 1958), 182.

33. Erik H. Erikson, *The Life Cycle Completed* (New York: Norton, 1998), 114.

34. Laura Mullane and Mary Beth Lakin, "Redefining the Golden Years," American Council on Education, January 29, 2007, http://www.acenet.edu.

35. Sue Shellenbarger, "Gray Is Good," *Wall Street Journal*, December 2, 2005. This fits with the findings of the Harvard study. See George E. Vaillant, MD, *Aging Well: Surprising Guideposts to a Happier Life* (Boston: Little, Brown, 2002).

36. *BusinessWeek*, June 27, 2005, 84.

37. Quoted in Paul Sullivan, "Not Working Can Really Ruin Your Retirement," *Financial Times,* January 11, 2006.

Index

About the Author

Michael Maccoby's book *The Gamesman* (1976) was the first bestseller to describe the personalities of leaders in high-tech companies. In his next book, *The Leader* (1981), he proposed as models leaders who developed both their organizations and people. As a result of his research, writing, and pioneering projects to transform the workplace, Maccoby—a psychoanalyst and anthropologist—was hired as a consultant and executive coach by companies such as IBM, AT&T, Volvo, ABB, and government organizations such as the World Bank and the U.S. Commerce and State Departments. From 1970 to 1990 Maccoby was a research associate and program director at Harvard's Kennedy School of Government. Currently, he is president of the Maccoby Group in Washington, D.C., and teaches leadership at the Brookings Institution and Oxford University's Saïd Business School. He has authored or coauthored twelve books, the most recent being *Narcissistic Leaders*. He serves on the boards of the Washington School of Psychiatry, Shanker Institute, and Nuestros Pequeños Hermanos. His BA and PhD are from Harvard.